Desperate Venture

Desperate Venture
Central Ontario Railway

James Plomer
with Alan R. Capon

Mika Publishing Company
Belleville, Ontario
1979

For Frances

ISBN 0-919303-35-8
HE2810.C46P56   385'.06'5713   C79-094588-6
Printed and bound in Canada

Cover illustration by George Nott, Saint John, N.B.

FOREWORD

Most people are of the opinion that railways had their origin in England. This is true as far as commercial railways are concerned — witness the rise of the Stockton and Darlington in 1825 and the Liverpool and Manchester in 1830. These were the first practical applications of a variation of a system of guidance that went back for many centuries.

Two intrinsic qualities, not known to other modes of transport, make railways unique and superior. One is that they are designed to carry heavy loads on relatively small bearing surfaces with a minimum of frictional resistance and gravity drag. The other is the track that provides a systematic method of guidance that obviates the necessity of steering lines of vehicles in confined spaces. Eighteenth-century mines in Germany and Great Britain proved the worth of this principle.

The Romans spent hundreds of years charging around Europe conquering other armies and building their famous roads of flat stones laid on surfaces 10 feet in width. Centuries earlier the Greeks had found it more practical to provide a relatively friction free running surface for vehicles by carving guideways or rutways in stone that existed near the surface.

The Industrial Revolution in Great Britain provided the impetus from which these primitive rutways grew into plateways and eventually into the modern concept of railways with a flanged wheel travelling along a raised steel rail.

After the resounding success of the two primitive English companies, railway building burned with an intense fervor for the next 100 years. The widest proliferation of these narrow steel guideways occurred in North America at the turn of the 20th century when railways literally by the thousands were built often impractically and needlessly across the maps of the United States and Canada.

In *Desperate Venture,* Jim Plomer, with the collaboration of Alan Capon, provides an absorbing account of the rise and eventual decline of the Central Ontario Railway and gives the reader a clear insight into events during the mad and reckless days of Railway Mania.

The shrill whistles of the early Prince Edward Railway trains as they probed northward from the County to a junction with the Grand Trunk Railway presaged the burgeoning growth of Trenton as a railway centre. The book provides a fascinating record of this period as well as of interesting later events that led to the coming into the area of the Canadian Pacific and the ill-starred Canadian Northern.

The author's detailed and sympathetic treatment of the dreams and the genius of Samuel J. Ritchie, the Central Ontario Railway's President, is ably done. His account of Ritchie's dedication to construction quality and his determination to push this tenuous steel trail further north from Coe Hill to Bancroft — and then on to Lake St. Peter and Wallace — but never to the elusive dream of a joining with the Canada Atlantic — provides a rare insight into the scheming and plotting among the early railway barons.

This distinguished retired naval officer and world-recognized rail fan, who makes his home at Milford, Ontario in Prince Edward County, has brought to life, with his newsman partner, in this exciting account of the building of the Central Ontario Railway all of the drama, intrigue and commotion of railway building at the turn of the twentieth century.

Today, paved roads and the ascendancy of the internal combustion engine have made a mockery of the brilliance and dedication of Samuel Ritchie and his beloved Central Ontario Railway. Weeds and rust now obliterate the once proud main line and only ghostly echoes of the past resound on Ormsby grade.

But again the winds of change will not be stilled and the same forces and new transport systems that led to the demise of the Central Ontario Railway are now themselves being weakened and their future threatened by the growing spectre of a world energy deficiency. Although the rails of the Central Ontario Railway are now stilled, the author suggests that a rebirth is possible — and who knows — smoke may still **rise** again on Ormsby grade.

J. Robert Burns
Rideau Area Manager
Canadian National Railways
Belleville, Ontario

Belleville, Ontario
June 14, 1979

PREFACE

The advantage of writing a history of a smaller railway is that one can come closer to covering the many facets of such enterprises. Those who have written histories, to their everlasting credit, of the Canadian National Railways and its major components, or the Canadian Pacific, have subjects so vast that they have had to sacrifice much that they would have otherwise included. The other options are to focus on some particular period or facets such as corporate history, motive power, equipment, stations, steamships, airlines and so on.

Railways have grown isolated from our daily lives, much different to the generations who lived in the Great Railway Age. The Central Ontario Railway finally disappeared in 1914. It was very much of its age. In keeping with its means it served the people from the comparatively prosperous Prince Edward County in Eastern Ontario, to the northern limits of Hastings County, a land of many broken dreams. The railway shared them.

In the course of early research the name of a forgotten man, Samuel J. Ritchie, appeared in the local press as 'an American financier'. There were no interviews, no personal details. Pictures of him are so scarce that only one so far has turned up. He was a man that disliked personal publicity.

At this stage by unusual good fortune an article appeared in the biannual publication of the Railway and Locomotive Historical Society of Boston, Mass., giving a list of all material of any consequence in the archives of various United States institutions. The list was an extract from a government publication. There it was, the Ritchie papers relating to the Central Ontario Railway held by the Western Reserve Historical Society of Cleveland, Ohio.

Here one learnt that the Central Ontario Railway was Ritchie, and he was the railway. A full biography of this extraordinary individual, important in Canadian history, waits to be written.

For a sense of reality one can only attempt to live with the people of those times. These were the years of that most endearing of all machines, the steam locomotive. These hauled wooden passenger cars of strange styling and low-capacity freight cars over light rail. At first these lines were built by men and horses; later by clumsy steam shovels. Morse code controlled the movement of trains. The railway was in the hands of hardy, resourceful men — your fathers and grandfathers.

The book started, and was researched, over a number of years with Alan R. Capon. When he moved to another newspaper it was not possible for him to devote time to continued research, but since then he has continued both with criticism and with the typing of the manuscript, and this has been much appreciated.

There are so many people that have helped to make this book possible that I hope I have not missed any names among the acknowledgements, if so I tender my apologies. Another gentleman I must mention is David Hanes of L'Amable, professional photographer and self-taught industrial archaeologist, who has been particularly generous of his time and local knowledge.

The financial assistance of the Ontario Arts Council has made the considerable research necessary for this book possible. I hope the Council will feel these funds have been well spent.

ACKNOWLEDGEMENTS

Having received so much friendly assistance this seems to be a small appreciation. For a great deal of help I must thank the following institutions: —

Akron-Summit Public Library, Ohio
Canadian National Railways, Headquarters Library Montreal
Canadian Pacific Railway, Corporate Archives, Montreal
Corby Public Library, Belleville, Ont.
Hale Farm Museum, Akron, Ohio
Hastings County Museum, Belleville, Ont.
Ontario Archives, Queens Park, Toronto, Ont.
Public Archives of Canada, Ottawa, Ont.
Trenton Memorial Public Library, Trenton, Ont.
Western Reserve Historical Society, Cleveland, Ohio

And these newspapers: —
Bancroft Times, Bancroft, Ont.
Madoc Review, Madoc, Ont.
Picton Gazette, Picton, Ont.
Trentonian & Tri-County News, Trenton, Ont.

And the following people: —
(1) For a great deal of assistance:
Mr. Roy Cornish, Trenton, Ont.
Mr. J. Robert Burns, Area Manager,
  C.N.R., Belleville, Ont.
Mr. Ray Corley, Toronto, Ont.
Mr. Omer S.A. Lavallee, Montreal, Que.
Mr. J. Norman Lowe, Montreal, Que.
Mr. and Mrs. Malcolm Love, North Marysburgh, Ont.
Mr. Andrew A. Merrilees, Toronto, Ont.
The Late Willis Metcalfe, South Marysburgh, Ont.
Mrs. Jack Milne, Brampton, Ont.
Mr. and Mrs. Lloyd Thompson, Picton, Ont.
Mr. Ross Weaver, Picton, Ont.
Mrs. Murray B. Wiltsie, Wellington, Ont.

(2) Others who were of considerable assistance:
Mr. Henry Black, Kingston, Ont.
Mr. H.R. Botting, Belleville, Ont.
Captain Walter Bowen, Trenton, Ont.
Mr. L.A. Courtemanche, Belleville, Ont.
Mr. Charles Fraleigh, Bloomfield, Ont.

Mr. I.A. Graham, Belleville, Ont.
Mr. Stirling Grimmon, South Marysburgh, Ont.
Mr. Earl Hawley, Bancroft, Ont.
Mr. Winston Hicks, Glenora, Ont.
Mr. Gerard Kavanagh, South Marysburgh, Ont.
Mr. Joseph Lavalley, Wallace, Ont.
Mr. Donald MacDermaid, County Museum, Picton. Ont.
Mr. and Mrs. Stan Maxwell, Madoc, Ont.
Mr. Lawrence A. Meagher, Belleville, Ont.
Mr. Willard Metcalfe, Athol, Ont.
Mr. Herman Snider, L'Amable, Ont.
Mr. Harvey Young, Belleville, Ont.

Chapter One

If we could fly backwards in time to the year 1879 when the first railway train arrived in Picton, we would have seen the same frenzy and excitement as occurred in communities throughout Canada since the days of the first railroad boom here in the fifties.

Canadians were preoccupied with railways for many years and many citizens and politicians believed, with the promoters, that fantastic profits could be reaped if only the steel rails could pass through their community.

With unthinking enthusiasm, towns, townships, villages and counties loaned monies and guaranteed bonds, and rail lines spread willy-nilly through the country, particularly in Canada West. Although in some cases prosperity accompanied the boom, in other places the laying of the rails was to lead to bankruptcy for the promoters and a shock to the citizenry.

Railroad fever existed in Prince Edward County, Ontario, as elsewhere, and for many years people speculated on the possibility of building a railroad but nothing substantial took place until 1873, when a modest, 32-mile line from Picton to Trenton to connect with the Grand Trunk line was proposed.

Branch line railways, whether in the early stage of their independence or in the later stage as part of one of the two big transcontinental systems, are very much part of the region they serve. A great number of the branch lines were once independent concerns.

In other years they played an important role in the social life of a community. The biggest daily event was, of course, the arrival of the passenger train. Then, an almost standard make-up was of two short wooden coaches plus the inevitable mail-express-baggage car. Everyone seemed to find a reason to be down at the depot for the train's arrival. Now the branch line passenger trains are all but gone.

Most of the branch lines that survive do so on a freight only basis, operate at a loss, and remain open at government insistence, different from the lordly main lines that run through miles of barren country without fear of abandonment.

This book is about a line that has not quite disappeared. Its history, like its environment, is highly individual. Because of its dependence on the community where it was conceived one must first relate briefly something of the history and geography of the area that both have shared.

Prince Edward County is one of the most individual counties in Ontario, in both people and geography. Many years ago when the Murray Canal was cut through to the Bay of Quinte this peninsula jutting out into Lake Ontario became an island. True, the canal is of modest dimensions and is restricted to smaller vessels, but an island the county became.

Physically most of the county is a limestone plateau, much of it two to three hundred feet high. The soil varies from marginal to good, and is sufficiently fertile to support a number of orchards and many herds of dairy cattle. Its most famous feature is the miles of sand dunes on the western shore which attract thousands of visitors annually.

In the distant past the biggest and most profitable crops were barley, rye and hops, and these were exported across Lake Ontario to United States ports. This long-term prosperity came to an abrupt end in 1890 when the United States government stopped the trade with high tariffs. As a memorial to those earlier years there remain a number of fine stone and Georgian brick houses. Only in recent years has prosperity returned to the county.

The shoreline extended many miles by numerous points, bays and inlets; a maritime economy and way of living was inevitable. In every sheltered stretch of water could be found docks, warehouses, and even a sprinkling of grain elevators. There were a number of shipyards that built schooners. Here professional shipwrights and skilled farmers built, owned and often sailed these ships. Later there were also large and small operators of steamers. The passenger ships, most of them paddle-steamers, provided an extensive feeder service to Picton, the county seat, with its fine natural harbour. From there regular sailings were made to Belleville, Kingston, Toronto, and from these places were good connections to Montreal and to many United States ports.

The county men could be found manning ships on every lake and in every capacity. There was also a busy fishing industry. So far inland, this farming-sailing community was unique.

The county people have a strong sense of heritage. The oldest families are descendents of United Empire Loyalists with people of British and Dutch origin, and also German mercenaries who had fought for the British in the American War of Independence. These were followed by Irish and English settlers, but for many generations the number of newcomers was few. In 1873 the population was given as 27,366 inhabitants, this declined considerably over the years and even today is some 5,000 less than this figure.

Into an area so wholly maritime in its way of life the railway had to come in by the backdoor, and then after many difficulties.

The first attempt to build a railway was in May 1854 when a group of citizens met to promote the Prince Edward County Railway Company.[1] A partial map, crudely drawn, shows the proposed line running through Milford to South Bay where harbour facilities existed. The rest of the line is conjectoral.

Reaction in the County was not favourable and nothing more was done.

Among the directors (Appendix I) was Philip Low of Picton, later a successful lawyer and president of a regional telegraph company. Twenty years later he would be among those promoting a second railway.

Another argument against rail transportation, despite the fact that shipping was tied up in the winter months, was that notwithstanding the all year round capability of railways the biggest markets for Prince Edward County were then across the lake via United States ports. Here the railway could not compete.

In keeping with the Loyalist and military background of their forefathers, not so remote then, uncompromising support of the Tory party was traditional. Most of the railway supporters were Tories, but even that was not enough to overcome the local reluctance.

Chas. Bockus.
Deceased, Picton.

Charles Bockus

Historical Atlas — Mika Reprint

In the 1860's came the first positive hope for a railway, with a new leader of the railway supporters in the person of Charles Bockus, a wealthy and highly respected citizen. Born in Gananoque, east of Kingston, Ontario on December 30th, 1802, he had an unusual career. He came to Picton at the age of 27 years and opened a store, and according to the words of a writer for the Belden Atlas of Hastings and Prince Edward Counties "his business grew to immense magnitude". In 1836, at the age of 34 years, he was elected to the then parliament of Upper Canada. In confirmation of his considerable ability, in the second year of his first term he became chairman of the Finance Committee. To the general regret of the people of Prince Edward County, in 1843, "for reasons of business" he resigned his seat and moved to Montreal. After an absence of thirty years, partly spent in the United States, he returned to Picton, about 1872. His youngest daughter was married and lived in Picton. Apparently his family had never given up their association with the county.

Charles Bockus is said to have moved in high financial circles in Boston and had many contacts in that city, among them may well have been Jay Cooke, the J. P. Morgan of his day.

At seventy years of age, Bockus could have been expected to retire and enjoy the company of his friends and the peaceful life of the county, but that was not his style. The proposed railway caught his imagination and before long he made the cause of the "railway maniacs" his own. With great energy, much tact, and all his influence and prestige he led the crusade. Even when he felt that there was enough support to make a start, there still remained a significant and determined opposition, particularly from townships through which the railway lines were unlikely to pass.[2]

Bockus' deputy in the railway enterprise was Lt. Col. Walter Ross, M.P., a Liberal, whose son his daughter had married. Some seventeen years younger than Bockus he had an important part to play. A Scottish immigrant, like many others of his race he had worked hard and with considerable success. He began with a dry-goods store and eventually owned a big store in Picton.[3]

For many years Ross had been the chairman and largest stockholder of the Ontario and Quebec Navigation Company, so the prospect of a railway did not frighten him. His military rank came as Commanding Officer of the 16th Regiment of Volunteers, a militia regiment of high reputation. He had been the elected member from the area for several years and secured a place in Canadian history by having sat as a member of the Dominion's first parliament.[4]

Those who had been fighting the apparently hopeless railway battle for so many years were heartened by this new leadership.

In the early '70's, the first serious attempt was made to promote the railway company. This seems to have been, in part, a trial run to ascertain how much financial support could be expected from the county in municipal and county grants and in individual investment. Unfortunately the plan proposed was too grandiose. The hostile reaction was not entirely emotional, people were shrewd enough to see that much of the proposed

mileage was unlikely to be profitable. Indeed, had the line been built as proposed the company would probably have failed.

The suggested line was to run from the Village of Trenton, a few miles north of the projected Murray Canal. A mile and a half beyond that community there was to be a junction with the Grand Trunk Railway (now the Canadian National main line) whose first through train from Toronto to Montreal had stopped there on October 27th, 1856. This proposal was realistic but after that less reasonable proposals were made. The line was to continue through some small but active settlements to Long Point, the south-eastern tip of the county and the proposed terminus, of the 1853 project.

Colonel Ross

Long Point was a small fishing harbour. To turn it into a commercial port would have cost a great deal of money. That district had little else to offer in the way of traffic for the line. Cynically labelled even yet as "hungry acres", the land is marginal for farming, suitable for grazing only if there is sufficient rainfall. Understandably the inhabitants of that area were quick to take offence at such descriptions, after all they made a living there.

The surveyor offered two routes to Long Point, one located closer to the shoreline. The mileage figures were 48.75 and 50.62 respectively. The cost, presumably of the longer line, was given as $658,961, the odd dollars, by no means a forgotten custom, giving a misleading impression of scrupulous accuracy. The surveyor's name, appropriate for his profession, was Legge.

Whatever Legge's professional abilities, he was, if wordy in the style of the times, a high-pressure promoter, sufficiently so that the two local newspapers supported the project enthusiastically and County Council granted the considerable bonus subsidy of $87,500 when the company should be incorporated, and on the understanding that construction would be started within nine months.

Will Hume, a worthy character, a mate on schooners and a renowned balladeer, saw the Long Point extension this way. (Unfortunately only one verse has survived.) He figured two trains a year would look after all the freight from that area:

"One load in the fall this train will draw
    and one load in the spring besides.
The one in the fall to pull out rye straw,
    and the one in the spring, cowhides."

There is reason to believe that other verses were even less flattering to Long Point. The song had another purpose.

In those years Milford was one of the busiest centres in Prince Edward County. It was a rip-roaring settlement with four hotels, whose bars did a land-rush business quenching the thirsts of schooner-men and shipyard workers from nearby Port Milford, as well as lumbermen, millworkers and farmers for many miles around, including the citizens of Long Point. Now the county people were much given to feuding, and not by means of sullen silences and dirty looks, but as an opportunity for open, joyous donnybrooks with full community participation.

Will Hume chose Empey's Hotel for the first performance of his celebrated ballad and sang it lustily while standing on a table. Politely waiting for his song to end Will's supporters and the Long Pointers joined in battle royal. History does not record who won this epic battle but undoubtedly there was a bumper harvest of black eyes, broken noses and missing teeth and perhaps a cracked skull or two. Empey's bar was totally and completely wrecked.[5]

Our balladeer died comparatively young of tuberculosis. He left as his memorial some fine stone fences that he built.

What influence the ballad had is not known but the more practical of the railway supporters did reject the proposals for the extension to Long Point. Charles Bockus and his associates now prepared plans for a 34-mile line from Picton to Trenton.[6]

The Bill incorporating the company and the authority to build the line was passed by the Provincial Legislature on March 29th, 1873, a few months short of the sixth year of Confederation.

With the economy of North America at a new peak of prosperity this seemed to be the best of times to get started. Other promoters thought the same elsewhere in Ontario and Quebec. These proposals seemed to be numerous at the time, but the great railway expansion in Canada was yet to come. As to the public controversies over the projected Canadian Pacific Railway, these were of small interest in Prince Edward County compared to the proposed local line. In fact, the Canadian Pacific did not run trains through Trenton and Belleville until forty years later.

That summer an accurate survey was made under the direction of a Mr. Hayes. Apart from one deep cut, and three lesser ones in the vicinity of Consecon, the engineering would be light and the grades easy. A difficulty that was encountered during construction was a swampy basin in the limestone rock, known as Hillier swamp. It would be forty years before it would be finally stabilized.

That summer a contractor was selected, William Macdonald of Kingston. He began assembling his equipment on the docks ready to ship it by water to Picton as soon as he got the go-ahead.

On September 8th, Col. Ross' wife appropriately turned the first ceremonial sod. It seemed the Prince Edward County Railway would soon be under construction.

A week later came disaster, not only for Prince Edward County, but for the entire North American continent. It started in the United States when Jay Cooke, the man financing the Northern Pacific, their second western transcontinental railroad, went broke. He had believed he could succeed. The bubble burst on September 18th and his bank closed its door and the railroad went bankrupt. The depression that followed was the worst North America had yet experienced.

The repercussions spread, and as with many bigger projects elsewhere, work on the county railway, little as it was at that time, stopped completely. The Kingston contractor held on for a while before he withdrew from this commitment.

On November 5th that year John A. Macdonald, Canada's first prime minister, resigned over the Pacific Railway scandal. On January 22nd, 1874 the Liberal opposition took office. It was a gloomy event for many people in the county although the event does not seem to have had any direct influence on the fortunes of the local line. Also, Col. Ross happened to be a Liberal.

Tired of waiting and having second thoughts in those hard times, County Council repealed the by-law in order to cancel the bonus. Charles Bockus, the company's principal shareholder with some of the other shareholders, Col. Ross, Robert Boyle and Philip Low, countered through the courts but lost their case.

Sadly, Charles Bockus who had done just about everything to promote the railway died on January 10th, 1878. A short street in Picton is named after him.

The hopes for a railway line to Picton seemed to have ended.

Chapter Two

The world of the 1870's was almost as uneasy as it would be a hundred years later. That decade had started with Bismarck's army overrunning France with ruthless efficiency.

In 1877 Britain had annexed the unwilling Boer republic of the Transvaal, a happening of considerable future consequence. But nobody worried overly much about these things, particularly in Canada. The British empire was by far the strongest single world power.

The only reservation, a bitter thought to many, had been the British governments indecent haste in giving way to United States demands on extremely important border disputes. Nonetheless, the loyal people of the County held neither the Queen, nor the Union Jack accountable, and remained as proud as ever of the might of the British Empire.

In Canada railways were in an early stage of development compared to the United States. One could travel from Windsor through Toronto and Montreal to board a transatlantic liner at Portland, Me., all on the Grand Trunk Railway. The first through train to Halifax did not make the journey until 1876.

By 1878 the Canadian Pacific Railway was now under construction from what is now Thunder Bay to Winnipeg. The main line west from that Manitoba city had also been started.

In Prince Edward County, when 1878 came round, times were a great deal more prosperous. Although rumours abounded, for and against, the railway cause seemed to remain hopeless. When Charles Bockus died in the early months of that year it had seemed this was the end of the idea. His kinsman, Col. Walter Ross, M.P., now took over as the leader of the "railway maniacs".

The first sign of renewed activity, sufficient to start another hubbub of rumours, was an advertisement. On March 29th, in the Picton Gazette, "The Prince Edward R.R." wanted "100 Cords of Beech and Maple Body Wood for which the Highest Market Price would be paid."

Before long the promoter was soon pressuring County Council to extend the time limit on the bonus (now reduced to $60,000) from October 15th, 1878, by one year. Otherwise construction of the line was obviously impossible. The weight of the rails was already stipulated as 56 lbs. per yard, standard for all recent construction of branch or country lines, and not a few more important routes.

County Council met in the Shire Hall, Picton, where it still meets, on June 15th. It was a long and troubled meeting. The majority representing those townships that would not be reached by the railway were dead against it. Here was their chance to fight again where they had been defeated seven years earlier.

Another meeting was held on June 25th to continue what had become a bitter wrangle.

One impressive argument of the promoters, though it was not part of their brief, was that in summertime when travel was easy it would take longer to travel by stage coach and ferry to Belleville to catch the train for Toronto then it would be to go by train from Picton to Toronto.

The railway case was finally won by a single vote, and only because W. R. Dempsey, Reeve of Ameliasburgh, an anti-railway township, believing sincerely that the County generally would benefit in the end, "crossed the floor". The amendment to the by-law was passed, but one-third of the line would have to be graded by the old deadline, October 15th, 1878.

The following night the promoters gave a banquet to celebrate their victory at Picton's Cosmopolitan Hotel.

Hoping to heal some recent wounds the

guests of honour were the members of County Council. Conspicuously absent was W.R. Dempsey. This event was hosted by Philip Low, Q.C., long a shareholder in the enterprise and who with others had been pressing for this line for so long. Others present were Col. Ross, Warden Samuel N. Smith of Sophiasburgh and many other still well-known County names, (See Appendices) sat down to the "well-filled festive board."

There followed innumerable toasts and speeches. Warden Smith, who had been in opposition, accepted the defeat graciously. Philip Low read a telegram from a new contractor accepting tentative conditions. His name was Alexander Manning of the firm of Manning and MacDonald of Toronto. The last of the toasts "The Press" was responded to by S.M. Conger, the respected editor and publisher of *The Picton Gazette*. Next day his paper would describe the evening as a "feast of reason and a flow of soul." Next day it is likely that many souls sincerely regretted the flow and found reason an intolerable chore.

Mr. Conger certainly does not seem to have been affected. The same edition of his newspaper headlined joyously "P.E.C.R.R. AT LAST" and "WE ARE AWAKENING FROM OUR RIP VAN WINKLE SLEEP". There was, however, an unfortunate sequence to that single deciding vote of W.R. Dempsey.[1]

Apparently as soon as the voting was completed he had been accused of taking a bribe from the promoters. An honourable man, he was profoundly shocked. Belief in his guilt soon spread through the county. It was also said that others had received inducement to vote for the railway. Dempsey was defeated at the next election. Inevitably this began to prey on his mind.

According to George W. McMullen (who was to take an active part in the railway), when he spoke to the press of this matter some 36 years later (March, 1914) at the time of Dempsey's death, he said that he was able to intervene on Dempsey's behalf.

By 1881, McMullen was to be in a position to know all the transactions of the railway company. As he now said, "... beyond doubt questionable means had been resorted to for the purpose of securing the needed votes to amend the By-law." He said that this knowledge was "pretty general", and although defending Mr. Dempsey noted that if Dempsey had not voted the

way he did probably many more years would have passed before the railway was built.

Some two years later, McMullen had encountered Dempsey in Trenton, and Dempsey had told him that the vote he had made had cost him dearly. Now he could not attend a single public meeting without feeling the finger of scorn being pointed at him. He told McMullen, "you are probably the only man who can clear up this matter and put me back where I was." McMullen promised to see what he could do for him.

Without saying anything to Dempsey, McMullen attended the Township of Ameliasburgh's next nomination meeting. Dempsey was not present and he gave those at the meeting the truth, pointing out it was hardly right to condemn Dempsey for a far-sighted proper course! He concluded "... that they should make him feel that he was restored to their confidence."

Dempsey was, of course, delighted when he learned of this. The following year he was elected reeve again, and by acclamation. He held that office for three consecutive terms. Later he ran for the Ontario Legislature and won by a large majority.[2]

The next event, and it was an important one, was the first public meeting of the Prince Edward County shareholders. It turned out there were only thirteen of them. A great deal more information became available to the public for the first time.

Most early Canadian railways started off desperately short of capital. All depended on public funds from various levels of government, but few companies could have had so little ready cash at the close of a decade of hard trying.

At this meeting, already public knowledge, the amount of $700,000 had been the capital needed. The first business of the meeting was to reduce this to $300,000, because, so it was earnestly maintained, it would now be much cheaper to build the line. The truth was, that amount of money could not be raised. Their only hope would be some bank or bond house would take this amount in debentures, the equivalent of a first mortgage — if it could be built, and that their stocks take second place. The list of stockholders* and the amounts subscribed, also released at this meeting show the harsh realities of their financial situation.

See Appendices

17

The list starts with the largest single holding and this is something of a mystery. It was held in trust by Robert Boyle, publisher and proprietor of *The Picton Times,* for an unnamed owner; 810 shares of what all the shares were, $100 certificates. Walter Ross held a hundred shares for the estate of his late father-in-law Charles Bockus. His father, the Colonel, and Philip Low, Q.C. held a modest ten shares apiece; as did nine others. A total of thirteen shareholders.[3]

This represented a total of $102,000, not very much money to build a thirty-mile railway and to equip it. But in cold cash this was a good deal less. Only 10% had been subscribed, the rest being hopefully on call basis at another 10% each time. Their real capital then was $10,200 and out of this, considerable amounts must have already been expended — including, possibly, "votes purchased".

Plainly the purchase of the stock was considered more of an act of faith in the county than a shrewd investment.

Three more sources were being combed for financial assistance besides the Village of Wellington. They were the Ontario government, the Town of Picton, and the Village of Trenton, the northern terminus of the line.

Alex Manning, the contractor, was present at this meeting. According to a newspaper report he "very kindly rendered valuable assistance in all arrangements." This is the first intimation of an engaging personality.

Several important motions were passed at the meeting:

(1) The $300,000 debentures to be used as cash by the contractor (when raised).

Original 42 lb steel, P.E.C. Rly. — And not badly worn! 1978   *Photo, Author*

(2) The directors were authorized to enter into a contract with Alex Manning.

(3) All aid, bonuses etc., be turned over to the contractor.

Manning now proved that he was the man to get things done. He promised to be back in a few days with his surveyors so that by the time the Picton and Wellington bonuses became law he would be ready to put his men to work grading the line.

He had little choice for he would have to work fast to get one third of the grading done by the October deadline set by the County — even to minimum standards.

The directors met afterwards and voted for a further call of ten per cent on the shares.

These historic meetings closed, to quote the editorial version, on a problem, concerning one W.S. Macdonald of Kingston "... and last, *but not least,* was a preparation for shutting off the *wind* of a *pretended* stockholder, who has at various times and occasions caused more or less trouble." The steps taken were more mundane, the formation of a committee to take legal action. Was this Macdonald the contractor of 1873, who was left stranded with his equipment on the docks of that city?

The Picton Gazette, likely with inside information, remarked in the same editorial, "In all probability as soon as the road is built Mr. Manning will lease it to the Grand Trunk Railway for a term of years." This was normal practice; building a short line and leasing, or selling, it at a profit (or at a loss to escape a greater loss) to a bigger company. This long editorial ends appropriately: ". . . and the result is beyond peradventure."

From now on the newspaper would refer to the line as "Our Railway".

The appointment by County Council, not by the stockholders, of Col. Ross, as president, his son Walter as secretary, and Stephen Niles as vice-president showed where the power was — but only at this stage.[4]

When the question of the weight of the rails came up before County Council is not recorded. There are some interesting pine rail patterns in the Shire Hall, part of a switch, which may well have been the evidence used in making a future petition. It is known the Provincial Legislature cleared the matter first. Manning's case, and there is good reason to believe him, was that there would be no railway if money had to be found for 56 lb. rail. He now requested the by-law be modified to authorize 42 lb. rail, which was pretty light, even for those years. With the smaller locomotives to ride this rail, loads would be smaller and operations costlier. County Councillors seemed to have given in quickly.

In Picton, as the vote on the bonus came closer, there was much argument as to where the station should be located. There were some that advocated that this should be located down at the harbour. While it would have involved a steeper gradient than existed anywhere else on the line, it was feasible. The line would have to be located through or past the town cemetery, along the bank of a small stream. Others advocated one in the centre of the town. The railway company thus would have found the line cheaper to build, no gradient to operate, but freight transshipments to and from the steamers would be costly, which would mean less revenue for the railway. Most

seemed to have favoured the centre of town, as more convenient to passengers.

On August 16th, the *Gazette* editor was pleased to observe, "In the meantime McMurdock and his staff of surveyors are pushing on the work of locating with a view to an early start with the grading of the road, showing that the contractor is going on with the work in good faith."

A week later came news that diverted attention from the railway. There was to be a Federal Election on September 18th, and Col. Ross had decided not to run this time.

Tory Prince Edward had high hopes that John A. Macdonald, Canada's first Prime Minister, out of power these past five years, would be elected this time. There was a personal touch to this, for years before John A. had practiced law in Hallowell (Picton), and here had held his first public office, as secretary of the town school board.

The famous scandal over the incorporation of the Canadian Pacific Railway had been Macdonald's downfall. The Liberals had charged that the charter to build the Canadian Pacific Railway had been given to Sir Hugh Allan in return for large campaign contributions. A Royal Commission found the charges to be true. According to Pierre Berton, in his book "The National Dream" one of the leading figures that brought about the political disaster was George W. McMullen of Picton. Berton does not offer a very attractive portrait of him.

During the weeks before the election the *Picton Gazette* focussed again on the controversy over the location of the town station, and took a much sterner line. "Now, the question of paramount importance is first to secure the building of the railroad and in due course all matters of detail will assuredly follow. But what is now apparently agitating the minds of many is the location of the depot: and we might say it is the intention and wish of the Board [of Directors] as well as the Contractor, to make the station as convenient and accessible as possible for all concerned, and if the natural obstacles in getting to the water can with any reasonable outlay be overcome, most assuredly will be done." This editorial concluded "if the cost was in excess of the town's bonus, it was presumed that no one would be so unreasonable as to insist upon it."

Towards the end of August, Wellington passed its bonus by-law, a modest $2,500. There was a rider, and an understandable one, that it would not be payable until the line was finished and equipped with rolling stock. This was, however, not the kind of security the railway company could borrow against.

The Picton bonus was ratified by a vote on September 6th; $20,000 was a useful contribution to the line. Nothing was stipulated about the site of the station. Alex Manning had also gained the reputation of an honest man. For the ratepayers, in terms of what a dollar was then worth, they were paying a good deal more than the rest of the county residents for the line — two mills, or one dollar for every $500 of investment.

When the federal elections were over John A. Macdonald was once again in power. Whatever the rejoicing, this made no difference to the fortunes of the county railway.

In the same edition that listed the election returns, September 20th, the Gazette carried the heading "CLEAR THE TRACK WHEN THE BELL RINGS!" It was announced that the contract had been signed with Alex. Macdonald and the work of grading commenced early in the afternoon and evening of the same day, Tuesday.

The Monday before, the steamer "Empress of India" had docked in Picton and unloaded thirty-two horses and the necessary and complete outfit of carts, wagons, scrapers, and other tools, belonging to Alexander Manning. By Friday, the grading had reached a mile past the town limits, the day before the newspaper published on September 20th.

(FOLIO I) Pattern of 42 lb. rail preserved in The County Hall in Picton. These pine patterns were used, it is believed, to convince the County Council of that day that this light rail was a practical substitute for 56 lb. rail.

Photo, Jack Chiang, Courtesy Tom Walker, County Secretary

A low-key admission of error which would eventually become a storm, "Our only regret is that the Contractor finds it is impracticable to comply with the wishes of a large majority of the townspeople" to put the station near the centre of the town.

Instead it was now to be sited on the town's outer limits, south of the town, the remotest corner from every facet of the town's business. But the editor refused to admit anything more than that, maintaining the new site was "the next best thing." His ending to the editorial this time was "Look out friends for the iron horse, early next spring. Hip, hip, hurrah!" He was optimistic.

By October 4th, as the deadline became closer, grading was underway over Waring's Farm, near the stone house, which still stands at what is still known as Waring's Corners on County Road One and Highway 33. It was also reported that the surveying party had met with obstacles (unspecified) of more or less magnitude between Wellington and Melville, but had at last found "a very eligible route crossing the stream a little east of Melville." Not long after, the grading was reported to be five miles from Picton, short of the deadline.

In the same issue, the editor of the Gazette took time off from railway matters to give the Colonel the back of his hand over some political happenings. In the last days of the Liberal government he was off to Ottawa to ask Prime Minister Mackenzie for a seat in the Senate (in Canada a political appointment, not an elected office). ". . . we cannot believe that that gentleman had the cheek to ask for government office. The country has paid him well for all the services he ever performed, and does not owe him anything. His son has been well provided for in the Customs here, and we cannot believe his mission to Ottawa had a sinister object in view." With this punch line the editor concluded ". . . that coveted Senatorship, which he is not likely to get."

By October 16th the line does not seem to have been one-third graded. Neither The Gazette nor County Council seems to have objected. By October 11th, he had twenty-five teams of horses at work and the grading crew had grown considerably. If the County was to have a railway there was nothing to be gained by ruining the contractor. More likely County Council had enough other business to look after and did not want any more showdowns like the last one.

The same month the contractor announced that plans had been made for the winter. A little under three miles from Picton, 90 acres of woodland had been purchased. Houses for the men and stables for the horses would be provided once the ground was too frozen to work. Already the woods were being cleared at the rate of one acre a day to provide timber for the following year. The site, so it was planned, would provide for the shops, etc., for the railway.

By mid-November, thirteen miles had been graded, more than the third demanded. The only ungraded part of the route was on which side to pass Lake Consecon; inland, or on the Lake Ontario side which contained Consecon village of that name and a natural harbour? The latter seemed the obvious choice and was the one taken. Maybe this was an attempt to shake out another bonus!

The last news items reported for the year, 1878, was at the annual meeting of the railway company. There was good news. Fifteen miles had finally been graded. The Village of Trenton had not only granted a bonus of $10,000 but had also provided the right-of-way through the village. And there was some strange news.

The call for ten per cent on the shares already held had not been met. This included the President, Walter Ross (he did not get a Senatorship) and the vice-president S.P. Niles. Nonetheless both were returned to office.

The resolution was also passed, apparently without any debate, that their stocks should be forfeited. The real owner, as he seemed to have become earlier, was confirmed, Alex Manning the contractor. Evidently there had been a private deal beforehand. Ross and Niles continued in office, a useful front in maintaining local identity.

By then the workers and the horses were in their winter quarters, busy logging out the small forest. Like the ships in the harbour, there was nothing else to do but carry out repairs and wait for the spring.

Chapter Three

Through the winter months John Haney, the superintendent, had been getting ready for a quick start at the first sign of spring of 1879. This would be in strong contrast to the hurried improvisations of the previous summer. Now he could prove he was a man of exceptional ability.

Back in January on the first Monday and Tuesday, forty carloads of new British 42 lb. steel rail, (in those years rated in strength as the equivalent in strength to 50 lbs. of North American rail) had been unloaded at the Grand Trunk's Trenton station a few miles north of the settlement. On that same Tuesday another twenty cars arrived. There would be more to follow. The Trenton *Courier* observed, "We may shortly hear the whistle of an engine through our village."

While tracklaying was expected to start from Trenton sometime in May, it could have been earlier, for Picton harbour was open to shipping on April 26th. This work had been sub-contracted.

By June 2nd, progress had been rapid, several miles of track had been laid and even more important a junction had been made up a short, sharp gradient with the Grand Trunk at what became known as Trenton Junction. This layout has been much changed since.

The contractor's first locomotive arrived, it seems as soon as this rail connection had been made, that was the day Trenton residents heard their first locomotive whistle within the village. The engine house was ready, having been built by one McKillam McKinnon, but was not yet accessible to the locomotive, as the contractor had yet to finish the turntable and its pit — a hard task in mid-winter.

By the end of June, the long low pile trestle across the western end of Lake Consecon was well underway. It was around a third of a mile long and the costliest engineering project on the line. Some years later it would disappear under earth fill. Later yet a new road bed on a narrower crossing to the west, would be constructed. Once this was completed the locomotive would be able to haul the construction train carrying rails and ties to the end of the grading.[1]

Already the track gang had quite a way to catch up. In the meantime John Haney had taken his grading crew to Wellington to resume the grading to Bloomfield. This had ceased the previous year because of demands by a few farmers who wanted premium prices for their land. It had been planned for the track-laying crews to catch up by mid-July.

The stations were close to being ready. The one at Picton, said to be "a commodious structure", was built by two gentlemen whose descendents live in Prince Edward County today, T.G. Carson and Thomas Love. The other stations, staffed by agents, were at Bloomfield, Wellington, Consecon, and, of course, Trenton. There were also three flag stations. (See the reproduction of the first timetable.)

The last week of June had also seen the arrival of Manning's second locomotive. This should ensure there were no delays as far as motive power was concerned, whether by break-downs or for routine maintenance.

During the same month there had come "a cloud no bigger than a man's hand." If the County people had been aware of the news item there was little reason for them to be interested. In that considerable region north of Trenton, long believed to be rich in mineral deposits, the Belleville *Intelligencer* reported the owners (un-named) of a large and rich deposit of red hematite were negotiating its sale to an unnamed ironmaster in the United States. Railways covering part of this area had recently been opened under the control of the Grand Trunk, putting that company in the best position to further tap this area which also had considerable resources in timber.

Trenton had long sought to rival the bigger and more affluent Belleville. So the Trentonians were now looking north for the future, which at present was not encouraging. Plainly the Prince Edward County Railway was an end in itself, that would, if anything, take traffic away from Trenton's port facilities. In any case that company was not in a financial position to inspire even the most optimistic dreams for any northward extensions.

While the County railway could not be described as rich, plainly there were now sufficient funds available to finish the line properly. These additional funds had become available from the Province of Ontario in the form of a government subsidy, the Railway Aid Fund, at the rate of $4,000 a mile, a bonanza for this under-financed project. Manning seems to have had friends in the right places and knew how to treat with them. As was to be expected, this had caused much grumbling among jealous neighbours. Development lines were needed north of the Grand Trunk where in that rocky countryside construction was costly compared to the flat tableland of Prince Edward County. Anyway the government budget for subsidies had pretty well run out by the time others had got their applications in.[2]

Total subsidies for the railway now amounted to $7,000 a mile, which was a high figure for those years. The principal engineering works made a small total: the Consecon bridge, the four cuts, one of fair size and length, to be known by the railroaders as Taylor's, Consecon, Pettingill's and Pye's. These were narrow and in winter would quickly fill with snow to block the passage of trains. All were situated between Carrying Place and Hillier. The ruling grade was out of Consecon Lake towards Picton where the line climbed towards the limestone plateau that is the substance of Prince Edward County. Nearer Wellington, Hillier swamp gave a good deal of trouble to the construction crews, and would do so for many years. Double width ties would be tried. Even then the effect of passing trains was such that the fence by the tracks shook so much with each passing train that it was not possible to sit on it. This was eventually cured by mattresses of brush and gravel. The route had no sharp curves.[3]

Early in July the Trenton newspaper reported two small disasters. Patrick English had a rail drop on his foot and he lost his "large and next toe". The newspaper did not report what Patrick said when it happened. After that Engineer P.

Mayo "drove his hand through the window of the engine, getting his hand badly cut." This may have been an act of frustration from watching the clumsy trackworkers. The newspaper concluded cheerfully that both were doing well under medical care.

Apparently no lives were lost in the construction of the line, though it is not possible to be certain as complete newspaper files are not available.

It was not until the first week in August that the Hillier area saw its first train — thirteen cars. The sub-contractor laying the track had failed hopelessly after a first burst of energy, so the tireless Haney had taken over that task as well. It was estimated that the failure of the sub-contractor had delayed completion of the line by three to four weeks. Yet Haney, working night and day, had the rails laid to Wellington by August 19th — quite a feat.[4] What is more, when the line had been finished he would say he could have done it sooner had it been necessary.

By the end of August the line had been graded to Bloomfield where they met the right-of-way that had been completed the previous year. In a few days now, as *The Picton Gazette* exulted, the line would be "railed" to Picton and the "bullgine" could then be "closely examined and admired".

By September 27th, the line, buildings etc. were finished. Much of the line had already been passed by the inspectors of the Federal Government, only the newer sections remained to be approved.

For a new line the roadbed must have been good, even discounting the unprofessional enthusiasm of a Gazette reporter. He had travelled over the ballasted line in mid-September at the rate of seven miles in six minutes, 70 miles an hour and on a construction train at that! A couple of months later, after the line was in business, there was a strong rumour that a train had made fifteen miles in ten minutes — 75 miles an hour. Such claims can only be accepted for what they are, legends.

At some date, not known, it was announced the real owner of the line, Alexander Manning, would lease the property to the local company with its original officers. The headquarters would therefore remain in Picton.

October 7th, 1879 was to be the day of the official opening, a week ahead of the date to qualify for the $60,000 Prince Edward County bonus. Four days before this, with the exception of some "twenty or thirty" men needed for the finishing touches, all the construction crews were paid off. Regular scheduled services would come a little later, it was expected in another ten days.

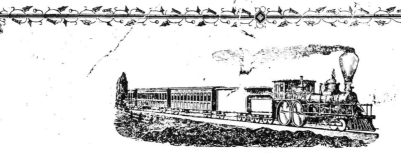

(Form No. 6.)

PRINCE EDWARD COUNTY RAILWAY.

TIME TABLE.

TO TAKE EFFECT ON

THURSDAY, NOV. 27TH, 1879.

(TRAINS RUN ON MONTREAL TIME.

MILES.						
		Leave	Kingston,			6:00 a.m.
		"	Montreal,		10: 0 p.m.	
		"	Toronto,			7:35 "
		Leave	Trenton Junction,		7:30 a.m.	1:00 p.m.
	1-6	"	Trenton,		7:37 "	1:10 "
6-6	5-0	"	*Carrying Place,		7:52 "	1:28 "
10-9	4-3	"	Consecon,		8:04 "	1:41 "
15-7	4-8	"	*Hillier,		8:23 "	2:07 "
17-7	2-0	"	*Four Corners,		8:28 "	2:15 "
12-2	3-?	"	Wellington,		8:40 "	2:38 "
28-0	6-8	"	Bloomfield,		9:03 "	3:00 "
31-8	3-8	"	Picton,	Arrive.	9:15 "	3:15 "

MILES.					A. M.	P. M.
		Leave	Picton,		9:45	4:00
	3-8	"	Bloomfield,		9:57	4:12
10-6	6-8	"	Wellington,		10:18	4:35
14-1	3 5	"	*Four Corners,		10:30	4:46
16-1	2-0	"	*Hillier,		10:35	4:54
20-9	4-8	"	Consecon,		10:54	5:18
25-2	4-3	"	*Carrying Place.		11:06	5:31
30-2	5-0	"	Trenton,		11:22	5:50
31-8	1-6	"	Trenton Junction,	Arrive.	11:30	6:00
			Toronto,	Arrive.		11:15
			Kingston,	"	1:55 p.m.	11:00
			Montreal,	"	9:00	

Flag Stations, stop only on signal.

The P. E. Co. Railway Company, while endeavoring to make close connection with trains east west at Trenton Junction, will not be responsible for any failure in so doing, neither will they be nsible for the times of arrivals and departures mentioned in the above table, at places beyond the of their Line.

JOHN HANEY,
General Manager.

1879 The First Timetable, Prince Edward County Railways

The stage was set for the grand climax — the official opening ceremonies. Instead it was anti-climactic. No bands, no processions, no banners, no V.I.P.'s, only local "notables", no ceremonies at all in Picton — instead there was a banquet in Wellington and this was in honour of the contractor. The Village of Wellington "did them proud" with good food served in a large tent erected on open ground near the station. The weather was perfect.

Two special trains ran from Trenton and Picton arriving in the evening, Wellington being, by coincidence, in tenths of a mile, the mid-point between the two towns. The train from the north carried the 'dignitaries' from such places as Belleville, made the journey with several stops in one hour to arrive just ahead of the train from Picton. The locomotive on the Trenton train was the "Toronto", the bigger of the two. There were reports that the track was exceptionally smooth.

The locomotive that drew the train from Picton was "Picton". Both may have been the machines used in the construction of the line. Some of the passenger cars were rented from the Grand Trunk. The invited guests, 200 in all, rode free.

The banquet itself seems to have been successful enough if one enjoyed hearing many speeches. It was expected in those days.

S.P. Niles, as Vice-President, started the proceedings with a short speech to be followed by the usual toasts and responses. Lt. Col. Walter Ross, the President, followed him. Then came Alexander Manning who had made the railway possible. Unfortunately the only newspaper report available for reference that gave an account of these happenings did not go into detail, as to what the speakers had to say. This was the *Daily Ontario* of Belleville, which ended its report with the observation that Wellington could become a popular resort with its miles of sandy beaches nearby, if suitable accommodation were built for vacationers.[5]

Perhaps the lack of ceremony or celebrations in Picton was because of a growing ill-temper over the station site. When the line came into use, and the inconvenience became even more apparent, this irritation grew. Their newspaper had besought them to trust the contractor. They had. Now they felt that they had been "conned" by the contractor who had scooped up their bonus fast enough.

Prince Edward County Railway.

Picton, 1 April 1881

Prince Edward County Railway Letterhead

More remote and somewhat acid was the editor of the *North Hastings Review* of Madoc which had only recently got its own railway. "Excursions are now the order of the day from Picton," and he sniffed, "The thing is new to them." Maybe he did not receive an invitation to the banquet.

The final government inspection of the line was on October 9th, by a Mr. Shanley, one of two brothers, among the ablest and most famous of many Canadian railway contractors. Which brother this was, none of the sources available have recorded. Anyway he passed the line without requiring extensive work before it could be opened to the public. In those years that was quite a compliment.

A few days later the Warden of Prince Edward County handed over the cheque for the much fought over subsidy of $60,000. This was believed to be the largest cheque that had been handled at that time by the Picton Branch of the Bank of Montreal.

More events were coming fast. On October 23rd, it was announced that John Haney would be the General Manager, an obvious condition of Manning's lease.

Next the station agents were appointed: Trenton: C.C. Dench; Consecon: W.M. Marrow; Bloomfield: Ab. Spencer; Wellington: N.S. Harrington; Picton: John Feehan. The flag stations were of course unmanned.

It is understood that there were three sections on the line, the section foreman for the Picton end was John Hyatt.

The line opened for public traffic on

Monday, October 27th, 1879. The first train at Picton was in charge of Conductor R. Hamilton. John Berry was the engineer. George Neunn fed the cordwood into the firebox.

The equipment owned by the railway company was minimal, said to be two locomotives, two passenger cars and two flatcars — just a beginning. The rest of their traffic needs would have to be filled by using rented equipment, including baggage cars.

From opening day business was brisk. Freight traffic "exceeded the expectation of management". The amount of passenger business was described as an agreeable surprise.

The bell was ringing, the track was clear! The two locomotives whistled, rattled, roared and snorted their way through the countryside to tell the world that the County had its railway — at last.

Chapter Four

We have at hand that much used but yet to be invented time machine. Let us go back to the early spring of 1880. It is 7:15 a.m. and the sun is shining. There is frost in the air and still some snow on the ground. The place: Trenton Junction.

You are, of course, invisible — with neither speech nor substance but you do possess all your other senses — at times with regret. It is cold waiting on the platform. The east and westbound trains of the Grand Trunk have met here and pulled out a few minutes ago. A dozen or so passengers from both trains are waiting for the Picton train.

Presently she can be heard to the east of the station as the sound of the Montreal train dies away, backing noisily up the grade to the junction itself. She reverses, and clanks and rattles towards us, a lean looking locomotive with a high diamond stack and with her tender piled with cordwood, pushing a baggage car and a coach. She slowly passes, bell ringing, to stop with much creaking of brakes and giving off a smoky perfume, that of maple logs, mixed with oily steam. The coach has open platforms at each end.

The conductor steps down from the rear platform, with its shining, brass handrails, splendid in his uniform and authoritative in manner, to welcome most of the passengers by name with such warmth that it is plain that this is where a homecoming begins. The brakeman helps the passengers aboard with their luggage. You make your own way aboard, thinking what unattractive clothes the people are wearing.

After the cold wind outside, the warmth from the wood stove is pleasant indeed. The smell of the hot stove enamel and fresh varnish mixed with wood smoke is not disagreeable. The small windows are disappointing, while the sight of the narrow, close-spaced, reversible seats make you thankful that you are without any physical presence!

A few minutes remain before departure time. The conductor has been assuring the passengers that the train should not be late today, for there have been complaints since the line opened. Through a window you can see the last of the mailbags, express parcels, and luggage being wheeled past to the baggage car. Most conspicuous among the several loads are some huge sample trunks that belong to a commercial traveller who is among the passengers. He is easily identified by being (it was demanded of him) over-dressed.

The conductor standing on the platform having looked at his gold pocket watch once more, nods to himself, and calls his "A-l-l a-board!" to a now deserted platform. He gives the highball to the engineer and steps on to the coach with a sure foot as the locomotive whistles and backs out from the station.

The brakeman drops off to throw the switch, waits for the train to take the Picton line, reversing the switch after it has passed, locks it with a stout brass padlock and then runs to catch up with the train. All this is nothing new to you for it is still part of everyday railroading on branch lines and in yards.

But you are at first puzzled by the size of the train crew, particularly for such a short train. When you sort them out, baggage man, mail clerk (a government employee), conductor and a brakeman, as well as the engineer and fireman, you wonder if they are all necessary. But you will be impressed by how hard they work, more so when you overhear a conversation and learn that sixteen and eighteen hour days are quite normal, six days a week.

As the train heads down the short steep grade through the Grand Trunk's small freight yard you watch the brakeman tightening up the brake wheel of the coach with a short club that he is never without. The brake wheel he is using is at the rear end of the coach, waist high on the outboard end of the platform. Throughout the journey, using strength and skill, he will apply these brakes for every scheduled stop. While the locomotive brakes would be sufficient to stop such a short train here with so many stops; applying the handbrakes saves time on a tight schedule. The flag stops and such emergencies as cattle or an obstruction on the track are communicated to him by the whistle signals from the engineer. Sometimes it can be children on the line, and a quick reaction and hard muscles may be the difference between life and death. The air brake, already invented, would not be in general use for many years yet.

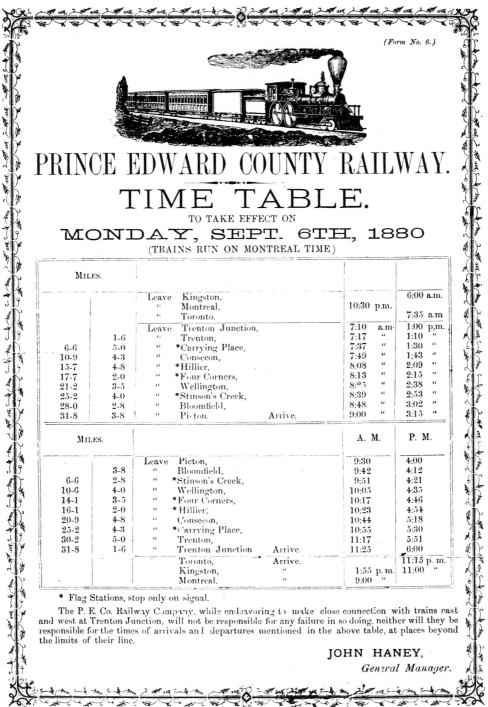

(Form No. 6.)

PRINCE EDWARD COUNTY RAILWAY.
TIME TABLE.
TO TAKE EFFECT ON
MONDAY, SEPT. 6TH, 1880
(TRAINS RUN ON MONTREAL TIME)

MILES.						
		Leave	Kingston.			6:00 a.m.
		"	Montreal.		10:30 p.m.	
		"	Toronto.			7:35 a.m
		Leave	Trenton Junction,		7:10 a.m.	1:00 p.m.
	1-6	"	Trenton,		7:17 "	1:10 "
6-6	5-0	"	*Carrying Place,		7:37 "	1:30 "
10-9	4-3	"	Consecon,		7:49 "	1:43 "
15-7	4-8	"	*Hillier,		8:08 "	2:09 "
17-7	2-0	"	*Four Corners,		8:13 "	2:15 "
21-2	3-5	"	Wellington,		8:25 "	2:38 "
25-2	4-0	"	*Stinson's Creek,		8:39 "	2:53 "
28-0	2-8	"	Bloomfield,		8:48 "	3:02 "
31-8	3-8	"	Picton.	Arrive.	9:00 "	3:15 "

MILES.					A. M.	P. M.
		Leave	Picton,		9:30	4:00
	3-8	"	Bloomfield,		9:42	4:12
6-6	2-8	"	*Stinson's Creek,		9:51	4:21
10-6	4-0	"	Wellington,		10:05	4:35
14-1	3-5	"	*Four Corners,		10:17	4:46
16-1	2-0	"	*Hillier,		10:23	4:54
20-9	4-8	"	Consecon,		10:44	5:18
25-2	4-3	"	*Carrying Place,		10:55	5:30
30-2	5-0	"	Trenton,		11:17	5:51
31-8	1-6	"	Trenton Junction	Arrive.	11:25	6:00
			Toronto,	Arrive.		11:15 p.m.
			Kingston,	"	1:55 p.m.	11:00 "
			Montreal.	"	9:00 "	

* Flag Stations, stop only on signal.

The P. E. Co. Railway Company, while endeavoring to make close connection with trains east and west at Trenton Junction, will not be responsible for any failure in so doing, neither will they be responsible for the times of arrivals and departures mentioned in the above table, at places beyond the limits of their line.

JOHN HANEY,
General Manager.

1880 Timetable & Operating Instructions

On freight trains, particularly on heavy grades, application of the hand brakes from the boxcar roof, a dangerous game, was all that prevented a runaway — and not always at that.

In those days each engineer had his own engine and, with his fireman, was responsible for all light repairs and general maintenance, usually after a long day on the road. The fireman had to keep the engine clean, and generally locomotives of the day shone. As far as the engineer was concerned it was *his* engine and usually there was enormous professional pride, further sparked by rivalry with his brother engineers. They often bought extra paint and brass fittings, including fancy and distinctive whistles out of their pay. On a free day they could be seen with their firemen giving their engines enough attention to make their womenfolk jealous.

RULES FOR EMPLOYEES.

Trains leaving Trenton Junction at 7:10 a.m., and Picton at 9:30 a.m., may arrive at Way Stations *three* minutes ahead of time, and leave on time.

Trains leaving Trenton Junction at 1 p.m., and Picton at 4 p.m., may arrive at Way Stations *seven* minutes ahead of time, and leave on time.

Enginemen and Conductors will use great caution at Trenton Junction, and while on the line of the Grand Trunk Railway, will promptly obey all orders of the Station Agent at that point.

Trains or Engines not to be run faster than at the rate of Six miles an hour through the Town of Trenton, and the Bell to be rung continuously while passing through, and the whistle to be used only when actually necessary, while passing through the Town of Trenton.

No Engineman to leave his Engine, whether on the main line or siding, except on very urgent necessity, and then he must leave it in charge of the fireman. and under no pretext whatever, must *both* leave the engine until it is given up to the proper person appointed to receive it. Any failure to obey this rule will meet immediate dismissal.

All trains must be run slowly over Consecon Bridge.

SIGNALS.

Two short whistles and one long whistle on approaching Trenton Station and the Junction from the East, to distinguish from G. T. R. trains.

One whistle to put on Brakes.

Two whistles, to start or let off Brakes.

Three whistles, to back up.

Four whistles, for Switch.

A number of short sharp whistles, signifying danger.

JOHN HANEY,
General Manager.

Rules For Employees

Early Excursion, P.E.C. Rly. May 27, 1880, Trenton *Courier*

Courtesy, Roy Cornish, Trenton, Ont.

For the fireman it was a long, hard apprenticeship. Feeding that load of cordwood was a back-breaker for it burned fast, and as a result brought him the extra task of re-loading the tender. Trains often stopped on the way to Picton to "wood-up." The saying was that all a fireman needed was a strong back, but that saying is supposed to have originated with trainmen who maintained a tradition of feuding with the locomotive crews.

Railroading was a dangerous occupation. Railway accidents were frequent on the entire North American continent. One contributing factor was physical exhaustion from long hours. Reactions slowed or even ceased when men simply collapsed into sleep in spite of rough-riding locomotives and cars.

There were other factors in this dangerous occupation. Look at the conductor's hands in the train you are riding as he takes the tickets. He has a

finger missing. The brakeman is worse off for he lacks two fingers and part of another.

When you boarded the train you may have noticed the couplers. Each had a bell-shaped casting with a slot in the centre into which a shackle was fitted to be held by a vertical pin that was dropped down from the top, the link-and-pin coupler, older than the steam locomotive. Beautifully simple, but the heavy link had to be lifted and guided into the slot by hand. An instrument was designed to do this but it was slow and clumsy, partly from bravado it was seldom used. Sooner or later one was almost bound to be a fraction of a second slow and another brakeman or yardman received the unofficial emblem of his profession.

Freight trains provided additional dangers, particularly in winter. Boxcars with their narrow catwalks with no handholds, only the brake wheel standing about a foot high. Failing to keep a foothold on the swaying, icy boards could mean a fall to serious injury or death; failure to set the brakes for a heavy grade meant a runaway train and a possible wreck.

More people got on the train at Trenton and a friendly, sociable atmosphere was noticeable. This camaraderie will grow all the way to our destination.

Those who have come from Toronto are eagerly questioned, for long-distance travel in those days was still not common, and a visit to the city was an event to be shared.

Those who have been away from the County for some time are even more eager to hear what had been happening there in their absence. There is a certain exclusiveness about all this.

A flag stop at Carrying Place, the site of the old portage road across the isthmus, brings up the subject of the projected Murray Canal among the passengers.

The stop at Consecon brought a lot more passengers aboard, many carrying baskets and hand luggage. At the head-end, the baggage and mail car, the railway employees were busy enough to delay the train's departure for a few minutes.

The train rumbled on across the long pile bridge, across the lake, and speeding up to tackle the grade, the exhaust echoed back from the narrow cuts that had been such a nuisance, plugging in with snow during the winter months. Although the hubbub of conversation increased many passengers, particularly the children, watched intently through the small windows, savouring every minute of the ride. For many it was still a novel experience. Some asked frequent questions of the train crew.

There are complaints to the conductor about how roughly the train rides, compared to when the line was new. He answers solemnly that the new road has to settle and that the start of the spring thaw has added to their difficulties. But Haney has the track gangs out and was already putting down fresh ballast as fast as the work train could handle it. Light cars with hard springing were not easy riding anyway.

It has begun to snow. The train rattles and clatters to the staccato syncopation of wheels and rail joints; never quite drowned out by the buzz of conversation.

A stout matron with a teenage daughter, not overly attractive, now gains your attention.

She is staring at the drummer with intense loathing and suspicion. He happens to be a respectable family man, but one suspects had he so much as remarked on the weather, she would have called the conductor. Such was the legendary reputation of the knights of the road.

What were our passengers talking about? Odds and ends of gossip, the past winter (not too severe), speculating when Picton harbour would be open, crop prospects and market prices in the United States, and so on.

You have also been watching the flat, though gently rolling countryside with a covering of old snow drifts and patches of bare ground. Not the best time of the year to see the County, but the many wooded areas and the well-kept farmhouses and barns still made it attractive.

Wellington catches your eye with its fine red brick, Georgian houses and its many trees, though bare of leaves now. The train is running parallel with the main street, along the backyards, before drawing into the station in the centre of the community.

There had been several good views of Lake Ontario, the beach fringed with broken ice and the blue water beyond. As the train leaves Wellington you get a quick glimpse of the famous sandbanks before you head inland towards Bloomfield, the last stop before Picton.

As we near the end of the journey the conductor takes a last look at his watch. He smiles proudly. The train draws in at 9:15 sharp.

You walk out of the station with the crowd making their way towards the town along a narrow, muddy road. Most are laden with bags and baskets, some are clutching children as well. Most of the horse-drawn liveries have already left. These people are too poor or too frugal to pay the fare.

There is one more conveyance to come; one of the hotel liveries, smart in paint and varnish and drawn by a matched pair of horses, the big sample trunk on the roof. As it passes our friends, the disapproving matron with her daughter, the front wheel hits a puddle to drench her with icy water. She looks up and for an instant her eyes meet those of the drummer. He receives a look of such profound malevolence that his self-confidence must have been destroyed for the rest of the day.

The time machine has run down. Your

invisibility fades and you find yourself somewhat dazed walking along Lake Street, a paved street nowadays. By the Prince Edward County garage you jump away just in time to miss being hit by a truck. A burly individual climbing down from a grader stares at you suspiciously — as if you were under the influence of alcohol — or worse. Oh well, what can you say anyway!

Chapter Five

If you had been riding the Picton train again in late November you would have found the conversation among the passengers a great deal more animated. The sole topic now was that two of the McMullen brothers, George William and J.B., members of a Picton family, had bought the line.[1] Although they were known to be well-to-do such a purchase was said to be well beyond their resources.

What would be particularly noticeable was the number of hot arguments that the McMullen name aroused. Plainly they were controversial people. But on one point there was general agreement, many new developments could now be expected but there were some strong reservations as to whether they would come to anything. One could only wait and see. The railway would continue to operate as it had during its recently completed first year, for the McMullens would not be able to exercise any control over operations for several months yet.

First Bloomfield Station, around 1900

Photo, Coll. Charles Fraleigh

Figures differ as to the first year's operations, but for a new railway business had been good with an apparent surplus over operating costs of around $2,000.

The capital structure of the line was unusual. Common stock stood at a book value of $102,000, but only $1,000 had been paid up. The preference shares, presumably all held by Manning, stood at $198,000 par value. The 6% debentures at $100,000 represented fixed interest that had to be paid. What was received by Manning for the sale of the railway is not known.

More unusual was the total amount of bonuses and subsidies received from various levels of government. These totalled $218,500, close to $6,890 a mile. Other groups seeking to promote their own railways had complained. At close to $6,890 a mile and considering the easy construction over the tableland of the County, this was a huge subsidy.

Hillier Station — 1910-12

Poor's Almanac, that compendium of information for railroad investors, from which much of this information was obtained, lists the equipment as consisting of: two locomotives, five passenger and one baggage car, plus nine freight cars (three box and six flat). For this fleet of elderly stock rent was paid — $5,400 annually — possibly to the Grand Trunk Railway.

Many years later one of the several McMullen brothers would describe the two locomotives as being worn out and practically useless. On December 2nd, shortly after the McMullens announced their purchase, the new locomotive shed in Trenton burned down. The smaller locomotive was hauled out in time, the other, the larger locomotive No. 2, was first reported as destroyed.[2] After several months, it was repaired — for better or worse.

Passenger business had been good during the summer. Excursions had added considerably to revenues. From May on, weekend excursions for half-fare return from all stations were advertised. Among the benefits claimed was that in the hot weather such a journey would prove "... an economical and pleasant restorative for invalids."

There would also be group excursions for church and fraternal organizations.

Freight traffic would develop less rapidly but again business had been good. With only the two ancient locomotives, schedules could only have been irregular. After the fire at the engine house one can only wonder why no extra locomotive was hired to help out. The passenger traffic had to have priority, however, because of the mail contracts. The future looked promising for increased freight loadings with the County's first canning factory under construction, the first of many that would be built at Picton, Bloomfield and Wellington.

Original P.E.C. Rly. Station at Trenton, Destroyed 1903   *From "Evolution of Trenton"*

There was also a contract for the coming winter of a hundred carloads of baled straw to be shipped to Boston. Providing the purchase price was within reason the McMullens had a line with a good future as it stood, given better equipment.

A problem confronting the railways of that age were train wreckers, illiterate people who feared for various reasons the fundamental changes brought by the railways. A local example came with an eight-column banner advertisement in the Trenton *Courier* that June offering the considerable reward (for those times) of $100 for information leading to the conviction of "certain evil disposed persons" who had "placed Spikes, Bolts, and other obstructions on the Prince Edward County Railway to the great danger of life and property. "WARNING: The Penalty for the above offence is from 3 to 14 years of Hard Labour in the Penitentiary." One outcome could have

been a rush of nervous individuals back to the steamboats. But they need not have worried for there is no record of any derailments that year, nor is there any record of the apprehension of any "evil disposed persons."

Ten years earlier, in 1871, George William McMullen, had been the centre of Canada's greatest political storm, the "Pacific Scandal", involving the formation of a company under government approval that would build and operate Canada's first railway to the Pacific Coast. More than anyone else, at the youthful age of twenty-seven, he would be responsible for bringing down Canada's first federal government of Prime Minister John A. Macdonald. This is fully described in Pierre Berton's "The National Dream."

It is a tale of financial skullduggery and utter ruthlessness involving Sir Hugh Allan, Montreal shipowner and the richest man in Canada. Behind him were an equally ruthless group of Americans that represented the Northern Pacific Railway, first United States railroad, in the north-west, then under construction and also aiming to reach the Pacific Coast. Their plans were to gain control of the Canadian project and use it as no more than a feeder line for their own system.

Consecon Station in 1979. Picton with Consecon are the only two stations still standing in Pr. Edward County. The short passing track is occasionally used for bad order cars.

Photo, Author

George McMullen's journey into this drama seems to have been almost a matter of fate. Born in Prince Edward County in 1854, he was too young to have known John A. Macdonald when he practiced law in Hallowell (Picton), but his father Daniel undoubtedly had. How friendly they had been is questionable. For there was likely to be little in common between a Methodist minister, of private means at that, who had produced a family of twelve and retired early, and that of a charming, hard-drinking, prankster of a young lawyer. Unfortunately nothing is known about this for the McMullen papers were lost in a fire many years ago.

George McMullen was, whatever his sins or virtues, an unusual man. He had an extremely active brain and even more active imagination. His energy was boundless. With considerable mechanical curiosity it was inevitable that he should have become an inventor. But inventions were not the reason that brought him to Ottawa.

All this really started when at an early age he had gone to Chicago where before long with his many-sided talents, he was running the *Chicago Evening Post,* having a controlling interest in that newspaper. How large the circulation of the paper was at that time is not known, but according to members of the family, his was the only paper that continued to publish throughout the Chicago fire. It was here that he became an American citizen; something that he treasured so much that after he returned to Canada he never gave it up. He was known around the County as George "Washington" McMullen. He was frank, his first loyalty was to the United States and he believed, all his life, that Canada would be better off a part of that country — an unpopular opinion in Canada, let alone among United Empire Loyalists.

With a lively personality and an immense sense of humour, he had made many friends in high places. Of his many interests the principal one was railroads, his considerable ingenuity compensating for a lack of practical experience, but to a degree.

Among the influential persons whose confidence he came to enjoy were those responsible for the management and financing of the Northern Pacific. Jay Cooke, the all-powerful Philadelphia banker was among them. When the Northern Pacific group, using Sir Hugh Allan as a Canadian front, proposed to build the Pacific railway, what better agent and go-between than the bright, personable, George McMullen. Allan and the other Canadians involved, like the Americans, all considered the buying of politicians a necessary part of their business. It is hard to say who was the least scrupulous. The world of big business and politicians of those days was no place for a young man to venture so boldly, indeed McMullen had walked into a veritable nest of scoundrels, whatever his own standards of integrity.

Nonetheless before it was all over he had among other acts, sold incriminating documents, some of them stolen, to the highest political bidder (the Liberals) to help recoup some of his financial losses, and testified with a complete disregard to the consequences to all those involved. As a result the Macdonald government fell. McMullen would be left with the reputation of arch-villain among the Tories. But like the rest of the McMullen family he happened to be a strong Liberal, in consequence, to many of that party he was a hero.

If there was nothing praiseworthy in the whole affair, one overlooked benefit was the greater circumspection of John A. Macdonald and the Conservative party when, after a term in opposition, they were returned to power. Their return being largely due to the yet greater inadequacies of the Liberals.

Now, ten years later, his own sense of humour long returned, George McMullen seemingly had his own railroad — if a small one. His busy mind was already planning many extensions; uppermost in his thought was an extension northwards past Trenton.

*   *   *

The winter of 1880-1881 that followed the McMullen purchase had been severe. Operating conditions had been extremely difficult on the railway, the line being closed for several days at a time. March saw the last snowstorm which had tied up all the railways of central Canada for periods governed by the depth of the snowfall and the amount of snow-fighting equipment available. With each snowstorm on the County railway the narrow cuts in the Consecon area had quickly filled, closing down the line for several days at a time.

According to Poor's Almanac the company did not own a plough, and this would have meant waiting until one could be rented from the Grand Trunk. Likely the well-packed snow had to be dug out by hand. In the deeper cuts this would have meant the snow shovellers had to work down in steps, shovelling it upwards in stages, a process requiring a considerable number of men. By mid-March it was estimated that snow had covered the ground for 120 days.

There was another problem. The Trenton newspaper had reported on February 4th that No. 2, the more powerful engine, had been repaired but was not yet in "perfect order". The line having been blocked once again in a recent storm, the paper continued, "... we may hope that the repaired engine will shortly come to the relief of the little engine that has been doing double duty since the fire, and the road will be able to make steady headway against the frequent storms."

Here was a tough challenge indeed for John Haney and his men; one small ancient, second-hand locomotive to buck the snow. More than that she likely needed a lot of work done at nights and on Sundays just to keep her going — all with limited resources for repairs. Operating expenses must have been excessive that winter. Shoestring operations mean high overheads.

Newspaper reports of the day record that in February one Robert Hamilton was "severely crushed last week being caught between two cars he was coupling." The paper said "He was confined to the house for a few days."

George McMullen was also busy that month, fighting what could be called the "Battle for Madoc".

Some background events. The first was the purchase of the Dufferin and the Nelson mines by two of the largest U.S. steel corporations, the Johnstown Steel Co., and the Bethlehem Steel Co.

The second, of more direct consequence, was the appearance in the mining area in the same month, when weather conditions must have made travel both restricted and uncertain, of George McMullen's brother J.B. McMullen accompanied by a J.B. Brown, a geologist from the Lake Superior District. The latter was the representative of a millionaire congressman, the Hon. J. Hubbell, a potential investor of large sums of money.

Finally the company's earlier announcement that they would construct a giant ore dock at Weller's Bay, about eight miles south of Trenton. The site was near the narrowest part of the isthmus between Prince Edward County and the mainland where a portage road had existed as long as people could remember. In its final days it had been a private line of hardwood rails and horses. The settlement still bears the name of Carrying Place.

Trenton harbour would have required much dredging; here there was plenty of room and all agreed, including the Trenton newspaper, that this was the best site. More than this the McMullens let it be known that the company would eventually be operating a steamship line of ore carriers from here.

Well-armed with all this information and bursting with optimism J.B. McMullen staged a meeting with the citizens of Madoc, one of the larger communities. George was likely away in the United States hunting for capital funds in large amounts.

This was one of the richer areas of the mineral belt, and it was already "served" by the recently constructed Grand Junction Railway, which now made its somewhat uncertain way from Belleville to Peterborough. Already there were rumours around that the Grand Trunk Railway was in the process of buying up this line. The McMullens' purpose was to build into the village, for which they wanted a bonus of $5,000 and a further $10,000 from the township. The tactic was to get the support of the village after which the township's support would likely follow.

On Monday, February 14th, the meeting was convened at Moon's Hotel and it was well attended. The proceedings started by the Reeve, E.D.O. Flynn being called to the chair. J.B. McMullen took the floor, announcing that he and his brother had bought the Prince Edward County Railway. He told the meeting that he had heard of the fine mineral resources in the area and said if proper facilities for its transportation existed, "a fine business would be done." He had therefore applied to the government for an extension of the line to Madoc, which had been granted. They

would have associated with them Mr. Hubbell of Washington, a member of the United States Congress.

J.B. McMullen then made his request for the bonus from the village, assuring them that they would get government aid if it was given to any railway. In any case the line would be built if municipal bonuses were secured. They expected a bonus from Marmora and another $20,000 from Trenton.

With a direct line to the ore docks at Weller's Bay, shipping costs, he told them, would be greatly reduced, while the road they would provide would be a first class one.

On being called on to speak, Mr. Munson, a mine owner, gave the opinion, "The present means of transportation [meaning the Grand Junction] was a serious obstacle in the way of proper development of the iron region, and they would never expect to do even a reasonable business with the present facilities. Cars were being continually called for that could not be supplied, which was in fact the case with many of the leading American lines, some of which were 2,000 cars behind order." He favoured the projected road, as the present dockage at Belleville was not adequate for the requirements of their district, and besides, in the case of his own shipments, a distance of a 150 miles out of the Bay of Quinte would be saved … "Even with three trains a day, the Dufferin mine (at capacity) alone could block this road. Furthermore, the Grand Trunk showed them no favour and very little courtesy."

Others present expressed strong doubts about J.B. McMullen's proposition, at times there was open hostility. The meeting seemed to be divided between the "iron men" and the rest. The latter supported the Grand Junction which had already received considerable financial support from both village and township. As a result of this division it was eventually decided to form a committee of seven to consider the matter, in the meantime the McMullens were to provide certain information.[3]

A week later the Reeve called a meeting at the Town Hall to hear the committee's report. J.B. McMullen was able to speak first. He expressed his conviction of the feasibility of the route by way of Stirling, Marmora and Malone; tapping the different ore beds and mines between the latter place and Madoc. As for the advantages of Weller's Bay, he said a lake captain had told him that he could make two trips from there to the American side for every trip from Belleville. He wound up assuring them that if the bonus was granted Madoc would be the terminus of the line.

The committee, apparently unmoved or unwilling to reopen their deliberations, made their report in the form of a series of resolutions. Briefly they were:

1. The present facilities for doing business at Belleville are wholly inadequate not just in shipping iron ore, but for the general good of the community.

2. The new connection with Weller's Bay and Trenton was heartily approved.

3. In the opinion of the committee the most desirable way to ensure this route was by using the Grand Junction to a point near West Huntingdon station, going via Stirling and Trenton to Weller's Bay. And from such branches of the Grand Junction north of Madoc as would give the mines every facility to ensure their development.

4. Accordingly the committee did not feel it was necessary to give any aid.

Then Mr. Wood, a member of the committee rose and gave further reasons for supporting the committee's resolutions, among them: He had discussed the matter with "gentlemen conversant with shipping ore by rail, and the opinion he gathered satisfied him that the railway already subscribed by us, by way of bonus, could do all the work for many years to come. But the facilities at Belleville were inadequate ... but McMullen is not an iron ore man; he is here as a speculator to extend his railway, making a new line; he asks us for assistance. It is not for us to consider Mr. McMullen's interests."

Mr. Wood continued that he "could not bear remarking that it did seem to him very absurd to ask us to support a line running through another section of the country to a point several miles to the north of us, and then, in order to have it avail, in any sense for the village, or mines surrounding, run back again to the south, spreading itself in the shape of distended fingers on a hand, one of the lines connecting with Madoc village. It required more credibility than he was possessed of to believe in any such proposition."

J.B. McMullen must have fairly jumped to his feet to counter this attack. More than Madoc, one would guess J. Hubbell's financial backing was

at stake, "In his opinion the resolutions had been framed in the interest of the Grand Junction Railway. He would like to know if the meeting was composed of stockholders of that company? He had come here to see if the people wanted a second railway, and he had come here to talk business, not nonsense. He thought the miners would prefer another road, as the present one was in notoriously bad condition. He did not think the people wanted to aid the same road twice, yet this was what the resolutions proposed. He asked them if they wanted to patch up the present road instead of aiding a new one. He asked them for a paltry $5,000; they would give it or not as they pleased. He had secured a charter to build into Madoc, but he was not bound to come here."

Mr. Wood replied that, he was more than ever in favour of the resolutions.

A further debate followed. The first to speak was Captain Mitchell, associate of William Coe, to express his doubts once more of the Grand Junction. He reminded the gathering that at the previous meeting he had pointed out the impossibility of getting cars. Since then "they had plenty of cars shoved upon them." He continued to support the new line as did other iron men who spoke later. But the debate that followed, though it continued for some time, contained nothing new.

Finally the resolutions were submitted to the meeting. The voting: nine for the railway, "about thirteen against."

The Madoc newspaper, *The Hastings Review* thought it was "a very unsatisfactory conclusion to such an important meeting, all must admit."

The Trenton *Courier* strongly supporting the new line, as to be expected, had this to say, "it believed the route to Madoc village would be too circuitous and the most direct line was required to develop the area. It would also be expensive even if the village gave double the amount. What surprised them was that Mr. McMullen should have gone there to ask for assistance."[4]

The *Courier* wound up its editorial suggesting that "the McMullens should start their own townsite nearby in a more convenient location for the railway, which as a real estate venture would profit them more than the bonus — in the hope that Madoc might see her interest and danger ... we throw out the suggestion for what it is worth, neither will we charge the Messrs. McMullen anything for its adoption."

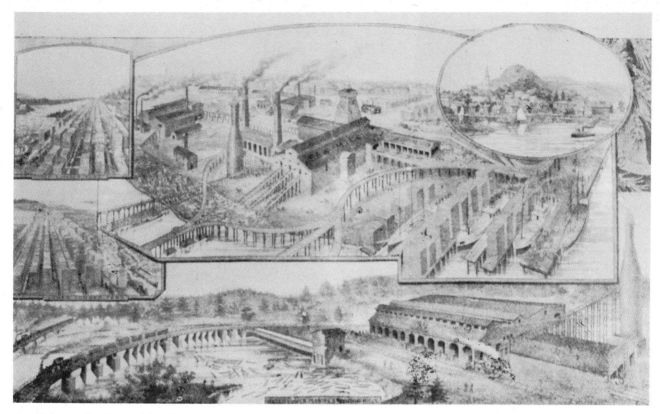

Old-time drawings of the Gilmour Complex. Note the Mill Train crossing the combined bridge and power dam.

"Evolution of Trenton"

But the editor of the *North Hastings Review* was in no mood for any facetious sniping. He responded with all the heavy artillery he could muster in a furious counter attack. Here is part of his barrage:

"SOME GRATUITOUS ADVICE"

"Our contemporary, the Trenton Courier, is in the enviable position of having a modern philosopher at its head ... this new Cassandra." Then referring to the new settlement that would bring in more than $5,000 in bonus money, "A wonderful scheme! Worthy of a great mind! Prophet or philosopher, which? Alas! Like the inspired daughter of Priam, he utterly fails to inspire hope at the proposed village location, or fear of such a dire calamity at Madoc." As to the Trenton editor not charging for that idea "... but we are of the opinion that these gentlemen will consider it dear even at that price."[5]

Neither editor wrote any more on the subject, perhaps both were satisfied that they had silenced the enemy. So ended the "Battle for Madoc". The McMullens' road would never reach that village.

As for the Grand Junction, target of many brickbats, the Madoc newspaper had reported earlier, "Quite a remarkable car has been attached to the Madoc train on the G.J.R. for the past week. Frequenters of the station pronounce it a new style of Pullman, but this would hardly be appropriate as it answers the purpose not only of a first-class passenger, but smoking, express and baggage as well. (Technically, a combine), a seat runs lengthwise on each side of the car, the windows being protected by wooden bars, and the whole being beautifully frescoed by whitewash ..."[6]

But better days were coming; on March 10th the same newspaper reported the delivery of two new coaches from Crossen at Cobourg similar to some new cars received a few weeks earlier. "The cars are handsomely finished, and are in every sense creditable to the road." This could not have been said of the cars of the Prince Edward County Railway at that time.

In March the Grand Junction Railway received further praise from the newspaper after a severe storm for managing to run all its trains on time. Likely the resources of the Grand Trunk were behind them now, for in mid-May sale of the line to that corporation was confirmed. The official takeover was delayed. Instead, in June, the company was taken over by the Midland Railway, an amalgamation of a group of lines to the west of the Grand Junction. The reason was a negative one, the purpose to keep the lines out of the clutches of the Canadian Pacific Railway — not to develop the area.

The Grand Trunk was evidently in the mood to co-operate with the McMullens who may have been hoping to sell the line to them. For in the same June edition of the newspaper Mr. Hannaford, Engineer-in-Chief of that corporation, had been examining the route of the proposed "Trent Valley Railway" (first known indication of a change of name for the Prince Edward County Railway). He reported favourably on the project, and favoured locating the dock at Weller's Bay.

Early in April there was an announcement that the County Railway would build the extension into Picton as soon as the frost was out of the ground. More costly, by far, the northern end would be extended to Stirling that summer.

Supporting this an advertisement appeared in the Toronto newspapers asking for tenders on 75,000 railway ties.

The year 1881 looked as if it might be a big year for Trenton and the mining industry.

Trenton had already become the operational centre of Prince Edward County Railway's activities. This was inevitable with much of the traffic coming from the two-way interchange with the Grand Trunk Railway, the volume diminishing all the way to Picton. John Haney and others had soon moved their offices there. The annual meetings would continue to be held in Picton, at first because of the provisions in the original charter, and later, it would seem, because the McMullens lived and ran the railway from there.

With Belleville, of the three communities, Trenton was the late starter having achieved the status of a town as recently as 1880, the year after the opening of the County railway.

At Gilmour's, the mystery engine. This may well have been Prince Edward Co. Rly. No. 1. Whatever her origin, she has lost her tender. She would be a poor yard loco with such high wheels. Note the plating over her boiler lagging is loose.

Photo, Hastings County Museum

All three settlements had been founded by United Empire Loyalists. There had also been a good deal of intermarriage among their citizens, but this did nothing to prevent a growing rivalry between Trenton and her bigger rival lying twelve miles to the east.

Over a quarter of a century earlier, Trentonians had watched enviously as the Grand Trunk Railway selected Belleville as a divisional point, and even more so when a busy engine terminal, freight yards, and a divisional headquarters were established.

There was a feeling among Trentonians that their community could one day catch up. They had some advantages. The Trent River made their rival's Moira look small though both carried vast log drives. Neither was presently navigable, but sometime in the future, after decades of lobbying, the Trent would become a commercial waterway. Government had already been planning such a system of canals, but it would be two generations later before small steamboats would be able to go all the way to Peterborough and beyond to serve rich farming areas and growing towns and villages.

Trenton also had a fair harbour. It needed dredging, but as a commercial port it was more severely handicapped in that all eastbound traffic had to sail many additional miles around Prince Edward County, whose coast was the most hazardous in the Great Lakes.

The only hope here for Trenton was the construction of what would be known as the Murray Canal across the County's isthmus. But the construction of this long promised project was always being postponed on one pretext or another. Powerful Belleville citizens more influential than the Trentonians had lobbied against it as a matter of local advantage. Behind the scenes, no doubt, was Grand Trunk management, for that company stood to lose traffic if the canal were built.

Trenton's recent growth had been due in part to the construction of the P.E.C. Railway, and the subsequent increase in the number of County people visiting the town and market. But the bigger contribution to the growth of the settlement had started in 1852 with the arrival of the Gilmour Company, whose big sawmill now stood on the east bank of the river. How many they employed at that time is not known but in another decade it was a thousand men.

The Gilmour's had moved here from Quebec bringing with them many experienced lumberjacks and mill hands. Their incentive had been the many thousands of acres of prime forest around the upper reaches of the Trent. The skill and ingenuity of these lumbermen was soon proven by such operations as damming up swamps to float the logs to the river. Here also was the promise of considerable rail traffic though the mood of the new railway owners was to consider anything but iron ore as incidental.

Gilmour's were the company that bought the County's mysterious No. 1 engine. She has already been described as being in poor condition; but the old locomotives were of simple and robust construction and could be repaired over and over again until little of the original locomotive remained. She becomes a mystery, but seems to have had a long life.

A large area north of these two rival towns had long been known to be rich, not only in iron ore but in many other metals, including gold. Small mines had been worked here and there for many years, but the general state of the roads, bad even for those times, had made production a marginal operation. Marmora was the iron ore centre.

The year after the completion of the Grand Trunk main line along the shore of Lake Ontario in 1857, Marmora Foundry was seeking a charter to build a "tramroad or railway" to a point on that system. In 1858 there followed another petition to build from Marmora to Belleville, in the same year for yet another line to be built from Marmora to Port Colborne situated west of Trenton. All died on the books.

Recently two railways had been constructed north of the two towns. There was only one of any consequence, the high-sounding Grand Junction Railway, though so cheaply built that its short life under that title was beset with serious operating problems. Construction took two years reaching Peterborough in 1879 at the year's end, a total distance of 53 miles. The route taken was generally south of the mineral belt before it headed north, passing some 12 miles north of Trenton, near enough to be insulting and too far to be useful. It was soon taken over by that conglomerate of small railways, the Midland, which in turn was bought up by the Grand Trunk lest the Canadian Pacific used this system to invade what the Grand Trunk considered to be its own territory. Negotiations had started in 1881 and were completed the following year.

Another Shot. Here she has a bigger fuel banker.

Photo, Marten Lewis Collection

The Grand Junction did have one feeder line into the mineral area, the Belleville and North Hastings Railway. It was no great asset. The title was misleading for it reached neither Belleville nor the northern part of Hastings County. It joined the Grand Junction 12 miles out of Belleville and ran to Madoc. The charter was to continue to Eldorado, but so far Madoc was as far as it had reached.

Madoc and Eldorado had been the scene of a real boom-and-bust gold rush in the sixties. Gold was still being mined in modest quantities, though only Madoc village could by now be called a busy community. One local enterprise dating back to 1837 was an iron foundry, unfortunately this was to close down in the next few years.

With the limited scientific and mechanical means available (magnetic readings and drills of limited depth) there were good reasons to believe there were considerable deposits of iron ore; further confirmed by the numerous outcroppings. This was the age when every fresh mineral discovery brought excited optimism and dreams of unlimited wealth. There were many more disappointments than fortunes. Here it seemed that all that was needed were transportation and capital funds. The United States with its expanding steel industry looked like an inexhaustible market for all the good quality iron ore that could be mined and processed.

The six principal operators, small as they might be, deserve mention.

The most important in this account was the Coe Hill Mine, belonging to William Coe, a prospector with both determination and faith in his discovery. The Coe Hill settlement must have been called after him. At present his mine consisted of no more than a cut and a 40-foot shaft. But a diamond drill at the depth of 230 feet had disclosed there was a solid bed of ore, 70-feet deep and of such high quality that it was considered to have the highest potential of any operation in the area.

The other mines, the Arthur, the Baker, the Emma, the Louisa and the Bentlifte, all were in varying degrees, promising. As an American mining magazine would sum it up after examining the assays of each mine, "Widely separated as they are, and yet all plainly connected by the geographical formations, it is fair to assume that they constitute but a small fraction of the valuable deposits of ore, that when the territory is fully developed it will not be excelled, and here is a breath-taker, by any other territory on the continent, not even by the wondrously rich deposits of the Lake Superior region."

Early in 1881, Samuel J. Ritchie, an American financier and industrialist, long before this report was published in 1883, had been busy in the area, often discreetly, buying up the mineral rights to more than a 100,000 acres of land, as well as obtaining partnership in the promising Coe Hill mine. He had every confidence that before many years had passed this would be the world's biggest iron ore operation — mining, smelting, and transportation.

Chapter Six

In June it was announced that the Midland Railway, an amalgamation of several lesser railways in the region, would take over the Grand Junction. Like the Grand Trunk this system was British-owned. That same year the sale of the Midland to the Grand Trunk was confirmed. This was finalized on December 15th 1881 at a shareholders meeting of the latter company.

Back in early April there had been news that the northern extension of the P.E.C. Railway to Stirling would be completed that summer. Proving they were in earnest were advertisements in the Toronto newspapers calling for tenders on 75,000 railway ties.

Of more immediate concern to the citizens of Picton, another early April announcement, was that the line would be extended into the town. A bonus of $1,000 had been extracted from town council as their contribution. Furthermore it was promised work would start as soon as the frost was out of the ground.

Then on May 27th, the McMullens announced that the construction of the line to Stirling would be delayed a year. The reasons given were the Grand Trunk's purchase of the Grand Junction, and the favourable arrangements made for reaching the mines at North Hastings, which meant the iron ore would be shipped through Belleville. This had been a helter-skelter promotion. Now there was a steadier hand behind the scenes.

On June 17th, 1881 at Wilson's Hotel in Picton there was a shareholders meeting of significance. The old directors resigned. Lt. Col. Walter Ross stepped down as president. In his place a new name to everyone, Samuel J. Ritchie of Akron, Ohio, appeared. Here was the money-man the McMullens needed to pick up their option. We shall hear a great deal of Ritchie but for a while the McMullens continued to hold centre stage.

George was now vice-president, J.B. a director; and H.C. secretary-treasurer. Only W.T. Yarwood and S.P. Niles continued to represent the county. Congressman J. Hubbell? He was not heard of again.

A later report in early June, off to a late start: "Messrs. McMullen have a large gang of men grading the track for the extension of the line into Picton." But not under the direction of the redoubtable John Haney. He had been transferred to the north "to look after the interests of the company." Likely he was to superintend the construction, which was then cancelled. He was also moved to make room for one of the McMullens. Likely he had remained on the payroll as Alexander Manning's representative until the purchase was completed. The McMullens were clever, ingenious people and knew a lot about railroads, but for lack of experience not much about railroading. John Haney would be missed.

Cancellation of the construction of the line to Stirling had the editor of the Trenton *Courier* worried and he exhorted everyone to do all they could to get the line built. In this state of mind, "that new Cassandra", now reversed himself on the planned Murray Canal, gloomily foreseeing its construction as a threat to Trenton instead. But he did brighten up when he learned of quantities of timber being stockpiled at Weller's Bay, which was followed by a statement from the McMullens that the work once started "would be pushed forward with all despatch."

There were many excursions along the line that summer, daylight, moonlight, group, family, often with bands. The people were happy with their railway. But there was a complaint that the coaches were uncomfortable and that the track was rough. The Trenton newspaper defended the railway vigorously against this complaint, then fired its own shot: the company rates were unfair, favouring Picton, and that the layover times at Trenton should be longer. This latter problem, it was suggested, could be solved by reducing the easy schedule of the trains 15 minutes each way.

But the editor of *The Picton Times* called this "complaining" and "very small". The schedules remained unchanged.

Original Prince Edward County Rly. Station at Picton after its third move. Now a duplex dwelling on Lake St., (1978 Photo)

Picture, Author

It was also reported that the "barbed wire fences along the line are not very much admired by the farmers along the line of the P.E. Railway, several horses and cattle having already been injured by coming in contact with it."

By November 1881 the site of the new terminal was nearly ready. There was probably an official opening of the station but no records are available. The site was a good train length, plus, from Lake Street and parallel with Main Street. The new freight shed was also located here. But the extension was too short, the passenger trains blocking Lake Street.

What is still remembered in Prince Edward County history was the arrival of the old station borne on flatcars. This turned out to be a far more memorable event, an amateur performance in low comedy, for the slow moving train came to a sudden halt at a structure called Crandall's barn. Nobody had checked the clearances beforehand. Thereupon the work force set to and dismantled a corner of that structure. So the station arrived, one might say, late at the depot — or vice versa. John Haney would never have let that happen. The relocation of the Picton station had been good entertainment.

Years later McMullen complained that the job had cost them $2,000 more than the bonus. Presumably the extra cost in removing the corner of the barn was included. He said nothing of reduced cost of operation or traffic gained.

In the fall, the manager (unnamed) of the railway told the press that a branch from Wellington to West Point, a resort area some three to four miles long was being "contemplated with favour". The track would run along the sand dunes and shuttle service would be provided. The village of Wellington was expected to contribute $3,000 towards a total estimated expenditure of $30,000, but this did not progress any further, though this project was included and approved in the next bill submitted to parliament.

Aerial photo by Lloyd Thompson showing roadbed of line to dock. Buildings, nothing to do with the C.O.R., were erected at a much later date. In the distance the C.O.R. (now C.N.R.) mainline can be seen crossing the Murray Canal.

Beyond surveying the spur line to the dock site at Weller's Bay, not much was accomplished during the winter of 1881. This did not prevent the newspapers of the region spending their winter in optimistic dreams of an extremely prosperous future for the two Counties — and there was good reason. The Bill for the northern extension had come up before the Ontario Legislature, in this the system was to be called the "Ontario Midland Railway."[1] On the assumption of its successful passage much was happening.

In January of the new year, 1882, Samuel J. Ritchie (who was beginning to make as many public statements as George McMullen) announced that 36 miles of line would be built that summer northwards from Trenton: a contract for part of the work had already been let. Plainly he was confident of the passing of the bill. Moreover, the line was to be built to the highest standards, the rail to be six pounds heavier per yard than the Grand Trunk's — the latter would not be so, but in all other respects he spoke truthfully. More important, he maintained, there was sufficient funds available to build the line without public assistance — though it was hoped to get a government bonus.

Other announcements followed, one after the other. The railroad had bought 2,600 acres of iron-ore fields from William Coe, on the basis of a three-quarter interest. (Coe was to receive a $50 royalty on every ton of ore that was shipped.)[2]

The company had a contract to deliver 400,000 tons of ore to Cleveland over the coming summer — all to be shipped over their own line, not via Belleville.

At Weller's Bay 125 acres had been bought for $6,000, not only for the dock area, but here there would also be a smelter and considerable railway plant, including a roundhouse and a repair shop.

The dock would be an impressive structure; standing thirty feet above high water and extending far enough into the bay to provide a minimum depth of twenty feet to the ships — a length of 2,000 feet. It would cost considerably more than the estimated $100,000.[3]

Later Ritchie let it be known that he was making arrangements for the construction of a Bessemer steel, rail mill in the area, a considerable investment in itself. He was also prepared to build car repair shops in the same locality, unless Trenton or some other place assisted in their construction. This north-western area of Prince Edward County now had the potential of becoming a highly industrialized area with a population of 50,000 to 100,000 people.

More information followed. The new line was to be built to the Township of Wollaston, the site of the railway's biggest iron mine, 84 feet wide, several hundred feet long, ten feet of which was expected to yield half a million tons of ore, more than enough for that first contract.

Confirming the high standards of construction of the line, all the principal bridges were to be of steel. A contract was let for 8,000 tons of 56 lb. rail for delivery by water to Trenton.

Late February the Bill was passed by the Ontario Legislature. There was only one change, the name of the company was changed to the "Central Ontario Railway", as it would be known for nearly 30 years. Authority had also been obtained to build "80 miles north to the great iron ore deposits." The Madoc newspaper commented, "While the Bill was passing its second reading in Toronto, Belleville gentlemen were passing resolutions to oppose it. The distress of these gentlemen at the prosperity of their neighbours is pitiable …"[4]

At the last annual meeting of the Prince Edward County Railway, William Coe and John B. McMullen were elected to the board of directors. The latter had overall charge of the construction of the new line.

At the first annual meeting of the Central Ontario Railway, more sabotage was reported — but this had been discovered in time to prevent an accident. The first incident was near Picton where "some miscreants" had "deliberately" driven some spikes between the rail joints. The other sounded ineffectual, for near Hillier, a plank had been laid across the track.

There was also more positive news for the board. Approximately 350 men were already at work, in spite of the demands of other railways under construction in the area, labour and teams were in good supply. Unlike Prince Edward County, no difficulties had been experienced in buying the right-of-way.

It was also confirmed that the Coe Hill Mining Co. with a capital of $750,000 had been formed with the same directors as the C.O.R. And a new director was elected, William Chisholm of Cleveland, Ohio, a wealthy steel maker and industrialist.

Headquarters were to be moved to Trenton, a move that was inevitable, but not happily received in Picton.

Old dock piling still survives.

Photo, Alan R. Capon

Much overgrown, the walls of the turntable pit remain.

Photo, Author

As spring came round, country roads became impassable, particularly in the northern areas. This was a season when railways were particularly welcome. One citizen of Eldorado became sufficiently depressed by the soft mud to offer to pay $500 from his own pocket if the C.O.R. would "touch at that place on their way north."

The choice of the route for the western entrance of the Murray Canal, on which construction was about to start, became the cause of yet another battle between the towns of Belleville and Trenton. The choice of routes lay between the old Carrying Place portage route, a few miles north of the C.O.R.'s new dock, and a potential bonus to the scheme. The alternative was further north closer to Trenton, and this was supported by Belleville interests, even if hardly in their parish.[5]

The Carrying Place route was also the boundary of Prince Edward County.

For once Messrs. Ritchie and McMullen maintained a public silence, but they must have been lobbying hard behind the scenes for both Prince Edward County and Trenton pressed hard, but Belleville proved to be the more influential. Finally, in late May, after 40 years of lobbying and bickering, the Federal government called for tenders.

One never knew what to expect from George McMullen. He and his brother stayed in the news by announcing that they intended building a glass factory on Weller's Bay. Likely the needed minerals were available "up north", for the list of minerals discovered there is almost endless. More practical was their opening of a wire factory in Picton to supply fencing for the new line.

Survey parties were working on the projected line by May, north through Marmora, another south of Wollaston. Grading had already started out of Trenton.

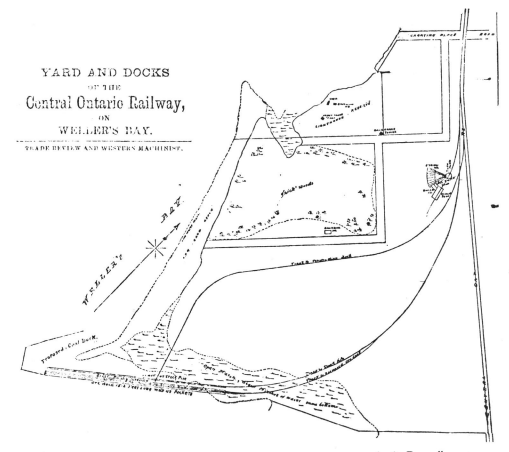

Map of Dock at Weller's Bay as planned. Coal dock extension was never built. Roundhouse was as shown.

Map, Courtesy Canadian Pacific Archives

One of the biggest obstacles in both cost and engineering was bridging the river above Trenton at Chisholm's Rapids, requiring a 500-foot long structure. Again the specifications were high for the times, best quality English steel, and to be guaranteed to carry the heaviest trains at a speed of at least 30 m.p.h. The Toronto Bridge Co. got the contract.[6]

No. 3, The first locomotive acquired by the C.O.R. Date of picture unknown, but note lack of airbrakes, and the link-and-pin adapter to the automatic coupler. Sold in 1891 to unknown buyer. She ran for only nine years on the line.   *Photo, Prince Edward Co. Historical Society*

Progress at Weller's Bay was also good. S.P. Niles, the director, had been appointed to superintend the work. Not surprisingly, considering the dimensions of the dock, 10,000 yards of fill would be needed and a 100,000 cu. ft. of lumber were among his first needs. The dredging would start in July and take 60 days. Two hundred and fifty men were already at work with another 50 to a 100 being hired each week as the work progressed. It was anticipated that the first shipments of ore would be made in early September.[7]

Madoc was where the action was, apart from the fearless editor and proprietor of the *North Hastings Review*, J.R. Orr, a major of the militia. William Coe, the man who had believed so long in the mineral future of the district, and at a considerable financial hardship, seeing all his dreams about to come true, made known his candidacy for the Liberal party in the coming federal election. (His opponent would be Tory, the Hon. Mackenzie Bowell, already a member of the cabinet, and owner of the Belleville *Intelligencer* newspaper.) In a long statement Coe forecast happily "... you will hear the sound of the locomotive whistle as it speeds through the woods and among the hills of North Hastings."[8]

Site of turntable and roundhouse can be spotted, confirmed by map. 1977

Photo, Lloyd Thompson

One of Coe's aims, was to import cattle from England to improve the local strain. Although he lost the election he kept this promise.

Then came a day, June 29, that brought joy to those on the County line, particularly to the mechanics and the locomotive crews; George McMullen ordered two new locomotives from the Kingston Locomotive Works. He said that fourteen locomotives in all would be required,

stating that if the first two were satisfactory, that company would get the remainder of the order.

On that day came news of the first recorded death on the line, though there may have been others. The victim was an elderly man who was first seen walking towards the train with his head down. He had been picking strawberries for his family and was returning home when he was hit. He lived for an hour after the accident. It turned out that the man was deaf. The McMullens paid all the funeral expenses. In August there was another fatality, this time on the new line when a young man named Mason was struck by a tree that he was felling.

On October 4th, grading was stopped, and wages were reduced to 25¢ a day for those who continued rock cutting and other work. Everything was just about ready for laying track. It was expected to have the line running to Marmora in a few weeks — all far short of the planned early September.

Three days earlier the "new" locomotives had arrived: No. 3, listed as built in Kingston in 1879 (see Appendix). Where she had been in the intervening three years is not known. Perhaps she had been repossessed? Ross Weaver of Picton, who knew the locomotive well, said she was a good engine but lacked power compared to later engines. The second Kingston engine, No. 4, arrived in November and was immediately named the "J.B. McMullen". The locomotives were likely identical, but all that is known today is that their cylinders and drive wheels were the same size. They were probably standard designs of the builders.

On October 19 it was reported that the new roundhouse at Weller's Bay was under construction, believed to be with 10 or 12 stalls, while one of the new locomotives making its first appearance on the Picton train, caused considerable interest.

Again, later than anticipated, track laying began on Monday, November 6th, 1882 with a new device. The Marmora newspaper claimed that this was the first track-laying machine to be used in Canada. Pioneering such an invention would appeal to both Ritchie and George McMullen — the latter, no doubt, would have preferred to have designed his own. This machine was the invention of G.F. Harris of New York, and had been assembled by the Crossen Co. of Cobourg (car builders). The track layer made a good start — a mile a day.[9]

Whether the tracks reached Marmora or not that year, no iron ore could be shipped as the bridge across Chisholm's Rapids could not be completed that season.

The Ritchie-McMullen team had spent a lot of extra money in vain as far as the year 1882 was concerned. The local press tactfully refrained from comment knowing the railway management had tried their hardest.

Nothing more is heard of the able John Haney, displaced by John B. McMullen. He must have left for other employment where his abilities and experience would be more than welcome.

With Samuel Ritchie now emerging from behind his Canadian front of the McMullens to assert himself as president, it would not be long before he became personally known around Ontario and the two counties. This was not hard for he was a genial man with an outgoing personality and a man of commanding stature. He was also a gifted storyteller and people gathered about him naturally. More unusual was that this easy manner and good humour never left him, even when he faced adversity and ruin. A fast growing interest in all things Canadian helped considerably.

Now that it was obvious that the railway was not locally owned but controlled by Americans, it seems that this was well received by people in the area. No criticism of American control seems to have appeared in the newspapers serving the Central Ontario Railway area, surprising in a Loyalist stronghold.

Paradoxically, George "Washington" McMullen was unendingly criticized for his passion for all things American. It is possible that the promise of a vast bonanza for the area made the nationality of control unimportant. Whatever the reasoning, Ritchie was the man to capture Canadian goodwill.

Ritchie's previous experiences had him well prepared for this enterprise. He was not long past his 43rd birthday when, with his fellow financiers, he had bought control of the line from the McMullens.

Born near Akron, Ohio, he had been raised on the family farm. After he had finished secondary school his first enterprise was in lumbering. From there and for an unknown number of years in some capacity, he was a railroader.

On June 15th, 1865, he married a Miss Sophronia Hale. It had been over her parents' land that he had conducted some of his earlier logging operations. He now settled down.

Within a couple of years he had started up a factory in the vicinity for making carriages. After a while, ambitious and innovative, he extended the plant and began manufacturing sewer pipe, a business that required political connections and at several levels. This project seems to have been highly successful. Unfortunately, eleven years later, in 1878, the plant burned down. He had no interest in rebuilding, instead, he looked for wider horizons and bigger challenges.

Over the years he had made many influential friends in business and politics, and not only in his own state. Among them was Andrew Carnegie, "King of Steel." This had become a close friendship. Later, Ritchie, possessing literary ability among his talents, would help Carnegie write his book, "Triumphant Democracy."[10]

As for the Central Ontario Railway, in spite of other more profitable ventures the line would become his great obsession. So much so that he would become an infrequent visitor to his own home.

Two greater individualists than Ritchie and McMullen have seldom become business partners. When this has happened, usually the partnership has been of short duration; although to an extent they complemented each others talents.

Site of Gardenville Station 1977

Photo, Alan R. Capon

Ritchie, if less brilliant, was more complex. He tended to be offhand in making agreements, becoming careless or overtrusting, and this led to serious misunderstandings with partners and colleagues; he then would become obsessively suspicious and sometimes vengeful.

The past year had brought many disappointments for Ritchie. The delays in finishing the bridge over the narrows had been costly, apart from lost traffic it had held up delivery of essential construction materials.

Construction costs had been much higher than anticipated. At a later date when Ritchie gave a $100 honorarium to William Ferguson, the construction boss for the section from Malone to a point an unknown number of miles past Millbridge, it was revealed that there were 87 rock cuts, some of them extensive. To this the Madoc paper commented: "... it is said that the road is one of the best in the Dominion. We believe this has considerably exceeded the company's estimate ..." There were rumours that the company was

54

Col. Ross House. Later purchased by George W. McMullen. Picture taken when first purchased by The Royal Canadian Legion. The gateposts have since been removed. *Photo, Alan R. Capon*

experiencing difficulty in raising capital.

Whatever the extent of these difficulties, Ritchie refused to lower the high standards he had set. Lack of funds dictated a drastic reduction in the size of the work force at the Weller's Bay docks for the time being, as the line would have to reach Coe Hill before any ore could be shipped.

Some small encouragement came on January 18th, 1883, with the start of regular freight service as far as the uncompleted bridge, roughly 14 miles from Trenton.

George McMullen was not, himself, stretched financially, for on the same date came the news that he had bought Colonel Ross' splendid mansion, though at a bargain price. It had cost $18,000 to build, he paid $7,000. This would be his home for the rest of his life.

Locomotive and roundhouse crews must have rejoiced when it became known that two more locomotives were on their way to Trenton with two more to follow shortly. This time the engines came from the United States. The same type as their predecessors, they were more powerful, if slower freight haulers. They were also heavier; more suited to the new line.[11] (See Appendix.)

These engines had been built in 1882. There was a gap of two years before their arrival on the lines of the C.O.R. They would appear to have been unsold stock. Evidently Ritchie was bargain hunting and looking for easy credit terms and the Rogers Locomotive Works was the most accommodating. The nearby Kingston company was at the time in serious financial difficulties and cash down was a necessary requirement. Ritchie and McMullen did negotiate with the Kingston works for two more locomotives, but nothing came of it.

The four engines were numbered 5 to 8, and named in the pecking order of "G.W. McMullen", "William Coe", "D.S. McMullen", and "H.B. Payne". Apparently the more permanent method of installing brass plates was not used, instead economy prevailed and the names were painted on the sides of the cab. Ritchie shunned such personal aggrandizement.

North and south of the C.O.R. the Grand

55

Trunk and the Canadian Pacific were occupied in a relentless war for position. The Grand Trunk had the advantage of being there first and being long established.

A big part of the battle was buying up smaller lines, often at bargain prices, a move the Grand Trunk had already made in this area. The C.O.R. must have had some interesting possibilities for both these giants, if for no other reason than to keep the other out. The C.P.R. who had the most to gain (it would be close to thirty years before it established its own lakeshore route) was then supporting a line inland to Toronto, known then as the Ontario and Quebec Railway, a company it would leave.

Later this year came the first of the take-over rumours to appear in print.

On November 22nd, the Madoc Review had a paragraph datelined Cleveland, saying that it was understood that the C.P.R.'s intention was to take over the C.O.R. In an interview Ritchie refused to confirm this but admitted that "parties had offered to purchase the road." It may be of some significance that soon after, the C.O.R. made application for legislative approval to extend their line northwards to make a junction with the C.P.R.'s transcontinental line along the Ottawa River and to issue bonds for this purpose. There the matter would rest for the present.

No. 6, The most photographed engine. Spent most of her life on the Picton run. Ross Weaver said she had a reputation as a good engine. Scrapped in 1913 as Canadian Northern No. 40 after 31 years at work.

The worst of news for Ritchie and his associates had hit them in the spring; news that would cool the interest of would-be purchasers and affect current financing of the line. This was legislation by the United States government in March imposing a tariff of 75¢ (roughly 10%) per ton on all imported iron ore.[12]

William Coe was interviewed immediately. He appeared unworried. He admitted this would stop the shipment of low grade ores, but said that their high grade ores would not be affected. He added, confidently, that these duties would be cancelled when the Democrats returned to power.[13]

A representative of the Bethlehem Iron Company visiting Belleville told the same newspaper that they would receive about 3,000 tons through that city, but hoped to get another 4,000 tons over the C.O.R. when the line opened. In the meantime they had closed down their older mine.

Later it turned out they had sold this mine with all its equipment to William Coe for $30,000, but on an advantageous arrangement that meant he would receive value for his money even if the mine yielded no further returns.[14]

By mid-May, the rails had reached Malone (milepost 36.4). The track-laying machine had hit its stride again at one mile a day, only to be slowed down by the C.O.R.'s first strike. The work force wanted more pay. A number were immediately paid off and discharged. The line would not open in 1883.

There followed persistent rumours that the company's finances were shaky — rumours strong enough for another strike to take place on August 2nd, the Madoc newspaper, quoting a report from the Intelligencer of Belleville, that the men had not been paid for two months. A fortnight later, The Madoc Review published a letter of denial from George McMullen saying there had been a delay in payment, because of the illness of his brother, D.S. McMullen. As the newspaper pointed out, many bankrupt railways had bred a well-founded suspicion among railway workers, who had need to protect themselves. The company then brought in a large number of Quebec workers and there were no more strikes.

In spite of these problems the rails did reach Marmora (milepost 30.4) in July 1883 and then Eldorado (milepost 40.7).

The latter months had also seen the company's first serious accident, although luckily there were no deaths or injuries. A train, loaded with rails, was climbing the grade near Rawdon when the coupling broke. With automatic air-brakes still in the future, the cars ran back down the hill to collide with some cars standing on the track. The result was that five cars were wrecked and four others damaged.

Another threat to further expansion by the C.O.R. came with a campaign supported by Bowell in his Belleville newspaper, deprecating both the C.O.R. and the Midland, claiming this would further isolate Madoc. But Belleville was their real concern. But the last lines of a letter signed by Billa Flint, a successful Hastings promoter and entrepreneur whose "Enterprise Steam Saw Mill" had been a first in this part of the province: "Let us take care of the interests of our own city, and if we succeed we will sweep the rich valley of the Moira, and all north into our own instead of Madoc business man's hands . . ."[15]

That fine gentleman Ross Weaver, former fireman, brakeman, and conductor who was brought up in this neighbourhood.

These periodic local hubbubs, without any discernible rhythm, came and went. Some were just causes, most served some particular interest, some instigated overdue reforms. The first months of 1884 saw one that led to the ending of a serious injustice.

The C.O.R. had already been morally guilty of piracy, but within the law, by expropriating near Coe Hill and its subsidiary mining company, a privately owned iron ore mine for a pitifully small sum on the basis of needing the land for their right-of-way and for a station site.

This time the syndicate was accused of expropriating crown lands for mining operations, then selling the surface rights to settlers. The correspondence in the newspapers grew considerably, nearly all letters written under nom de plumes such as "Interested", "A Farmer", "Hastings Road", and "Citizen". Before long there would be legislation amending the Railway Act.[16]

In the previous year Belleville had agitated against Madoc getting the regional business. This year Madoc whipped out its crying towels. It was becoming isolated with the C.O.R.'s settlements getting much of the trade that had formerly been theirs by road, more still would be lost as the railway was extended further north. Connections had yet to be made by the C.O.R. where it crossed the Grand Junction at Anson, near Stirling. Madoc supported the extension of the old Belleville and North Hastings (then Midland and Grand Trunk).[17]

The Ritchie-McMullen reaction must have been a big laugh at Madoc's predicament. However Ritchie wrote that they were "ready and anxious" to interchange traffic so that the C.O.R. could route traffic to Belleville as well.

The Picton line past Weller's Bay seemed to be just about forgotten when it was made known that the track would be raised six inches to one foot in the coming summer. The advantages would be, less snow on the track in the winter months, better drainage over the rest of the year, and smoother track.

There followed the news from Prince Edward County. To all intents the Women's Christian Temperence Union had been founded in Picton, by Mrs. Letitia Youmans, the temperance pioneer resident there. The C.O.R. supported the movement and when this fact was reported in the press, local publicans and saloon keepers gave notice that they would blacklist the railway and not permit them to haul their products. The threat does not seem to have been followed up, delivery by horse wagon over dirt roads was impractical, in winter — absurd.

Further away, the Kingston Locomotive Company was now in desperate financial straits. Of their 500 employees, 400 were abruptly laid off. This hit the City of Kingston hard, "the men having to leave the city for employment." Later it was made known that the Canadian Pacific would help finance the reorganization of that company.

Good news for the C.O.R. was the refusal of the government to subsidize the Grand Trunk (B. & N.H.) extension to Bancroft and the north, much to the chagrin of the citizenry of Madoc. The company was unpopular with the government.

If Madoc had no great liking for the C.O.R., the farmers along the line by Stirling made up for it. They organized a 'Grand Banquet' for the proprietors and officers on May 29th, to celebrate their section of the line being passed for passenger traffic by the government inspector.[18] But the biggest day yet for the C.O.R. was not far off — just three days away.

Success at last! The rails had reached Coe Hill mine in Wollaston Township, soon to be called Coe Hill, and on the following Monday, June 2nd, 1884, the first train of iron ore steamed out unsteadily over the roughly laid mine track for Weller's Bay. With much whistle blowing and a continuous ringing of the bell, the train was underway.[19] The last few miles through the hills had been quickly built. Little better than a roller-coaster, it was a headache for the train crews.

The work on the dock was now being completed in frantic haste.

Out in the bay two barges and a schooner lay at anchor ready to come alongside to receive the ore directly from the cars through the chutes. Soon they would be loaded and under way for the United States.[20]

On Thursday, a special train hosted by Samuel Ritchie, George and J.B. McMullen left Picton for Coe Hill. On board were a number of V.I.P.'s, mostly from the United States; also the manager of Molson's Bank in Trenton, that institution having a more than casual interest in the company.

That only 30 miles of the line remained to be

ballasted was in itself above average for that time, when many other short lines could wait a generation or more for such benefits. The telegraph line would soon follow.[21]

It would seem that Samuel Ritchie and his associates deserved to live happily ever after in ever-growing prosperity. Surely, nothing could go wrong now. The ore was there in unlimited quantities; an excellent railway had been built; and the high capacity docks were ready for quick, economical loading.

Chapter Seven

As a line built to standards that were unique in Canada during the past century, the extension merits some description, in a way that is not possible with giant systems whose tracks can extend in excess of twenty thousand miles. It is hoped this might help as a guide to those who may visit the area. While much has changed, and few stations remain, most places of interest on the line can be visited by side roads. For the industrial archeologist this is also a fascinating and neglected area. First, before visiting, it is suggested you read Gerald Boyce's book "Historic Hastings."

The high standards of construction were not only superior to the Grand Trunk main line, but more so compared to the brand-new Canadian Pacific's O. & Q. line, hag-ridden by lack of funds. Completed in May, 1884, this was the main line of the C.P.R. from Ottawa and the East to Toronto.

Frankford, early in the century. Believed to be an Orange Day Parade. A rare picture showing a passenger coach of that era.
Photo, Mrs. Christie Bates. Kindness Mr. Peter Johnson of Scarborough.

Frankford Station in 1977 as a Senior Citizens Club sponsored by The Lions Club. Both pictures looking north.

Photo, Author

An important feature of the C.O.R. line, but for the last miles into Coe Hill, was that there were no gradients over one per cent in either direction. Except on the plains this is rated "moderate" on any main line. A gradient percentage, incidentally, is the rise in feet per hundred linear feet. The detailed information given as to grades, sidings, etc., is from an official C.O.R. gradient profile, undated but identifiable as drawn up in 1906 or later.[1] The original sidings and passing tracks and their lengths in the years immediately after the opening can only be hypothetical.

An interesting comparison is the Prince Edward County section, a shorter line in easier country which had one gradient of 1.172% northbound, and two southbound of 1.286% and 1.25%.

Curvature is important in operations. To reduce curves can be costly in initial construction costs. The justification for curves is to reduce gradients. Otherwise, not only do curves increase distances, take more time and use more fuel, but sharp curves reduce speed and increase resistance to require higher power (or smaller loads) the same as a gradient. Severe curves increase wear and tear on wheels. Combine sharp curves and heavy gradients and a railroad has permanent high operating costs.

Railroad curves are measured in degrees (from a 100 foot chord of the circle represented by the curve, measure the angle between the two radii.) A standard U.S. authority[2] considers a one degree curve (5.730 ft. radius) as relatively flat, and a 10 degree curve as sharp, though they are to be found on trunk lines on this continent in mountainous areas. Ritchie's line, though high speed was not a requirement, contained only five 3-degree curves and one of 4.04 degrees near milepost 31.

Bridges and culverts, large and small, in keeping with several brick stations of permanent construction, were stone or concrete with steel I-beams. Smaller culverts were of concrete or tile pipe. Out of 95 such structures there is only one of timber and this was probably a later addition, to be compared with the thousands of timber structures on railroads elsewhere at this time. These were vulnerable to fire; and with wood preservatives non-existent, subject to rot after a short life.

Once clear of Trenton the country is thinly populated. The further north one goes the rockier it becomes, and the fewer the people. North of Coe Hill, roughly half the length of the County of Hastings, most of the land was untouched wilderness.

The majority of the population were of United Empire Loyalist descent or immigrants from the British Isles. Others had come from Quebec. A minority, often of strong character, were from Continental Europe. The native Algonquin Indians, people of the lakes and forests, seemingly stunned by the destruction in a single generation of their infinite past, living with nature, were too bewildered to adapt easily to such changed circumstances.

While the people of Prince Edward County tended to identify themselves with "The County" first, here, because of distance and a small population, "identification" was more by individual village or hamlet. In a harder environment (for many it had meant endless toil just to exist), this bred a hardy people.

The C.O.R. had been designed as an iron ore road, bulk haulage, but every effort was made to encourage local traffic. Stations were built where there were any traffic prospects, most were flag stops. Some would close in the years to come. Others remained open only to house an operator, a lonely life, and many quit the job after a short while. With a passing track, and a stop signal for train orders received by the operator in morse, the safety of the passing trains was entirely in his hands.

North of Frankford, typical of the well-graded, easily curved line built to Ritchie's high standards, and without government subsidies.   *Photo, Author*

Trent Bridge, original steel superstructure, Swing Bridge in distance a later substitution for last spans when Trent Canal was built. 1977 Photo.

Photo, Author

A hot day at Bonarlaw Station. The section crew are C.P.R. men. The station was C.O.R. property serving both lines. Time? Early twenties?

Photo, Heckman, Courtesy Canadian Pacific Archives

From the beginning there were many passengers in the summer months when the woods were busy. Hunters and fishermen were also numerous. Flag stops were not listed in the early timetables, but it is believed that the train would stop just about anywhere for a passenger, light freight or express packages. The expressmen would often undertake small purchases as a favour. Occasionally some unfortunate medical crisis would arise and an engineer would take calculated chances to get a patient to a hospital in time. With the roads no better than narrow, grassy cart tracks it certainly meant great, new opportunities for those living near the railway and it also meant a better standard of living. The impact of the arrival of the railway is hard to imagine now. For these people economic benefits came not so much

from the iron ore, but from the increased production of sawn lumber and cordwood. There was also the cordwood to be cut and sold for the railway to fuel the locomotives. In the farming areas, mostly grasslands, there was now a better outlet for dairy products; cheese factories were enlarged and new ones built.

If the new line had few communities as neighbours, a paradox lay in the number of railways it had as direct neighbours or nearby ones. This was because the C.O.R. travelled northwards across the main east to west routes.

Leaving Trenton (Population at that time 3,042 and Belleville 9,516) the C.O.R. follows the natural route of the Trent Valley along its west bank. Across the river are the huge Gilmour mills, joined by a causeway-dam. Likely as not you could have seen the former No. 1 engine of the Prince Edward County Railway switching cars. She had lost her tender, if this was the engine illustrated, but an extension of the frames at the rear carried a box, sufficient for a limited supply of water.

The village of Glen Miller (4.8 miles) is next, a paper mill is there to this day. The Trent River runs fast over its last miles. Here and there, where there is an island, are dams for water power; some built by private funds, others by government authorities. In those days many small industries grew around those sources of power. Frankford (milepost 7.9) is such a settlement, and after Trenton was the largest settlement on the line. Here the fall of water is sufficient to support lumber, flour, wool and paper mills. (Nowadays the headquarters and main Canadian plant of the Bata Shoe Company is at nearby Batawa.)

Past Frankford the line swings west, for the valley has broadened, cutting across a 45° bend in the river to the west for the easiest river crossing at Chisholm's Rapids, site of that critical 400-foot bridge. At the south end of the bridge is the station "Chisholm's" for a community that has barely survived since. The station lasted until the last few years of the century to be replaced when the Trent Canal was under construction many years later by a station on the north bank, Glen Ross. Here was an agent operator. There was also a passing track and a water tower.

Between the island and the north bank was another series of power dams, with the usual collection of mills and an iron foundry. The number of mills would be diminished by the construction of the canal, though two survived until 1913. Part of the 400-foot bridge was removed and in 1905 a second-hand swing bridge section was installed.

Before the railway came, Glen Ross had been called Rossford Station, it is said after John Ross, an early Grand Trunk president. An earlier line had been projected, an ancestor of the Grand Junction which would have crossed the river here on its way from Belleville to Georgian Bay, but that part of the line was never started.

At mile 15.4 we came to a station tersely called "Anson" in the timetables though it is often called today more appropriately 'Anson Junction'. In the late '80's, just to add to the confusion C.O.R. timetables referred to it as "Midland Railway Junction."

The line completed the same year as the Prince Edward County Railway, the Grand Trunk, was senior and had the right-of-way over C.O.R. trains at the level crossing. They also had to maintain the installation. This meant that Ritchie's trains, from time to time, had an aggravating wait.

The junction would be important to both lines then, giving the C.O.R. an outlet for lumber and pulpwood shipments to Belleville, and the smaller but higher paying general freight in return. But it was many years before the connection was made. In its obstinate way, the Grand Trunk would not make the connection. Until it was done there was no direct rail connection for the long-suffering Village of Madoc with the C.O.R. Hence the terse 'Anson'.

Perhaps the most valuable business here for the C.O.R. was from the Village of Stirling, less than two miles to the east, one of the bigger settlements in the area (population 874) and one of the more prosperous. A short journey to Anson by horse, cart or sleigh and Trenton was in easy reach.

Anson station was north of the cross-over. Here was another passing track, 800 feet long.

The station, built in open country, was not called after the famous British admiral, but after Anson Street near the site. The street, in turn, was called after Anson Cummings, who farmed there.

After leaving Anson, mile 198, the line crosses Squire's Creek with a 50-foot span. This waterway saw many log runs. The next station at mile 2039 is Rawdon, called after the township, whose entire population numbered 3,500. The station was built on a flat section, with a long, 200-foot passing track, part way up the longest northbound gradient. Before air-brakes were in general use this was the scene of several runaways. Locomotives short of steam had to double the grade.

There was no community at Rawdon, so the agent operator had a lonely time. The nearest settlement was at Wellman's Corners, two and a half miles due west. This was named for a well-respected United Empire Loyalist family. One of the earliest cheese factories had operated here. Later there was a sawmill.

Rawdon station was closed, as far as can be traced, between 1910 and 1912. By 1914 a new station had been opened .4 of a mile south, to be called Wellman.

Bonarlaw (Junction) looking south along C.O.R. 1977   *Photo, Author*

Bonarlaw looking west along C.P.R. tracks 1977   *Photo, Author*

First Regular Train Into Marmora Station, in wood burning days. It was first called Wolf Station after a man who was killed there.

Photo, Miss Grace Warren and Hastings Co. Museum

After reaching the summit the line runs down to Springbrook at mile 22.8; another small but busy settlement with saw, grist and shingle mills, whose activities were greatly increased with the coming of the railway. Here too was another cheese factory. The 800-foot passing track was much used.

The next place of importance, exactly at mile 25, is the diagonal level crossing with the Canadian Pacific Railway (ex O. and Q.) There is also a 1,100-foot passing track, and a connecting spur.

The C.O.R. had reached this point early enough to ship a considerable tonnage of construction materials for the C.P.R. More important, this became the means of regular traffic interchange for as far away as Picton to the benefit of both companies. The Grand Trunk too long used to a monopoly, had accepted delays in shipments complacently and not without occasional arrogance. The aggressive CPR, on the other hand, was after all the traffic it could get.

The O. and Q. represented one of the final victories in the all-out war between the two giants

that had ranged from the Grand Trunk buying up every possible independent line to hinder the CPR's invasion of their territory, to spreading malicious rumours in the City of London to prevent their rival obtaining new capital. By then, neither company had any extra cash to buy the C.O.R.; their executives may also have been less optimistic about its golden future.

At this time the CPR's transcontinental line was yet to be completed. The Riel Rebellion came in the early months of 1885. As everyone knows it was the unfortunate Riel who did more to save the CPR from bankruptcy than the company's sponsor John A. Macdonald — though nobody seems to have been particularly grateful. To keep the considerably lesser affairs of the C.O.R. in perspective with current railway happenings, the date of the driving of the last spike at Craigellachie completing the C.P.'s transcontinental line was on November 7th, 1885.

* * *

Marmora Station in 1977. Line no longer used, but station use by section crew. Heavy rail was extended just past station, Marmora Mine then being worked; south and west of station.

Photo, Author

Eldorado. Date unknown. Southbound passenger train. The Great Goldrush just a memory.

Photo, Ontario Govt. Archives

There was another enterprise of Ritchie's that had brought him into contact with Cornelius Van Horne. That was Ritchie's interest later in 1885 in the copper deposits discovered at Sudbury during the construction of the C.P.R. He would organize the mining syndicate that would become the Canadian Copper Company.[3]

The early community that developed near the junction with the Ontario and Quebec Railway was called Big Springs, although earlier it had been referred to as C.P.R. Junction. This could have been a bigger and more prosperous community, for the C.P.R. intended to establish their divisional point here. But these prospects faded rapidly when, unimpressed by local land disputes the company decided on Havelock, a short distance to the west, outside Hastings County.[4]

Maybe, from embarrassment, Big Springs changed its name when drowning its collective sorrow, to "Bell View" in honour of the local publican, John Bell. Then, in 1897, the community firmly resolved itself against any such observance of past disappointments, and voted dry. John Bell had to close his hotel, though "Bell View" the community remained for the next quarter of a century. The railway had long ignored whatever a community chose to call itself for the station remained "C.P.R. Junction." On maps and for a number of years this was also sometimes referred to as C.O.R. Junction, even after that company lost its corporate identity.

Not long after the First World War had ended the station agent decided it was more than time for a change of name and circulated a petition to this end. The community approved, and the village was renamed "Bonarlaw" after Great Britain's one and only Canadian-born prime minister. The C.P.R. was also agreeable and finally changed the name of the station.

Not yet built, leaving the C.O.R. line 1.8 miles from the junction, would be a short line to the historic Marmora Iron Works.

From that future junction point the railway heads in a north-easterly direction to Marmora Station, a short two miles east of the iron works and settlement. Marmora is the Italian word for marble, high grade marble being quarried here.

To the east, in easy walking distance, is the first of the gold mines in the Deloro area. The first gold discovery had been made in 1886. Since then several mines had opened and closed, as would be the case in the future. Some would be ambitious,

costly and unprofitable enterprises. Overall the C.O.R. probably gained more than the miners. In earlier years, Marmora had been the second biggest community in Hastings County, when Trenton was a small settlement.

At mile 37.6, after the line had changed direction to due east, the line reaches Malone. Here there was much cordwood and cut lumber to be shipped, common sight at all the more northern stations. Cordwood was locomotive fuel. While coal was coming into general use as a fuel elsewhere, the C.O.R. found wood to be cheaper for a few years yet, with wages low and the trees growing in the vicinity of the line.

Malone's sawmills were powered by the Moira River which ran through the town. There were a couple of small gold mines nearby.

Less than a mile out the line crosses into Madoc Township, to continue westerly to Eldorado, mile 40.7, site of the 1866 gold rush. This happening, complete with mounted police to keep some semblance of order, was an event — Ontario's first gold mine. Few profited, for it is said that no more than $100,000 worth of gold ever came out of here. Gold was still being mined when the C.O.R. arrived, but in small quantities.

If matters had gone according to local expectations, Eldorado should have been at least the northern terminus of the Belleville and North Hastings Railway, ready and waiting to interchange traffic with the C.O.R. More than this, the company should have pre-empted much of the route the C.O.R. now occupied north of this point. For this was the line that the 1,400 inhabitants of the village of Madoc, plus the 1,800 remaining in the township, had so confidently supported, anticipating a profitable flow of commerce to and from the north.

The directors of this line had included the Honourable Mackenzie Bowell, D'Arcy Boulton, builder and operator of smaller railways in southern Ontario, and a contractor and engineer of high reputation, Francis Shanley. Either he or his brother had given the final inspection of the Picton line on behalf of the government.[5]

Mackenzie Bowell, a federal cabinet minister, and owning a Belleville newspaper, used his influence to obtain what must have been a record $459,000 in subsidies, which included $150,000 from the City of Belleville, even though this line would start 12 miles out on what had been the Grand Junction at Madoc Junction. From there it was only 15 miles to Madoc, and another seven miles to Eldorado.

In spite of the talent available (and the money) this can best be described as an adventure in which incompetence and skullduggery were harmoniously combined. First it was planned to build the line as a narrow gauge railway; not only would construction have been much cheaper, but as such systems were now recognized as obsolete in Canada, rails and equipment were available at close to scrap prices. There must have been a good deal of behind-the-scenes fury, particularly in Madoc, and plans were changed to build the line to standard gauge. Madoc was in Bowell's constituency.

Colonel Stevens points out, in his history of the Canadian National Railway, this project 'was no more than a stalking horse,' a covert means, to obtain control of the shaky Grand Junction, whose common stock at the time could be bought for a pittance. While control was not obtained of the Grand Junction Railway, one cannot but wonder if there was considerable profit for this group when the Grand Trunk bought the line. Colonel Stevens remarks that there are no surviving records. Today, these happenings would bring serious charges of conflict of interest against Bowell, but not then. He was also chairman of the Belleville and North Hastings Railway and a director of the Grand Junction. Later he would become Prime Minister. However it must be said of him that such standards were normal in those days of financial and political buccaneers.

Old Wooden Boxcar Used For Stores, 1977   *Photo, Author*

The concrete platform and the station sign were all that was left in 1977. A short distance further east was where the Madoc line once joined.   *Photo, Author*

Looking west towards Malone in 1977. The rain made the tracks.   *Photo, Author*

The B. & N.H. itself, whatever its success as a 'stalking horse', was a poor railway. In its fifteen miles to Madoc its one engineering need was to cross Moira Lake. This was done by two timber trestles which had to be replaced by the Grand Trunk after it took over the line.

The line never owned any equipment and was operated in turn by the Grand Junction, Midland Railway, and the Grand Trunk. In its early years it was accident prone, tardy, and there were frequent complaints about the wretched equipment — all targets for the sharp wit of the Madoc newspaper's editor.

Madoc, ambitious and ready to develop its resources (it had already rolled rails for the Grand Junction railway) had become frustrated. The charter of the line had been obtained in 1875, construction began in August, 1876. Then in 1877 the line had suffered a set-back of some kind and work ceased. Having crawled and staggered the fifteen miles to Madoc it was finally opened for traffic on January 1st, 1880, and there it collapsed. Construction had averaged 3.3 miles per annum.

Soon to be returned to the forest. Roadbed midway between Ormsby Jct. and Coe Hill 1977   *Photo, Author*

As Colonel Stevens records, only token payments were made in buying common stock. It would seem likely that payments in director's fees, etc., were considerably in excess of these amounts. Madoc finally took legal action in 1906 to recover part of its subsidy.

Earlier the town had been rejoicing that it lay on the route of the projected Toronto and Ottawa Railway but little had been done before construction ceased.

The final blow for Madoc had been when there was every likelihood of the Ontario and Quebec Railway building through their town, the Grand Trunk had threatened to build a parallel line, and the Ontario and Quebec turned south through Tweed instead.

Returning to the C.O.R., the line heads north from Eldorado to Bannockburn, a distance of five miles. The countryside is becoming rockier, with less land to cultivate, and the settlers largely dependent on lumbering. With few easements the line climbs all the way. North of the station the line crosses Jordan Creek, which delivered the spring log drives to the Moira River through Malone. Rathbuns and Gilmours used to interchange their logs delivered by these rivers which flowed to different destinations, by log rafts towed along Lake Ontario. The railway changed much of this. Bannockburn at one time was known as Mumby's Mills. At this date there was both a grist and a sawmill there.[6]

Then another four miles, which seems to have been a standard distance between communities here, to Millbridge, situated a couple of miles to the west of the station. As a result of this distance, a new settlement would develop in its vicinity, Hogan. Millbridge, though small, was famous for its annual fair. This was an important event in those days when for the rest of the year people had to entertain themselves. They came from miles around and the C.O.R. coaches and stock cars carried capacity loads.[7]

Five miles more! And a station that may not have been even a flag stop when the line was built. McDonald's was near some beautiful lakes surrounded by forests. Summer traffic, as at other points, included many fishermen. Here they arrived in numbers complete with camping equipment, braving the blackflies, to return home with big catches.

The next station, Gilmour, at mile 59.7, also resulted from the building of the railway. A namesake of the operators of the Trenton mill, it has survived after the lumber company has been all but forgotten.

The arrivals and departures of the passenger and mixed trains represented the only communication with the outside world, except for the telegraph used for urgent matters which was located in the station building anyway. There was the mail, the railway express, which handles most parcels, and people coming and going on business and pleasure.

Waiting for the train was a time for news and gossip. Then, in the distance, the engine could be seen and heard, whistling for a farm crossing, a staccato exhaust, then the sound of her bell ringing as she approached the station.

Old roadbed of Coe Hill sub-division near Ormsby Jct. 1978   *Photo, Author*

Gilmour around 1912. The station is there yet, a credit to the good people of that community, unvandalised. The water-tower complete with windmill is long gone. Inside window is M.K. Baker, Agent.
Photo, David Hanes, L'Amable & Hastings County Museum

Coe Hill Station. Now located in the Coe Hill Fairgrounds and well maintained. 1977
Photo, Author

An old concrete structure. Can be seen from the highway north of Bannockburn.   *Photo, Author*

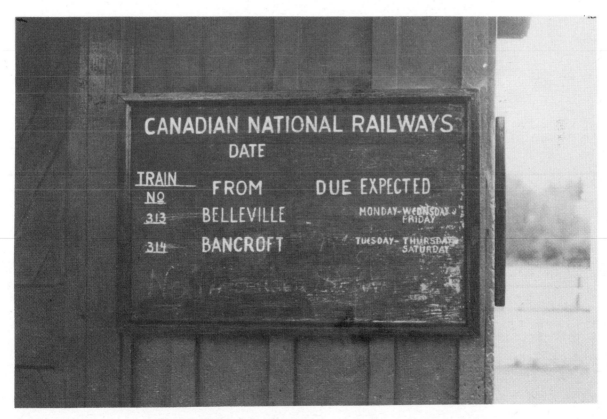

Sign Board Coe Hill Station 1977   *Photo, Author*

Part of Gilmour's, Trenton

"Evolution of Trenton"

The Still Waters of Beaver Creek. Here the logs were flushed down the
river by opening up the dams.   *Photo, Author*

It was the same all the way along the line, some stations would be more crowded, but if one visited often, one would discover there were differences in character and temperament in each settlement, more so then than now. In those days of isolation, and with the limited resources available, the people had to be gut-individualists to survive, let alone prosper. Most communities, like individuals, had good reputations, others were less exemplary. But in all, neighborliness, a necessity, was a normal, spontaneous reaction — seldom calculated.[8]

Just across the township line from Gilmour is the station for St. Ola, mile 62.5. This is in Limerick township, not incorporated until 1886. St. Ola, called after a Scottish saint, lies nearly three miles to the east, situated on Beaver Creek, and became the administrative centre for the township. With this distance to walk to the station the number waiting to greet the trains must have been smaller than elsewhere. The lake above the town had been dammed by the Gilmours and held sufficient water to flush the log drives down the sluggish creek, through Marmora to the south. The railway crosses Beaver Creek a few miles south of the station. With this water power available the village contained what seems to have been the almost standard selection of mills. A mile north the ruling gradient northbound begins;

cursed by locomotive crews since the railway was opened. The summit is the second highest point on the line.

Not many more rivers to cross, or station stops. The country is rougher and rockier; the stations are farther apart. The gradients steeper. The Ritchie standards had to be dropped before Ormsby. At mile 68.9 is a station called Rathbun, after the logging, manufacturing and railway magnate who ruled over his considerable empire from Deseronto, east of Belleville. A year later its name was changed to Ormsby.

Now the railway heads mostly downhill due east to the hard won goal, 79 miles from Trenton: Coe Hill. This last stretch was a heavy pull for outwardbound trains.[9]

Naturally, at Coe Hill, there was a handsome station, of frame construction. At this time, scattered among some spur lines, the community consisted of mining buildings, a number of small wooden dwellings, with some bunkhouses, against a background of mounds of iron ore and tailings. The area was heavily wooded.

The C.O.R. would expand further. There would be extensions and further development. But the line from Trenton to Ormsby would remain a masterpiece, if a minor one, of railroad construction.

St. Ola looking north. The pooch seemed to be trying to say "No Trains Running Anymore!"
Photo, Author

Gilmour in 1977. It is a couple of years since a train polished the rails.

Extension past Coe Hill to ore mines. 1977

Chapter Eight

At the end of summer, late August, 1884, the northern line was passed for passenger traffic. Service started a week later with two trains running each way, one called 'the express', carrying passengers, mail and express; the other a 'mixed'. All trains connected with the Grand Trunk Railway at Trenton, and at C.P.R. Junction where passenger service would come later.[1]

The Trenton merchants were delighted by a rush of new customers, most of whom had never visited the town before. Even Madoc found business better, customers taking the stage from Eldorado, where the passenger trains crossed.

The line must have been busy from the beginning, already 12,000 tons of ore had been shipped from Weller's Bay. Six schooners and a fleet of casual callers had carried the ore across the lake. One of the six was the "St. Louis". She had been purchased by the McMullens and was one of two that had returned with cargoes of coal, possibly an experiment. What was satisfying had been the discovery that with this volume of ore there was a saving of 50¢ a ton compared to shipping from Belleville.[2]

The boom was on. At Coe Hill the mining subsidiary was building more housing for the miners, anticipating an increase over the 73 men already employed.

Work on the Murray Canal was progressing. Five dredges and derricks were hard at work. Two steam pumps were emptying the canal at the sites for the two swing bridges, one for rail, the other for road traffic.[3]

The editor of *The North Hastings Review* was now pressing for the completion of the Belleville and North Hastings Railway to Eldorado.

October 8th, saw the C.O.R.'s first excursion north of Trenton (presumably it started from Picton), to Coe Hill. The visitors were given three hours to see the sights. Unfortunately it rained all day.

The same month saw the first recorded correspondence between Ritchie and Cornelius Van Horne, then vice-president and general manager of the Canadian Pacific Railway. Ritchie's handwriting is an interesting study in itself.[4]

Ritchie's letter, datelined Montreal on the 3rd, requests of Van Horne that he visit him at Trenton, "... not later than the next Tuesday morning as there is a matter aside from what I have been talking to you about that I desire to see you there before returning home [Akron, Ohio]." Considering Van Horne's position the tone was peremptory, but this does not seem to have given offence. Van Horne's replies were always courteous. One would gather that whatever Ritchie's tone he admired Van Horne greatly and patterned his future very much on that lion-hearted man's style in the development of his transportation and mining interests, except he found it harder to accept cheap construction.

Not unexpectedly Van Horne was too busy to come at such short notice though the letter or wire of answer is not recorded, but Ritchie telegraphed him on the 9th rather plaintively. It began, "Special reason why you should have come tomorrow..."

Van Horne was there two weeks later, arriving at what is now Bonarlaw in his business car to be met by Ritchie waiting with a special train. The likely sequence was that Van Horne's business car was switched to the C.O.R. tracks and attached to the rear of the C.O.R. train.

If Ritchie had yet to acquire his own business car, the C.O.R. locomotive and whatever cars were attached would be in superb condition. Locomotives were always beautifully maintained under Ritchie. That day the equipment would have been better turned out than when it had arrived from the builders.

Van Horne, always a believer in the highest practicable standards, would have been impressed, and frankly envious as they rode over the beautifully engineered C.O.R. tracks, after the rickety rails of the Ontario and Quebec.

The special first ran north to Coe Hill to see the mines. From there they ran south to Weller's Bay to inspect the dock.[5] Returning to the C.P.R. Junction in Van Horne's car there would be good food and drink, the best of cigars, and excellent conversation.

This left Ritchie envious of Van Horne's business car, and determined to have his own. When he purchased his car is not known, likely it was bought second-hand from the Grand Trunk. The first recorded date of its existence is on October 28th, 1885, a year plus two days after Van Horne's visit.

Ritchie, still at Trenton, wrote Van Horne on the 29th, "I forgot when I left you to refer to Andrew Carnegie who is head of the steel firm of Carnegie Bros. & Co., the largest steel manufacturers in the United States. They will be large consumers of our ore this coming season . . . I want you to fully satisfy yourself that there is not the slightest question about our being able to market *all* our ore even should there be no improvement in the iron market."

The follow-up to Van Horne's visit, Ritchie wired him, "Do you expect your men to be here this week, if so what day, answer." The C.P.R. officials arrived on the 30th to inspect the line. Ritchie had another special train for them.

This special was not so fortunate. At Eldorado the train ran through an open switch. "The engine and one or two cars plunged into the mud. The party . . . were delayed until the next morning, but the officials made themselves happy and comfortable at Harris' Hotel in the meantime."[6]

How did the C.O.R. look to Van Horne and his advisers as a viable proposition? That is if they could find the money to buy the line, and there were many higher priorities. Certainly the port of Weller's Bay had potential, primarily for handling coal imports from the United States, the only source of coal for Eastern Canada. At present their only economical route was by rail through Montreal. Without including commercial deliveries the railway was then consuming 80,000 tons annually in the east. With this facility all their requirements could be brought in during the navigation season. As yet the C.P.R. had no lake port in this region.

While ideally situated on the map, Weller's Bay had some disadvantages. The docks being designed only for discharging bulk cargoes, for bulk-unloading either extensive alterations and additions would be necessary or an additional dock would have to be built. If steamers of higher capacity, which with lower costs per ton were already a reality, then a heavy dredging programme would be essential. (As it was Weller's Bay being on a lee shore for the prevailing winds nobody seems to have realized that with the constant silting this was a less than ideal harbour site.) Against this was the advantage that with even half the volume anticipated in ore shipments, loaded trains in both directions would boost net revenue impressively.

These comings and goings inevitably resulted in a flood of conjecture. The Trenton Courier was cautious. "The people of Trenton are anxious to know what this means. Possibly we may soon have more perfect connections with both the great through railways."

The Madoc newspaper was more definite. "The rumour has been current around this village for some days past that the Canadian Pacific had secured the Central Ontario road, and would soon take over its control, and operate it under the management of the Ontario division . . ."

The mining subsidiary of the R.O.R. now confirmed the presence of another rich ore bed. It would appear to have been carefully timed.

After this everyone waited — and waited in vain. There is no record of the C.P.R.'s decision or their reasons. Likely Van Horne told Ritchie personally. Ritchie made no public statements on the subject. That was the end of the matter at least for the present.

There was other bad news. As with all newly constructed railways, the C.O.R. was having operating problems. On Thursday, the 27th November, the company had its first serious accident near Gilmour, unfortunately it involved the mixed train carrying 90 passengers. The rails spread under the locomotive, likely they had not been properly spiked, and five freight cars and the crowded passenger coach were overturned.

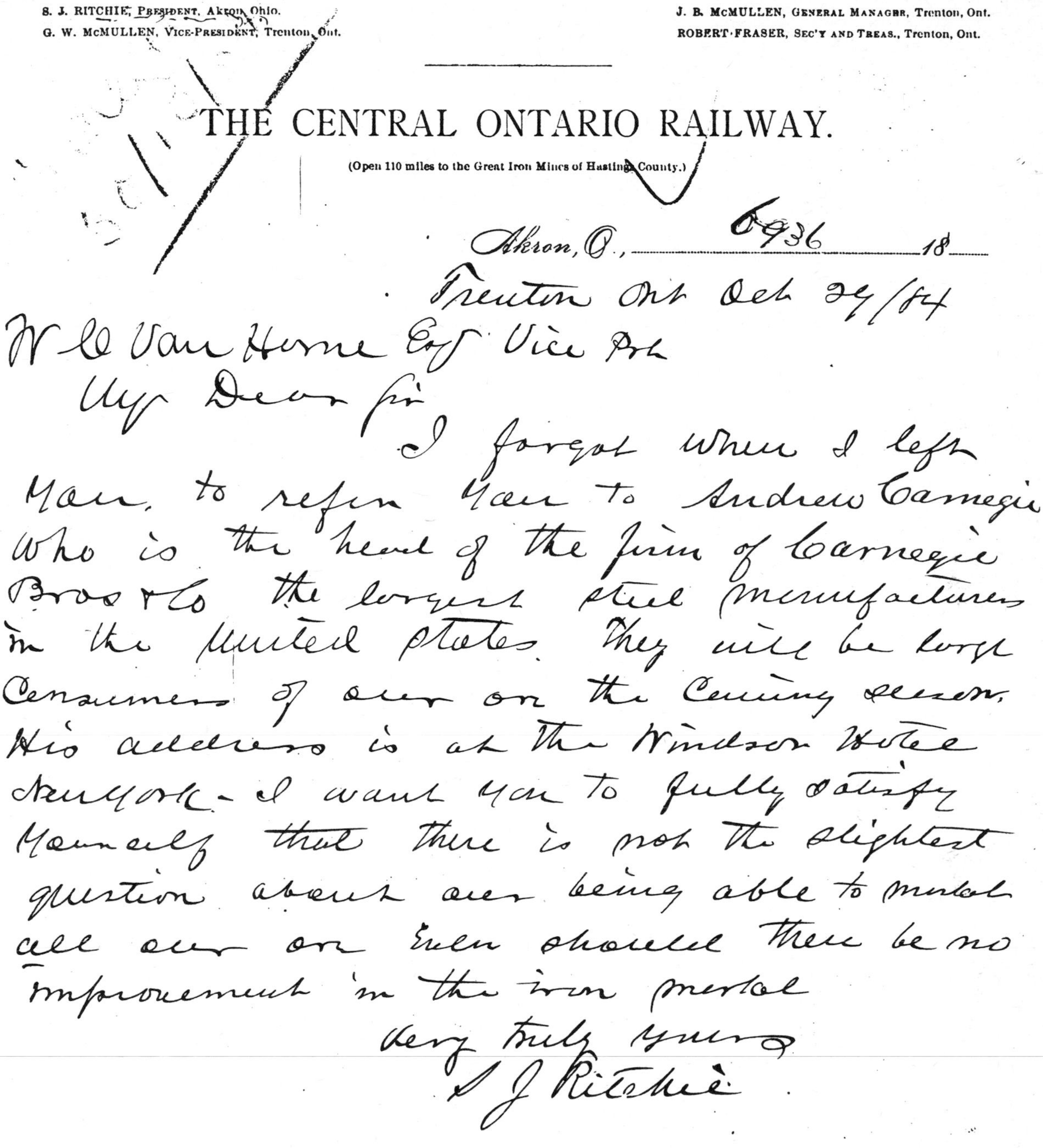
S. J. RITCHIE, President, Akron, Ohio.
G. W. McMULLEN, Vice-President, Trenton, Ont.
J. B. McMULLEN, General Manager, Trenton, Ont.
ROBERT FRASER, Sec'y and Treas., Trenton, Ont.

THE CENTRAL ONTARIO RAILWAY.

(Open 110 miles to the Great Iron Mines of Hastings County.)

Akron, O., 6936 18

Trenton Ont Oct 24/84

W C Van Horne Esq Vice Prs

My Dear Sir

I forgot when I left you to refer you to Andrew Carnegie who is the head of the firm of Carnegie Bros & Co the largest steel manufacturers in the United States. They will be large consumers of ore the coming season. His address is at the Windsor Hotel New York - I want you to fully satisfy yourself that there is not the slightest question about our being able to market all our ore even should there be no improvement in the iron market

Very truly yours

S J Ritchie

Letter Ritchie to Van Horne.

Corporate Archives, Canadian Pacific

This might have been a disaster. As the wooden coach went over a can of oil upset by the stove and blazed up. Conductor Robinson, quickly and courageously, smothered the blaze with a blanket. As it was, one passenger was critically injured, another had severe burns, and three others suffered lesser injuries. "A married woman and a child, the only females, miraculously escaped."[7]

On the same day there had been the potential for another serious accident when a sink-hole was discovered. It had been quickly filled. Later piles had to be driven into the swampy ground to secure the roadbed.[8]

Every so often Prince Edward County was back in the railway news. Early December there was some excitement when J. S. McCuaig, former M.P. for the County, gave notice of application for a charter to build a line from Picton to Peterson's Point (site of a long-established ferry) with a swing bridge and a short length of traffic line into Deseronto on the mainland.[9] This was a revival of George McMullen's earlier dream and in the light of subsequent events he may have been behind it.

The southern section of the C.O.R. was doing well. Traffic was increasing. The benefits of rail transportation to the community are well illustrated by one particular example. The railway had become a commuter line, not only for those working in the various centres, but now a new generation could get a high school education hitherto denied them. Before the line, unless one's family could afford to pay board and lodging in Picton, and be spared the daily chores on the farm, one's learning was likely to terminate at Grade 8 in a one-room school. Now, from all along the line, students were travelling daily to the Picton Academy.[10]

Sometime after the construction of the new station in Picton, a turntable was installed. Up until then the locomotives must have hauled their trains backward in one direction — a cold exercise in winter. The site, south of the main tracks at the end of a siding indicates that it was built after the new station site was constructed.

According to Gerard Kavanagh, who as a boy lived near the turntable, and Andrew Jarvis, for many years town clerk of Picton, this was a unique structure. The turntable was roofed-in with a hole for the smoke to emerge. This saved a lot of snow shovelling in the winter. Also unusual, there was no shed for the locomotive. A small square structure attached, served as a tool house.

The routine was for the locomotive to back the train out of the station to one of the sidings, after which it ran round the train and on to the turntable. The engine was turned. The engine crew had a coffee break and a smoke. They then backed the train into the station ready for loading.

The turntable fell out of use in the mid-twenties when a wye was built. The locomotives had outgrown it. Decay started and in time the roof fell in. About 1932 it was dismantled,[11] but not before it had given many Picton youngsters a great deal of entertainment.

Being roofed it was invisible to the outside world. Being hand-operated, it had two spars protruding at either end by which it was propelled around. A group of youngsters used to go there together for it took a number to get it moving. Once underway it would revolve for quite a while — the only free round-about for many miles.[12]

A proper roundhouse had been built at Weller's Bay, just off the main line. The number of stalls round the turntable is believed to have been seven or eight. Construction seems to have been completed in the late '80's. An adjoining machine shop was able to make heavy repairs on the locomotives. Cabs and other wooden parts were repaired at Trenton where the C.O.R. had a small car repair facility. The old turntable pit remains to this day, long overgrown by the surrounding woods.[13]

By year's end there seemed to be a good future for the C.O.R., even if there was not much ready cash around. William Coe, reviewing the year's operations, explained that shipments would have been higher but that there was already a surplus of a million tons of ore piled up at various docks in the United States. In spite of this, they had shipped 30,000 tons from the Coe Hill mine alone. He expressed optimism that once conditions improved in the United States they would be ready to ship in considerable volume. In proof of this he described the plant being installed and the shafts being sunk at their properties.[14]

This optimism was to be succeeded by disaster. In the summer of the following year, 1885, the news came from the United States that the Coe Hill ore could not be smelted. The sulphur content was too high, and as yet there was no known means of separation.

Ritchie and his associates kept this a secret

as long as possible. The local papers, as if by self-imposed censorship to keep local despondency to a minimum, at first made no mention of this.

Operating at the limit of their financial resources this looked like ruin to Ritchie's associates. Logically it was. But not to Ritchie, he was off to Sudbury to see if somehow his copper claims there could be developed quickly and at the same time save the C.O.R. It looked like a wild gamble. It was.

At Combermere, a small settlement in Renfrew County, a meeting was being held just before the Christmas of 1885. This county, as Hastings' northern neighbour, had invited representatives from across the county line to the meeting. A repetition of other similar meetings in that age, their purpose was "to devise means by which some railway company would be induced to open a line of railway into the free grant lands of Ontario." This area was mostly wilderness, but as the principal speaker, a Mr. Johnson pointed out, "In addition to mineral deposits and large timber forests ... the farmers were now raising more produce than they could easily find a market for." He was of the belief that although the Ontario government had ceased giving land grants to railways because of criticism, in their case the government would come to their assistance.[15]

With everyone convinced, a committee was appointed to approach three local railways to enquire what bonus per mile they would seek.[16] These lines were the C.O.R., the Irondale, Bancroft and Ottawa, and the Kingston and Pembroke (the "Kick and Push"). The K. & P. was geographically well-situated, but still under construction and had enough troubles of its own, and does not seem to have even considered this proposition. The I. B. & O. with construction barely started was already having serious financial problems. Ritchie, on the other hand, whatever the state of his finances, was interested — in fact, very interested. But his building fever had cooled sufficiently that he now refused to consider any further extensions without generous subsidies.

Ritchie was ready with his proposals, so soon, that he must have already had such a line planned. His plans were bold, even exciting. His first step was to recruit the influential J. S. McCuaig to lead a deputation to Ottawa to plead the cause of the extension with particular need for a mileage subsidy. It was an impressive group that McCuaig had recruited to accompany him, eight members of parliament from all over Ontario.

They met with the Minister of Railways, the Hon. J. H. Pope, on February 12th. Time had not been wasted.

The brief[17] of which a copy remains in the Public Archives, is plainly the work of Ritchie but it is signed by McCuaig. The big surprise was the extent of the proposed line to the Canadian Pacific transcontinental line to the north. He was, provided sufficient subsidy was available, ready to build the line in a north-westerly direction as far as Callander, approximately 150 miles from his present railhead at Coe Hill, or for a smaller subsidy or cash grant as far as Pembroke, the near point on the C.P.R. line, roughly half the distance. These two stations are 120 miles apart.

His purpose, not stated in his brief, was to ship his syndicate's copper from their mines in Sudbury to their docks on Weller's Bay; the shortest possible route, with the added advantage of the maximum amount of haulage for themselves. For inward bound freight there was great potential in coal and manufactured goods, not only to Sudbury but westwards to the prairies. This was hardly in the interests of the still expanding C.P.R. unless they intended to purchase the line. If not, they had no choice but to block this enterprise behind the scenes.

The Minister could give no decision at this time. As yet there was not even any general decision on railway subsidies, and as he told the delegation, their request would be considered, with others, according to their importance. He added that he himself was much impressed with the able exposition McCuaig had made.[18]

Other news that came as a surprise, "The Messrs. McMullen have retired from their connection with the road." No explanation was given. For the County it was no longer "Our Railway."

In spite of the possibility of a clash between two such rugged individualists, there is no evidence to support this, at this time. Any organization seeking favourable consideration from John A. Macdonald's government, would be taking a chance with "grits" prominent among their company, but with George McMullen among them — that amounted to a gross insult.

On March 24th, the Minister received Ritchie's formal application for a subsidy. This document was also a comprehensive report that contains new information, particularly on the mining operations upon which the railway depended so much. "The outlay for the equipment and successful working of these mines will equal if not exceed the expense of the entire railroad." Evidentally Ritchie and his associates also owned modern steel mills. "We have already used these ores in our furnaces at Cleveland for the manufacture of Bessemer steel rails, for locomotive Boiler plates ..."

"... The connecting lines ... necessary to build to connect the different mines will aggregate in length more than the entire main line." The application continued: "... the company has already expended nearly 3 millions of dollars ..." The extensive plant in Coe Hill "is not exceeded by any mining plant in the Dominion." And, they expected, after additional improvements, to "give employment to not less than 1,500 to 2,000 labourers." Evidently he still believed the Coe Hill ore could be marketed.

Ritchie also emphasized how generous the United States governments at all levels had been in granting subsidies in the development of the Lake Superior iron ore region, as well as in other states in rail transportation and other facilities.

Having made his case Ritchie asked for a subsidy of $3,200 a mile, the same as had been given earlier to other lines. He recommended the longer route to Callander. He concluded with the encouraging statement that, "negotiations are now nearly completed with iron producers in England, who propose to erect furnaces on our line for the manufacture of charcoal pig iron with the view of exporting the iron to England, as that class of iron has become very scarce in that country."[19] (Nothing ever came of this.)

Ritchie now had to wait not only for the current economic depression to lift, but for the government to decide. Meanwhile there were the daily operations of the railway to occupy his attention.

The C.O.R.'s passenger equipment was in trouble again. On an early March morning there was another mishap, this time at Coe Hill. Here the train crew had been preparing the 'mixed' for the run to Trenton. Finally having lit the fire in the coach they left for breakfast. When they returned the car was blazing away. It took them a while to extinguish the flames, but not before all the windows were broken and the interior was partially charred and the remainder of the coach scorched black. There being no other equipment available the passengers had to ride in this cold, draughty wreck to their destinations.[20]

A week later a mildly indignant correspondent to the newspaper complained (under a pen name) that this unfortunate car was still in regular service. Otherwise this Madoc resident had only good to say of the C.O.R. The line was "a great boon to the north country." The trains had run all winter "showing a spirit of enterprise not found in the Midland Division of the Grand Trunk Railway." He also stated that residents along the C.O.R. received their Toronto newspapers before the citizens of Madoc.[21]

The same writer observed an "almost unbroken line of cordwood, ties, sawlegs, timber and posts from Bannockburn to Rathbun which are being shipped as fast as possible."[22] Much of this was for the Rathbun Company of Deseronto.

Also in March, Ritchie took time off to write a three and a half page letter to Van Horne. While the subject of the greatly improved prospects of the C.P.R. since the Riel Rebellion did not affect the C.O.R., it is of interest in their personal relationship which did have a bearing of the fortunes of Ritchie and the C.O.R. Van Horne's reply was cordial, but brief.[23]

After the annual meeting of the Coe Hill Mining Co., held in Trenton on June 2nd, William Chisholm, already a director of the C.O.R. and a Cleveland ironmaster, was elected president as a result of Ritchie and the McMullens having sold their interests to a newcomer, James Maclaren. Ritchie, G.W. and D.S. McMullen resigned.[24]

There was restrained optimism, about this time, in Madoc and in Stirling when William Coe announced that Ritchie and Joseph Hichson, the Grand Trunk's influential executive, had come to an agreement to make the connection at Anson. Furthermore the Grand Trunk had also agreed to build the extension from Madoc to Eldorado if and when the C.O.R. would extend its line northwards to Bancroft.[25]

This was for a limited extension of the C.O.R., authorized by the federal government, not necessarily impeding Ritchie's grandiose plans, though it followed a different route. From Ormsby to seven miles short of Coe Hill, it is 19 miles to Bancroft. But Ritchie had already had the route surveyed and visited Ottawa to explore the likely extent of the cash subsidies available.[26]

Concurrently Ritchie wrote a letter to the Minister of Railways before he left Ottawa concerning the situation with the iron ore mines. The letter, dated June 16th, gives a strong hint of a certain desperation over and above the current economic recession. With typical Ritchie boldness he wrote "... I have been holding out special inducements to the large furnaces east of the Allegheny Mountains which have been getting their supplies of ore from Spain, Africa, and the Island of Cuba to obtain their supplies from Canada. The Pennsylvania Mills which have made very large investments in Cuba ... [have] been saddled with such excessive export and tonnage dues as to compel them to abandon that source of supply ... within the last few days ... have offered them a number of the mines or as many as they could work *free* should they erect suitable plant and machinery. If the Government will grant the aid requested by our company in my letter to you [not preserved] I believe we can direct nearly the whole of this Spanish and African trade to Canada. I have induced them not to make any foreign investments until I could know what your action would be. Such another opportunity ... is not likely to occur again." [27]

That same month the mining company announced they were closing the Coe Hill mine because of the state of the market. Over a hundred men would be out of work.

On the railway business must have been good in spite of this development for the passenger service was restored to two trains a day.[28] But this was also a tardy response to the C.P.R. which had, as far as can be traced, started their passenger train service with an announcement in the North Hastings Review of March 19th. Ritchie should have obtained new passenger cars sooner.

This was certainly a month of happenings, if little of the news was good. The C.O.R. had its first recorded head-on collision. Our Madoc editor's description was, "On Friday last two engines on the C.O. Railway, near Gilmour attempted to pass each other on a single track. They failed, and the result was both were badly wrecked. The accident was due to the agent allowing the passenger train to leave shortly before a gravel train was timed to arrived. We understand one brakeman was badly wounded, but no lives were lost."[29]

The Government proved to have acted quickly in approving the grants. The Madoc newspaper reported on July 25th that the C.O.R. had been authorized to build the line to Bancroft with a subsidy of $3,200 a mile, the total not to exceed $64,000 (20 miles).

For the line between Madoc and Eldorado, the Grand Trunk was granted $1,500 a mile, not to exceed $10,500. It had no doubt helped that Mackenzie Bowell was a cabinet minister.[30]

How much of the earlier Belleville and North Hastings line had been graded before, and to what extent this line north of Madoc had been used is not clear. Orr's editorial stated: "It now only remains to get the Grand Trunk to make the necessary repairs to the road ..."[31] The Grand Trunk followed up by sending an engineer with a contractor to the site.

That fall, on October 7th, Van Horne in a reply to an unrecorded letter of Ritchie's wrote "... we do not want 800 tons 56 lb. rail which you have on hand." (9.09 track miles in long tons). Ritchie had evidently prepared for a longer extension.

In the next paragraph Van Horne continued bluntly, "My movements are so very uncertain that I am unable to make an engagement with you as requested; in fact it is impossible to say when I should be able to visit your district again."[32]

Eighteen days later Van Horne was more gracious. He wrote in the first reference found to Ritchie's business car, "Referring to your letter of the 17th inst. I beg to say that we shall have pleasure in hauling your private car and party from Central Ontario Junction, and if you desire to Winnipeg and return." There followed the operating instructions.[33]

The seventh day of November was not a fortuitous day for the C.O.R. That evening in Trenton, in heavy fog, a gravel train stopped near the docks to allow a work train to run into the siding. Another train following pitched into the caboose, which was filled with Italian labourers. The men jumped off, but one unfortunate Italian was killed. The damage to equipment was reported as negligible.[34]

Chapter Nine

On February 12th, 1886, Ritchie wrote to Van Horne sending him a newspaper clipping on the new United States tariff bill that had the backing of the Democratic party and was expected to become law. Important for Ritchie was that iron ore would return to the free list. Less directly, but also important to the C.O.R., lumber had also been included.[1]

From Prince Edward County not long after, a lesser issue, the ghost of the projected line from Picton to Deseronto, crossing the Bay of Quinte, was resurrected. The editor of the Madoc newspaper optimistically believed that this project for "a small expenditure of capital would yield a rich reward."[2]

The public's mind was quickly taken away from this never to be realized dream of George McMullen's to another major law suit. One cannot do better than to quote the admirable Major Orr, owner and editor of the *North Hastings Review*, "A gigantic law suit will soon occupy the Courts between Messrs. Wm. Coe, of this village, and S. J. Ritchie, et al, of the Coe Hill Mining Company. Mr. Coe sues Ritchie for $50,000, amount due for the purchase of shares in the Coe Hill mine, and Ritchie returns the compliment with a suit for $500,000, for alleged wrong information regarding the resources of the above mine before the purchase took place. The trifling amounts involved in the above suits need not cause either of the litigants any uneasiness, we presume. It would seriously cripple the resources of the Review, however."[3]

In the same edition there was a report of many unemployed in the area as a result of the closing down of that mine. A month later Coe Hill would be described as "a deserted village." The railway, however, continued to be busy carrying the stock piles of ore to the docks at Weller's Bay. By May, the C.O.R. was moving forty car loads a day.[4] In October, before the close of navigation, 10,540 tons of ore had been unloaded at the docks.[5] The ore was probably sold at a cut price. This was a year of economic recession.

There was also a lesser law suit in April against the C.O.R. Mr. Billings of Billings' Farm (location unknown) had supplied the railway with water "to supply their tank pump." Mr. Billings demanded a certain remuneration, which the company refused to pay. He tore up the pipes. The company sued him. This was settled by the C.O.R. having to pay Billings a sum for the past supply, a certain sum yearly, and the costs of the case.[6]

As an interlude to C.O.R. events, the 104 route miles of the line might be put into perspective with the railway statistics of the Dominion Government at the end of 1885. There was then a total of 10,150 miles in operation. Casualties were 157 killed and 684 injured.[7]

Ritchie's determination to build north-west to Callender was undiminished. Having cultivated Van Horne's friendship he was ready to put it to the test. In May he received a reply from the great railroader that was cordial enough, but disappointing to Ritchie. To quote in part, "... While your proposed line would shorten the distance considerably it would still be too long to justify us in turning the freight away from the Northern if they should accept the earlier proposition. They have the shortest line and can afford to do the business cheaper than anybody else.

"We will be very glad however to see your line extended to a connection with us as proposed as I think such a connection would be very useful and while we would be glad to give you all the friendly assistance in our power, we could hardly promise you any of our Toronto business that way."[8]

Almost immediately Ritchie wrote to Sir George Stephen, president of the C.P.R., outlining his request to be forwarded to the federal government asking him to see the government and otherwise do all he could to support the new line.[9]

On June 3rd, Van Horne wrote to Ritchie that he "was unfortunately called to New York . . . and legislation at Ottawa was practically over on my return and I was not able to do anything for you.

"I understand that a large number of bonuses were provided for just at the end of the Session. I trust that you got one of them."[10]

Ritchie's request to the government had been for a subsidy of $5,000 per mile for the first 20 miles and $3,200 for the remaining one hundred. His chances of getting this money were considered rather slim by the Madoc newspaper.[11] The Napanee Express editor pointed out that Ritchie's line would shorten the distance to New York from the west "by several hundred miles . . . But there were some troublesome 'ifs' in the way".[12]

Ritchie did not get one of "the large number of bonuses," but he was not ready to give up.

A good dollar earner for all the railways in southeastern Ontario that year was the Orange Order's celebration of the 12th of July in Belleville, said to be one of the largest ever held in the area. In that city the many special trains were run down Pinnacle Street to Market Square. People also would come by steamer. Some four thousand Orangemen and their families attended. Among the special trains were those from Picton and Coe Hill.[13]

The Orangemen, they could not expect otherwise, had enemies. The Ottawa delegation on their return over the Canada Atlantic line luckily escaped "a dastardly attempt" to derail their train. The engineer was able to stop his train before it hit a heavy obstruction. Those returning to Picton and Coe Hill had no hostile acts to report.[14]

Ritchie had yet to inform the shareholders of his plans, apparently, for notice was given that there would be a general meeting of the shareholders of the C.O.R. on July 28th "to consider the advisability of extending the road to the Canadian Pacific Railway at or near Callender." The meeting was also to consider a resolution authorizing the issue of $400,000 in preference shares, and the payment or exchange of them for overdue coupons on the present bonds. If this worked it would also stave off the threat of receivership.[15]

Another projected railway was for a line from Carleton Place, west of Ottawa, to Carlow in North Hastings to join the C.O.R.[16]

Too late for the annual meeting, Thomas Bolger, assistant to Mr. Evans, the C.O.R.'s civil engineer, had explored the first 85 miles of the proposed route to Callender and gave glowing accounts of great stands of hardwood and pine. There were good prospects for the line based on these resources alone. With only a few small rivers to cross, construction costs were estimated as being less than the line already constructed.[17]

In the meantime both Evans and Bolger were also finishing off their surveys of the Bancroft extension.

Editor Orr, a strong Tory, wrote somewhat righteously of a recent event in Prince Edward County. "George Washington McMullen of Pacific Scandal, notoriety at large, and of local acquaintance by his connection with the building of the Central Ontario Railway, last week at a large public meeting in Prince Edward, spoke in favour of the severance of the ties that bind Canada to Great Britain, and annexation to the United States, as the only balm for Canadian hardtimes. His remarks created great excitement among the loyal people of Prince Edward, and brought down a storm on his unfortunate head. He was threatened with being mobbed, and it is said was treated with a dose of unhealthy egg. Annexation sentiments won't go down with Canadians."[18]

At least George McMullen deserved credit for his courage.

Setbacks in Ritchie's enterprises had the regularity of the tides, they only varied in their weight. There came one of the heavy ones. A letter from Dr. Selwyn of the Department of the Interior to Van Horne, dated January 7th, 1887, described Ritchie's vein of copper recently opened up at Sudbury as having promised to be a valuable source of traffic to the CPR, but his department having sent some samples to England for analysis they had been returned with the bad news that they contained such a high percentage of nickel and iron as to make smelting questionable. Then nickel had no industrial value and was held to be a curse in copper mining. In closing his letter Dr. Selwyn asked for a larger block of the ore for his museum! Van Horne forwarded this request to Ritchie.[19]

This was a winter of violent winds and record snowfalls. Early in February, T. O. Bolger returned from another field trip taking another route to the Callander area checking the forest resources and searching for a better grade. With a crew of three men they had tramped 160 miles on snowshoes, all took turns pulling two toboggans loaded with 550 lbs. of provisions. They met only a single person on the entire trip. They saw moose and deer in abundance but no wolves. The country was virgin forest with much tall hardwood.[20]

In his report, made personally to Ritchie, Bolger assessed this route as, "... very favourable for the construction of a railroad as although there are many hills and rocky ridges to be met, still there are always valleys to be found through which a track can be selected having moderately easy grades ... a good deal of curvature will be necessary."[21]

In a later report (April 9th) after returning to help Evans locate the Bancroft extension he found most of the distance that the magnetic attraction from the ore deposits was so strong that his compass was virtually useless.[22] The length of this line was to be 16¼ miles, from a point east of Coe Hill, Rathbun (later Ormsby). Coe Hill would end up at the end of a seven mile branch line.

The Irondale, Bancroft and Ottawa railway was also expected to start construction again in the spring in the direction of Bancroft.[23]

Editor Orr observed that when the line from Madoc to Eldorado was completed the citizens of Bancroft would be able to travel direct to Belleville or Trenton. As for Bancroft, with two railways and the numerous ore deposits in the vicinity of both lines, "that village would undoubtedly become one of the most stirring places in the Province."[24]

Ritchie was busier than ever. On March 18th, Orr more sanguine than he used to be, wrote, "A despatch from New York contains the following good news, if true: "An immense iron ore combination is being formed in New York which aims at nothing short of owning and controlling all the known valuable iron deposits of Canada, now being ascertained to be the richest iron country in the world. The Central Ontario Railway, which runs from Trenton, on Lake Ontario, through the centre of Ontario, and all the iron interests connected with it are to form part of the scheme. The road is to be extended 150 miles through the heart of the iron districts to a junction with the Canadian Pacific Railway at Lake Nipissing. The capital of the company is ten millions, more than two-thirds of which is already pledged. The syndicate, it is said, will own more than a hundred different properties at various points in Canada

and a mineral development, even greater than that on Lake Superior is predicted. Among the principal owners is Senator Payne, Stephenson Burke, S. J. Ritchie, all of Ohio, James McLaren of Ottawa, Erastus Wiman, A. B. Boardman and other prominent parties in New York".[25]

After this Ritchie wrote again to the Minister of Railways (still the Hon. J. H. Pope) requesting grants. New information here was that the first 35 miles from Coe Hill would require heavy engineering; and that five vessels could be loaded at a time at Weller's Bay.[26]

In May, John D. Evans, civil engineer, forwarded his plans to Ottawa as part of the procedure for obtaining the approved subsidies. Bureaucrats never change. One such has written on the file cover "The company should be asked for what purposes these are sent." (forgetting the question mark.) Another civil servant, more constructive, has added, "a gradient profile should be included." This correspondence would endure for some months.[27]

Another of those intermittent law suits came up. James B. McMullen sued William Coe, claiming a $3,000 commission on the sale by Coe of the Cameron Mine to the Cleveland Rolling Mill Co. The judge dismissed the action with costs to McMullen as having failed to prove an alleged agreement.[28]

So much for possible future developments and progress in the new line to Bancroft. This year the C.O.R. got more coverage in the Madoc newspaper than in any year of its history. This came from "a forlorn station agent" under the pen name of "Clifford." Unfortunately for posterity his contributions consisted largely of arch innuendoes concerning the courting habits of his colleagues, but the rest was of interest, supplemented by the reports of the newspaper.

The Review was the first with the news that the C.O.R.'s safe in Trenton had been blown open by a robber who had benefitted to the extent of $1,630 in cash. And that at Coe Hill there were still 50,000 tons of iron waiting to be shipped, part of the giant stockpile remaining when the mine closed.[29]

In "Clifford's" first report the C.O.R. telegraph system had been joined up with that of the CPR. As a result operators along the line were now doing a lot of commercial work, benefitting C.O.R. revenues.

On June 2nd, the newspaper reported how on the Southern Division a man was run over by a train. "The unfortunate man was under the influence of liquor and had apparently fallen on the track and was unable to rise. His name was Morgan."[30]

"Clifford" was back a week later telling the readers that a number of students were now at different stations along the line learning telegraphy, hoping to get employment when the line to Callander was being built. At Rawdon, unusual for that time, the student was a young lady.[31]

His next contribution was devoted to the farewell party given to the agent at Coe Hill, J. F. Chapman, who was leaving to work for the Rathbun Company at Deseronto. He was evidently highly esteemed. At a big party in his honour he was presented with a gift of a cane ". . . a beautiful ebony one with a massive gold head, richly carved and embossed . . . suitably inscribed." This was accompanied by an address signed by 35 C.O.R. employees, with their names and positions with the company recorded.[32]

In August he reported that operations had been resumed at the St. Charles mine and they were expecting to ship iron ore in a few weeks.[33] Later in September the mine was shipping ore daily. It also stated that shipments from the stockpile at Coe Hill were to start again.[34]

In his August column "Clifford" also had some news of new stations being built at Springbrook and Gilmour.[35] He described Gilmour as a booming settlement "as is no other place in the north." Not only did the settlement now have two "well stocked" general stores, but there was uncontrolled drunkenness, not only "on Saturday, even Sunday" with men under the influence "pitching quoits and shooting at a target . . . that women dread passing on their way to church."[36]

Throughout Canada in early years there were no liquor controls and it was cheap.

In November our columnist wrote the St. Charles mine had been closed and that "the miners had taken their departure." But if the mine had closed down other business for the railway was on the way. "Every day men may be seen wending their way to the station with a bag of clothes on their shoulder and the tassels of a red belt hanging conspicuously at their sides. They are the shantymen, going up to the woods up north to cut timber . . ."[37]

On the line, "we have been treated to four train loads of ballast on the Northern Division, and still we do not seem to get weary of excitement."[38]

Now the law suits were coming in threes. Among the Chancery Court cases being heard in Belleville late October were Coe versus Ritchie et al.; Coe versus Ritchie; and Ritchie versus Coe. There is no mention of the particular issues and no further mention of the cases is made in the newspaper.[39]

The last flyer for the year of projected rail developments was the statement that the Hon. Senator Billa Flint, local entrepreneur, would apply for a charter to build a railway from Belleville to Tweed, passing Bridgewater and connecting with and running on the C.O.R. to Coe Hill, then extending the said line to Bancroft. This appeared to be a hostile move with the C.O.R.'s line to that place approved for subsidy, surveyed and ready for the construction gangs. Belleville would gain.[40]

The outcome of one of the McMullen versus Ritchie suits resulted in March, 1888 in the McMullens obtaining a legal attachment on the C.O.R. for $283,000, a record amount for Hastings County.[41] This was by no means the end of the matter, and Ritchie seemingly continued about his business unfazed.

Almost at the same time the Hon. Mackenzie Bowell presented his petition for Senator Billa Flint's new railroad, part of which would follow the location to Bancroft so heroically surveyed.[42]

The following month Ritchie gave notice to the Commons of an amendment to the Act for the Callander line; even more ambitious, it was to be extended all the way to Sudbury. This, so Ritchie would explain, was a condition imposed by his new backers.[43] The syndicate's copper mines would then be able to ship over their own rails all the way to Weller's Bay. The C.P.R. could hardly approve. All that would be left for that corporation would be a lesser tonnage in the winter months over a shorter distance from what is now Bonarlaw. The amendment also requested authority to issue bonds for the new line at the rate of $30,000 a mile.

Ritchie's reason for dropping the short extension to Bancroft becomes apparent in his May application for a bonus for the new project. It would amount to around a million dollars. For this he asked that the Bancroft bonus be transferred to the new extension. He would not therefore be building the line to Bancroft.[44]

Swing Bridge over the Murray Canal 1977

Photo, Author

At the same time here was Senator Flint, with Bowell representing him in the Commons presenting a bill to build a new railway that incorporated running powers over the C.O.R. to that part of the route on the same Rathbun-Bancroft survey. He would inevitably seek a duplicate bonus.

It would seem to be a not unreasonable deduction, with the political ethics of the time, that this was Bowell's price for his essential support in parliament for the Sudbury extension. The Bancroft extension of that line was a potential money-maker and it would not be unreasonable to assume that Bowell had a financial interest in Senator Flint's scheme. Flint was also interested in the lumber round Bancroft.

The Bill for the Sudbury line was quickly passed by the House of Commons in the following May, Ritchie having stated he would build big copper and iron ore smelters.[45]

In April near disaster occurred outside Bannockburn. A pile of ties over a culvert was seen by an alert engineer. He could not quite stop his train in time but the damage to his locomotive was superficial, the local newspaper reporting "the cowcatcher [pilot] and headlight were smashed," and that was all. The company offered the considerable reward of $200,000 for information leading to the arrest of the villain.[46] How they could find that much money must have caused a good deal of rumination around Hastings and Prince Edward Counties.

Marmora Village, still without a railway, had a confrontation that same month with one J. B. Pierce when he told the council that he would build a new saw and flour mill there if they would bonus a four-mile extension to connect with the C.O.R. Otherwise he would build elsewhere.[47] Marmora lost.

Through spring and summer Ritchie's relations with the C.P.R., as might be expected, cooled. This would not have been helped by the reports of the poor quality of the copper ore. There

90

developed a strong reluctance to meet Ritchie's needs in the Sudbury area in the matter of spur lines and switches. Misunderstandings arose. Van Horne defended all this by stating the revenue from the mines was small. To this, Ritchie's manager there, produced strong arguments to the contrary.[48]

In the meantime Ritchie, with remarkable resourcefulness, encouraged by earlier experiments elsewhere, had discovered an engineer who had invented a process for smelting steel alloy with nickel as a hardener, and sold the idea to the U.S. Secretary of the Navy. Success would come at a critical time, to become one of the great metallurgical break-throughs of that century. There would be further difficulties but this was the beginning of the Sudbury area becoming the great nickel producer of the world.

Important to Canada economically, this changed the world for everyone. This new hard steel, apart from many industrial and commercial uses, would modernize in one stroke armour and armour piercing shells, particularly for warships, making contemporary navies largely obsolete.

This triumph of Ritchie's resulted in a resurgence of benevolence by the C.P.R. In September, the president, Sir George Stephen, cabled from England asking that Ritchie send "... a full statement establishing [the] success [of this] method ... Think can interest [the] very best people here."[49]

From world history and international finance, back to the seldom dull, everyday life of the C.O.R.

Construction of the Murray Canal had been progressing, but slowly — until, as editor Orr noted in April, "... more rapidly now that a Yankee boss was in charge."[50] George McMullen would have been pleased to read that.

The C.O.R.'s Southern Division grew more prosperous. Demorestville, north of Picton, now claimed to be the "hop metropolis of Central Ontario," providing new traffic. More important to the railway in volume was the shipping of canned goods to the extent of running special trains. Picton had become the largest fruit-canning centre in the Dominion.[51] Two large canning factories were near the station. Others were at Bloomfield and Wellington. The rest were scattered about the county.

The sinkhole near Eldorado was suffering

from lack of attention, and had become noticeable to train passengers.[52]

The Hon. Billa Flint had a letter published in Bowell's Belleville newspaper, *The Intelligencer*, in July, complaining that it had taken him two hours and seven minutes to travel by train the 27 miles from that city to Madoc. He considered this "better than going on foot or with a slow team." On the other hand, he noted, he had owned pony teams that had taken him, without using a whip, the 30 miles from his house at Bridgewater to Belleville in two hours.[53] The B. & N. H. did not seem to have improved at all since the Grand Trunk had taken over.

Gilmour seems to have settled down as the problem settlement on the C.O.R. line. In late July, "Attempts at train wrecking have been made several times recently at Gilmour Station ..."[54] The excitements of Sunday quoits and target shooting must have lost their novelty.

In August the largest iron ore deposit yet discovered in the area was made known, located in the vicinity of the Coe Hill station, but 300 feet below ground. The land was privately owned by Messrs. Jenkins and Chambers.

The rest of the year was uneventful, or did not make the local press. The year 1889 started off with good news. A new mine of William Coe's had already produced 2,000 tons of fine ore,[55] while the Gilmour Company were shipping logs at a rate of 1,500 a day to Trenton.[56]

A new development with potential for the railway was the Ledyard Gold Mine "over the border" from Hastings County, a few miles distant from Marmora Village. When discovered the previous year Coe had offered $10,000 for the claim but others had bid higher. Both the C.P.R. and the C.O.R. now offered to build a connecting line, a distance of six or seven miles. If the C.O.R. built the line Marmora Village would at last have a railway. A Cleveland company were by now owners of the mine.[57]

The Grand Trunk and its B. & N. H. branch took another hammering, this time in the House of Commons. S. D. Burdett, M.P. made his theme the misuse of public subsidies and the inconvenience to the local population. It was a long speech and with this approach he finally singled out that unfortunate line as a prime example for the Madoc-Eldorado connection.[58]

Apparently the line had been built, but so

poorly, that the government inspector refused to pass it. Yet $21,888 had been paid to the Grand Trunk, more than double the earlier authorized bonus the previous December.[59]

In May a letter from the general manager of the G.T.R. (equivalent of president in that company) was received by the Belleville City Council in response to further criticism by that body on the same subject. "Completion of the branch line to Eldorado for public service was suspended for some time owing to a misunderstanding as to the conditions to be imposed by the Department of Railways. This difference being at length removed, it became desirable to negotiate for a connection with the Central Ontario Railway ..."[60]

Back in February on that unhappy line the train from Belleville had been snowed in only a few hundred yards from Madoc Station.[61]

The Belleville and North Hastings did not have a corner on misfortunes. In mid-March there was an expensive derailment on the C.O.R., once again fortunately without any loss of life. A southbound "train of 16 cars loaded with cord wood left the track near Springbrook. Twelve cars were completely wrecked and several lengths of track torn up."[62]

In April, Coe was in the throes of another bout of development fever. This time he was attempting to interest the people of Belleville and Trenton in forming a new syndicate to develop the mineral resources around Port Arthur (now Thunder Bay) on Lake Superior.[63]

One of the early signs of spring on the C.O.R. were a hundred men leaving Trenton "for the north to work on the [log] drive for Gilmour [Co.]"[64]

Madoc Station. Freight only. The comfort stations were not intended as part of the composition. (Belleville & North Hastings section.)

Photo, Author

92

Wallridge Hematite Mine, Madoc, Ont.   *Topley Photo, Public Archives of Canada*

For most people the most important event that spring was the unofficial opening of the Murray Canal — at last! The construction dams were all removed, the water flowed in, and smaller lake boats were able to pass through.[65]

Gilmour was in the news again; though the publicity was not good, it was not the fault of the village. A "noisy" and "annoying" drunk who had been bothering the passengers all the way from Trenton, when only a couple of miles from that station, toppled off the train. The train was backed up. The crew searched for a corpse. Instead, covered in mud and sand, they found the man, sitting on a fence, singing "Whiskers, five a bag." As the newspaper concluded, "Moral, don't jump the express when sober."[66]

Ritchie was making progress lobbying for his new line to Callander. In May he had an interview with the Prime Minister, Sir John A. Macdonald. He pressed for mining machinery to be allowed in duty free.[67] Ritchie could speak of his new route with confidence for he had since walked it himself.[68]

The pressures from working with Ritchie, or a disagreement, caused his superintendent to resign that same month. G. W. Dench, formerly a conductor on the C.O.R., must have been popular for he received a tremendous farewell from the employees.[69] His successor was Robert Fraser, once a bank clerk.[70]

Dench was another example of the big

turnover of C.O.R. employees. Railwaymen were restless in that age. For single men there was little incentive to remain. Then there was the loneliness of the northern division stations, resulting in an almost continuous stream of agents and operators, once proficient, to move elsewhere. Most went to the C.P.R. where the wages were higher and the prospects for promotion better. Train crews tended more to remain with the company.

At last the general superintendent of the Grand Trunk for that area arrived at Eldorado and was reported as having come to a satisfactory agreement with the C.O.R. for a junction, and that the Madoc train would connect with the C.O.R. runs both north and south. Madoc rejoiced,[71] and looked forward to the arrival of the Napanee and Tamworth line.[72]

By July 11th, 1889, the connection to Eldorado from Madoc was open with two trains a day.[73]

By October, the citizens of Madoc had lost their enthusiasm for the Eldorado connection. Editor Orr described it as "a perfect farce." He noted "When the G.T.R. is a few minutes late the C.O.R. won't wait, and, to retaliate, the G.T.R. won't wait." The whole thing was "a dismal failure."[74]

In December the Minister of Railways received a stack of petitions from those in the two counties of Hastings and Prince Edward who thought the Sudbury line ought to be built. These had been rounded up by Ritchie who had even provided a printed resolution for each community.[75]

Long before these last events Ritchie had hurried off to England to sell his nickel hardened steel, and to try and raise more capital.[76]

Chapter Ten

The year 1890 began with a severe 'flu epidemic, then known as "la grippe." Thousands were absent from work; hundreds died.[1] At the height of this plague, possibly with a high temperature himself, the editor of the Toronto "Globe" decided that Ontario's Conservative leader was a "Blackguard, weak-minded, unscrupulous sneak, hypocrite and humbug."[2] But he forgot to blame him for the epidemic. These matters set the mood for the coming disputes over the control of the C.O.R., and they would last longer than the epidemic.

The earlier legal attachment of George McMullen's had been forgotten by the press, and apparently had been ignored by Ritchie. But it had been to deal with such matters that Ritchie had brought Judge Stevenson Burke of Cleveland onto the Board. Burke, his title a courtesy one from his early years when elected to a junior court, was a brilliant and astute corporation lawyer specializing in railroads. He was wealthy. A short term as president of the Hocking Valley in which he seems to have raided the treasury of that company before leaving to finish building a rival line.[3] Ritchie left these legal problems to Burke and set about his many projects.

These months, Ritchie was, if it was possible, busier than ever searching Europe for the best of the early experiments for combining nickel and steel. He now controlled three-quarters of the world supply. This was the year he received an offer from Germany for the entire nickel production from Sudbury. He turned it down for patriotic reasons.[4]

Ritchie had been corresponding with an old friend, Thomas Edison, arranging to try out a new and promising invention that might be the answer to eliminating the high sulphur content from the Coe Hill iron ore. This was based on electro-magnets.[5]

Not much had been heard from the railway itself for except over the past winter there had been good revenue from hauling cordwood.[6]

All this time the McMullen attachment on the railway was in reality the tip of a volcano, and the beginning of one of the more extraordinary adventures in railway litigation on the North American continent. It would last close to twenty years. The cataloguing of individual evils and weaknesses that followed would leave the Globe's liverish tirade against the Tory leader as no more than a puff of steam.

Railways have always been the targets for law suits. Disputes between the tycoons, between stockholder groups or between both, fill many law books. Proportionate to the size of the C.O.R., no other line appears to have been involved in such lengthy or costly litigation to be further complicated by being fought in the courts of both Canada and the United States.

Still in the mood of the first months of 1890, an item datelined Cleveland, February 27th appeared in the North Hastings Review and it was headlined: "Ritchie-McMullen". The sub-heading read: "The wicked partners make a big haul."

The news item read: "President S. J. Ritchie, of the Central Ontario road, entered suit here to-day against B. and G. W. McMullen, directors of the road, for $181,500. President Ritchie states that they were directors in the road, and deliberately took possession of 210 first mortgage bonds, worth $1,000 each, and $2,375 coupons of $30 each. These. so Ritchie claims, "they converted to their own use, and have wholly failed and refused to account for, except $100,000, and there is yet due $131,500. The books of the company were in the hands of the defendants, and so obscurely kept that they fail to show clearly what amounts the defendants have paid over to the plaintiffs, or to what use the moneys received were accounted for."

"The McMullens were in Cleveland to-day, and sheriffs deputies endeavoured to serve the papers on them. They left, however, and returned to Canada before service was obtained. Some time ago they got judgement against President Ritchie for $238,000, alleging that he had agreed to buy bonds and coupons off them, and had failed to do so. Ritchie denies this, and filed to-day's sensational suit."[7]

For all this there was more scheming and plotting going on behind the scenes than the press, or even Ritchie had any knowledge. There were other developments.

That fall there was a strong rumour reported in the Napanee Beaver that E. W. Rathbun had received an offer from an English syndicate of $4-million for his company. He was asking $6-million. Another despatch from the same source reported that Rathbun had an option at $10,000, open until January 1st, 1901, to purchase the Gilmour interests for $1¼-million. An interesting comparison as to the possible values of these two enterprises.[8] The Trenton mill had a capacity of a thousand logs a day. There would be much speculation on the outcome. The previous spring (1889) Rathbun's had been enquiring as to the possible purchase of the C.O.R. No further correspondence appears in the files.

In the press Ritchie had received considerable support from the sharp-spoken editors of the Globe. By November, Toronto's out-and-out Liberal newspaper had reversed itself and was now attacking the Sudbury extension and all that went with it. Ritchie's friendship with Ras. Wiman of the Standard Oil Company qualified him to be labelled a "Yankee monopolist," while the subsidies were considered as gifts of $1½-million outright and half a million annually. The Montreal Gazette more soberly concluded that such amounts should be raised by private capital.[9]

By now the addition of James MacLaren of Buckingham, Quebec, a man with considerable lumber interests, to the Board of Directors brought Canadian representation back. Unlike other directors he invested in the company and had political influence in Ottawa.

Throughout 1891, this rush of possible mergers, outright purchases, and other happenings, local and national, grew into an epidemic.

A report in January was that Rathbun would build a car works in Trenton.[10] This would either be a transfer or a duplication (more likely the former) of the plant he was already operating in Deseronto, some 14 miles to the east. The same month the newspapers announced that he had offered Gilmours $850,000 for their interests. Anti-climax came on February 5th with the news that the deal was off.[11]

Across the Dominion 1891 was an election year. The aging Sir John A. Macdonald now made his much quoted, patriotic appeal "... a British subject I was born — a British subject I will die." He was elected on March 5th, only to die on June 7th. Mackenzie Bowell of Belleville was re-elected and became Minister of Railways.

Before and after the election Ritchie was organizing all the support he could find. In Prince Edward County, both County Council and the Board of Trade formally petitioned that the line to Sudbury be built.[12] Hastings County did the same with a big "but" for the benefit of Belleville and the Grand Trunk, the "Belleville and North Hastings" should have running rights over the new line.[13] A "heavy", but otherwise unspecified deputation also waited on the premier of Ontario.[14]

From Sudbury came the news that, on good authority, the extension would soon be approved by the government and its early completion would follow.[15] The mines were having a slack time there. This was followed by more good news that "Andrew Carnegie had received an order from the War Department and the contract to supply $5-million of nickel steel for the new American cruisers. He will order the nickel from Sudbury, and mining will be by the Harvey process."[16] (The Harvey process was in the nickel-steel.)

In August the Rathbun deal having fallen through, Ritchie was negotiating with the Crossen Company of Cobourg, a bigger operation, to open a car works in Trenton.[17]

In the same month, on Sunday the 23rd, William Coe died from a stroke. He had no longer been active in either the railway or the mining industry. He did not die poor. The North Hastings Review estimated his worth as a quarter of a million dollars.[18]

There was no stopping Ritchie. In October he let it be known that he would establish a smelting works in Trenton — provided the Town gave him a bonus of $75,000.[19] The reaction was one of excitement. As the months went by it became evident town council would approve this request with a clear majority plus popular support.[20]

With Bowell now Minister of Railways Ritchie had to do business with him. From the tone of his correspondence one would gather their relationship was not particularly cordial.[21] Some years later Ritchie would learn that he had already incurred the considerable displeasure of Bowell, Flint and others for building the Trenton-Coe Hill line without subsidy.[22]

This greatly harmed the "spoils" system of subsidies for rail construction for it had reached the stage of an unwritten understanding among promoters, no subsidies, no railways. This was much to their benefit. Some had delivered little and made fortunes.

Ritchie wrote to Bowell in October. He pointed out, logically enough, that the Murray Canal had no docking facilities; being Ritchie he prescribed the best way this could be done. The letter ended, "We are about adding some improvements to our dock at Weller's Bay, but if the government would at once make these improvements so that we could use the canal we would not make any further outlay on our docks."[23]

By then to all accounts the Weller's Bay docks were little used, if at all. Herbert M. Love, for many years station agent in Picton, in his reminiscences published in a Picton newspaper, said the level of the lake rose after the iron ore business collapsed and the dock was submerged for an unspecified number of years.[24]

Love remembers that when the dock re-emerged from the lake, the railway, on a fetch-and-carry basis, sold off the superstructure. Ross Weaver of Picton, who lived in the Weller's Bay area, said a lot of the dock disappeared after dark. The largest part of this lumber, whether obtained by day or by night, went into neighbourhood barns and drive houses.[25] The government never built Ritchie's suggested improvements to the canal, Trenton being rival to Belleville and not in Bowell's constituency.

So far Billa Flint and Bowell had done nothing to build their Bancroft line, and the $64,000 grant had lapsed. Ritchie came up with the suggestion that this be restored and he would use it for a new survey for a length of nine miles starting instead from Coe Hill in the direction of Bancroft.[26]

Now the wretched former Belleville and North Hastings Railway brought further anguish to the citizens of Madoc. The Grand Trunk reduced the Eldorado service from daily, except Sundays, to twice a week.[27] The C.O.R. was not handing over any of its east-bound freight there, whether for Belleville, Deseronto or Montreal. The company Ritchie and Collins had no intention of losing the freight mileage round by Trenton. Probably the GTR gained by the inbound traffic, but that was a small percentage.

News continued to be sparse about the operations on the railway. The worst of the news had been the derailment of a freight train near Feeney's Mill, on February 12th by a "foul" switch that ran the locomotive and six or eight flatcars into the ditch. There were no injuries, the damage was not extensive though the line was tied up for several hours.[28]

Also recorded was a head-on collision on September 3rd, between a velocipede (a light track vehicle like a tricycle, the rider pedalling over one set of rails) and a lorry (a four-wheel car either pushed or pumped by hand). George Phillips of Malone had his nose badly smashed.[29]

There was also what must have been a splendid spectacle indeed! The arrival at the October Fall Show at Coe Hill of a double-headed Special hauling thirteen crowded coaches.[30]

The past spring had seen the completion of the road bridge from Belleville across the Bay of Quinte to Prince Edward County. It had been a big undertaking. This had little effect on C.O.R. traffic. The northern townships of the county gained but they were some distance from the railway. Not until the age of the automobile and the paved road would the C.O.R. and the Town of Trenton be affected, and that was long after the C.O.R. had passed into history as an independent line.

★ ★ ★

The puzzle remains how Ritchie remained so optimistic through 1891. Obviously he was an egotist with a confidence and imagination that too often overcame logic and reality. His integrity, not to be underestimated, contributed to his problems. More than most honest individuals he believed and trusted the dishonest to an extent that is bewildering. For a man with his experience and achievements he had shown himself to be unsophisticated, and extremely careless to the extent that he could accept evasiveness as an affirmative, even from politicians.

As one unknown thought (the letter is unsigned) during the following year: "Your knowledge of Mr. Ritchie is, I am sure too accurate not to overlook, or to consider as a serious offence, anything he may say in his compulsive way when the matter at first impression strikes him as a personal affront to himself, or a wrong to his interests ..."[31] (How did the letter get into Ritchie's personal files?)

Where Ritchie's enemies underestimated the man was in his iron determination.

Since the death of Sir John A. Macdonald, Ritchie now treated with his successor Sir Charles Tupper, one of the Fathers of Confederation. He had already supported Ritchie's original projected line to Sudbury, the blast furnaces, etc., but insisted reasonably enough, that the Ontario government contribute $4-million.[32]

In July Ritchie visited Tupper in Toronto and explained to him that, he had "had a consultation with Mr. Van Horne on the question and that a very strong altercation had taken place between them."[33] Apparently, on a different occasion, Ritchie confided to Tupper, "Van Horne had said some very uncomplimentary things about your government ..."[34]

Tupper replied to Ritchie: "I told him that I did not think he would expect the Government of Canada to quarrel with the Canadian Pacific Railway on his behalf."[35]

Ritchie should have known that. The Conservative Party had created the C.P.R. Inevitably this had become a close political alliance, not always based on mutual admiration, and this would last many decades. Later this would become more partisan when the Liberal Party would sponsor, and even build, rival transcontinental lines.

Tupper had in consequence asked Ritchie "to modify your application so that the extension of the line would not come into competition with the C.P.R."[36]

Ritchie followed Tupper's advice, he had no choice. A new line was projected to Burke's Falls, near Huntsville.[37] This was on the Northern line over which the C.P.R. was routing its Toronto traffic. This was shorter by 106 miles. According to Ritchie this met with Tupper's unofficial, but "cordial approval."[38] The traffic potential of such a line would seem to have been questionable.

On September 1st, never one to sulk, Ritchie wrote to Van Horne that the C.P.R.'s opposition to his line and the Ottawa and Toronto had made investors cautious of financing operations anywhere the C.P.R. had control. He suggested some public assurances from him might be appropriate.[39]

On the same date he wrote Senator Payne. "Briefly the Canadian Pacific have beaten us both at Ottawa and Toronto ... they have compelled the Grand Trunk people to abandon all attempts to get to Sudbury. The question comes up what to do with the railway — nothing so far as the Grand Trunk is concerned except to lease it to them."[40]

In an earlier letter to Superintendent Fraser he was blunter, "... and I have been humbugged and beaten by a corporation which openly threatens defiance of the government and which have invariably made these threats good."[41]

Ritchie had been experiencing other serious problems. Among them negotiations over the rights to a particular nickel process.[42] And there was now the need to build a large plant for Edison's magnetic process.

The principle that Ritchie had followed as far as his means permitted was that all raw materials mined in Canada should, as far as was practicable, be processed here. On this he had advised John A. Macdonald. Canada had a friend here who believed in this, past the point of personal gain. He deserves to be remembered. And it was this policy that brought on the first rumblings of serious trouble for him.

Back in April, not long before the Prime Minister's death, Ritchie had written to him that one reason for "war with his associates was that they wished to reduce the ores to the crudest shape possible in Sudbury and in that form ship them out of the country to be finished." Ritchie then publicly urged the government to tax all such exports: "... to the great anger of my associates and resulted in the Secretary Mr. McIntosh sending out a letter ... statements of vilifying character. ... I am now and always have been much the largest owner in the Sudbury nickel properties, although the stock does not stand in my own name."[43] The last sentence has much bearing on the future. McIntosh was, of course, Stevenson Burke's man.

Early in July, Ritchie wrote in a letter that he

and Burke had "stormy disagreements" at the latter's office.[44]

In another undated letter to the president of the Bethlehem Iron Company, "There was apparently the most cordial acquiescence on the part of Judge Burke and Senator Payne, and others interested in our side of the line, in my efforts to solve this much vexed iron question and with it success and salvation of the railway as well as my own salvation, but just as soon as success was in sight and to be made immediately available their true position of hostility, treachery and conspiracy became open and aroused. In this they are only consistent in their whole past history in making and availing themselves of opportunities to destroy my interests."[45]

What had happened was on October 9th when the Village of Trenton had sufficient signatures to grant the C.O.R. the sum of $75,000 for his new reduction plant, "Just as this had been done Burke and McIntosh arrived and told the citizens that no money was desired from them and that no work would go on, this of course set the town in an uproar. I have concluded to proceed at once against the Copper Co. and the Iron Co. for the damages to the Railway."[46]

On the same day he wrote to McIntosh: "Dear Sir, I demand that you immediately surrender and return to the Secretary of the Central Ontario Railway the stock books, minute books and the Company's seal which you unlawfully carried away from the Company's office yesterday. Yours etc. S.J. Ritchie, President, Central Ontario Railway."[47]

* * *

Unknown to Ritchie, a special meeting was held on March 24th, 1892 by George McMullen at his home in Picton (now the Legion hall). Among those present were Judge Burke, H.P. McIntosh and Senator Payne. The names of the others present are not recorded. At this meeting new directors were elected and others were dropped. MacLaren stayed on, his interests could not be disputed. Ritchie was not re-elected, a devastating blow. Furthermore he was voted out of the Sudbury company. By this act he was ruined — penniless.[48] The C.O.R. would now be controlled by others, and, as he saw it, his beloved line "destroyed."

The shock must have been extensive.

Several months would pass before Ritchie was back to writing letters again. He had seemingly been destroyed by those he had trusted as friends and associates. Lesser men would have accepted defeat or escaped by suicide. His position was hopeless. They had made full use of their considerable legal skills and native cunning to be in a strong enough position to justify their action. As well, Payne and Burke had the financial resources to overwhelm Ritchie in any foreseeable litigation.

How could Ritchie have let this happen? Briefly Ritchie had left a proportion of his stocks or bonds with Burke as security on a loan. He does not seem to have made any written agreement on the conditions. The money so borrowed had gone back into the C.O.R. These securities were not even registered in his name.[49]

Senator Payne was politically powerful and wealthy. He owned what was then one of Cleveland's largest office blocks. Not necessarily by choice, most of the individual railroads represented in the city were there as tenants. He was also rich enough to put up enough money to save one of the larger railroads in that region from bankruptcy. Like Burke he had loaned Ritchie money against more of his unregistered securities, in both cases this had included the potentially profitable Canadian Copper Co.[50] Their real investment in these enterprises had been nominal.

For the past few years Ritchie had been endeavouring to amalgamate all four companies, his main purpose to compensate those holding the valueless stocks in the Coe Hill mine and the C.O.R. by sharing in the growing prosperity of the Canadian Copper Co., this meant James MacLaren, William Coe's Estate and the McMullen's.[51] Now he could understand, however, why he had not got any support from Burke and Payne.

Apart from the methods of those two robber barons, one can understand their fear of losing their loans to Ritchie. His reckless adventuring frightened them. They had a case, being in a position similar to that of a bank holding collateral on an unpaid loan.

For that matter the Bank of Ottawa also held some of Ritchie's C.O.R. securities against such a loan. Here they would be registered in his name.[52]

The McMullens were now evidently on their way back into office in the C.O.R. The letter quoted from in the previous chapter from James

MacLaren to lawyer John Bell of Belleville, dated November 12th of that year is worth quoting further: "... I saw in Toronto two weeks since, George W. McMullen, and he told me that he had an agreement with Senator Payne, whereby the latter had contracted to give him for a nominal figure, after Ritchie's interests shall have been wiped out, enough of the stocks and securities of the road to enable him, McMullen, to take over and run it, which he then proposed to do. The *quid pro quo* passing from this contract was his institution of the two suits in the nature of creditor's bills in the Federal Courts in Cleveland by means of which Ritchie was to be carved up, and incidentally, I suppose, the carving knife was expected to sever the interests of your clients from the McLaren's. Your work in commencing the Chancery suit in Canada necessarily has the effect of interfering with the prosecution of this enterprise, so Mr. McMullen proposes pushing it to a hearing without delay."

"McMullen's contract was in writing, so he said, and he declared that he was prepared through the Senator's co-operation, either to control the road himself, or turn it over to a certain Messrs. Rathbun, whom I don't know. He said the McLaren interest was nil, on account of their not holding any of the early coupons, and but a smaller amount of the later ones." Payne must have had second thoughts for the McMullens remained in the background.

Another important sidelight on where the McMullens funding had come from over the years was discovered in a letter of Ritchie to one of his lawyers, almost a year after that momentous March meeting, "... McMullen has in every way in his person aided Payne and Burke to get complete possession and control of the Central Ontario Railway and in furtherance of this effort he has had suits in attachment brought in Canada in the name of his principal and backer, one C.S. Wilson, his neighbour, and who is probably the real owner of the McMullen judgment as well of the bonds and coupons ... In this suit he has caused a seizure to be made of the stock in *the C.O.R.* standing in my name."[53] This had been the prelude to that meeting.

C.S. Wilson, "Banker" Wilson as he was known in Picton, was the man that had financed the McMullens when they bought control of the Prince Edward County Railway. Although he remains off-stage he was an important influence in some of these events. With so many villains around

all that has been missing is a real life Uriah Heep. Here he is:

On the surface he was a successful businessman with his own private bank, an impressive building faced by white columns in the best banking tradition. It was situated between the present United Church (then Methodist) and Main Street. Some years later a fire damaged the structure. It lay empty for a while before being torn down.

He owned many properties and businesses, among them the small Phoenix Foundry, and the big Glenora Mill. His private bank was a formal description for what too often amounted to loan-sharking. He would lend money to farmers, home-owners, and merchants. The day a loan fell due, if the borrower was unable to meet it, he had the bailiff ready to sever the property as soon as the law allowed, a more frequent occurrence in hard times. On a quick sale such properties often sold at a fraction of their real value and "Banker" Wilson would be the buyer; then to be re-sold or rented at considerable profit. Straight Victorian melodrama, but no record whether Wilson hissed when he spoke. But he was smooth and unctious of manner.

Such a tragedy nearly happened to Malcolm Love's family farm in a year of poor crops. Fortunately his father, unlike others, was able to borrow the money that day from a friend he accidentally encountered outside the bank.[54]

As Ritchie expressed it seven months later, "I am beginning to find out something of the conspiracy and intrigue entered into for the wrecking of the railway."[55]

Power had changed drastically at board level. The next man to go was in May, Superintendent Fraser. Whether he left out of loyalty to Ritchie, or he was fired for the same reason one can only guess. His successor, given the title of Manager, was George Collins.[56] He would remain as the senior executive for the rest of the C.O.R.'s life.

Collins would prove to be exceptionally able, both as a railroader and as an administrator. That he was a local man was also much in his favour, coming from Ameliasburg Township in Prince Edward County. He knew no other railroad but the C.O.R. having started working for the company as a clerk in 1882.[57]

Chapter Eleven

The C.O.R. had become since the iron ore failure in 1885, an expand-or-die enterprise. Lumbering had kept the line operating but with the area being logged out fast this could only be a diminishing industry. New revenues had to be found. In the shadows of an uncertain future it is time to consider the state of the railway both physically and financially. Indeed, in spite of continuing penury, its resources had grown.

It had been six years since the line was completed to Coe Hill; eleven since the line from Picton to Trenton was opened. To this summary future activities and crises can be referred. The figures are taken for the greater part from Poor's Almanac for 1891. The accounts and the statistics are for the year ending in June, 1890, and from material in the Archives of Ontario.

James MacLaren of Buckingham, Que., recently elected to the board, was vice-president. According to Ritchie he had purchased a quarter interest in the company; the rest, according to Ritchie, at a later date, was almost entirely his money. The other directors, whose financial interests were at best controversial were Stevenson Burke, G.G. Allen, of whom little is known, and H.P. McIntosh, an associate of Burke's. All three resided in Cleveland, Ohio.

The route mileage was given as 104 miles and all was of 56-pound rail. What Poor had not been told was that the 42-pound rail remained between Picton and Trenton. This continued to limit the size of locomotives and the tonnage of trains.

Equipment had increased considerably. Locomotives had numbered ten in 1889, but only nine in 1890. Number three had been sold in that time. There are no further details as to her disposal. This could also have been the Gilmour locomotive illustrated.

In 1889, there were five passenger cars, "box and stock" numbered 24 and flats, essential for hauling logs, numbered 92. The extent the installation of airbrakes and mechanical couplers had been carried out at this time is not given. Former fireman and conductor Ross Weaver of Picton remembers that well into the present century many of the flatcars were "barefoot", (railroadese for cars with only hand-brakes). But most of these were probably captive on the road, hauling to Gilmour's and did not have to pass inspection by other lines. Money being scarce, it is likely that most of the time such modernization was considerably delayed.

The obvious conclusion over the past years, except for the brief boom before the iron ore failure, is that the C.O.R., not unlike many of its neighbours, large and small, lived in a state of penury. So it continued. In 1889 there was a surplus over operating costs of $5,441.34. In 1890, with a big drop in traffic receipts, there was a deficit of $3,663.64. Also to be taken into account, the C.O.R. paid lower wages than its bigger neighbours.

The extent of the line's lack of profit may not be fully realized until it is known that the company had yet to pay a "proverbial" cent on any of its bonds, stocks, etc. Ritchie, furthermore, had always paid his own expenses and had not received any director's fees. He certainly saved on paper for most of his voluminous correspondence is written on hotel stationery. It remains to his credit that he managed comparatively high standards on the line, often more than funds permitted. Others under these circumstances have milked a company into bankruptcy.

Summing up the earnings for 1890:-

Passenger	$26,916.19	
Freight	52,373.74	
Mail & Express	7,292.22	
Other	1,343.47[1]	$87,925.52

Operating expenses were: 91,588.96

To leave a deficit of: 3,663.64

An interesting footnote is that mixed train mileage was greater than that of passenger and freight trains combined.

The 1889 capital structure, which will be of future significance was:-

Common Stock $450,000.00

Preferred Stock   350,000.00

(No mention here of bonds or coupons)

                 $800,000.00

P.E.C. Rly. Provincial aid   126,500.00

Municipal Aid   93,500.00

                              $1,020,000.00

Floating Debentures   3,000.00

                              $1,023,000.00

These stocks were not listed on any stock exchange. Plainly their market value was negligible.

The cost of the railway was given as $1,494,000.00.

Somebody must have put up a lot of capital, and that was Ritchie.

A table of earnings to the end of 1914 is shown in an Appendix.

After such high drama at board level, the everyday events of the railway might seem less dramatic. And so they were. For the next seven years a stunned apathy seemed to settle on the line, a reaction to the atmosphere of hectic expansion that had left with Ritchie.

No statements exist of what the employees thought, whether train crews, operators and agents, clerks or section men. Because of the insecurity of the times and the financial problems of the company, first concerns would be job security and continuing wages.

Whatever the times Picton could thank the C.O.R. for a spectacular event on January 8th, 1894. This was the arrival at Picton yards of a new boiler for the steamer "Aberdeen" a scruffy little freighter, then refitting at the docks.

No weight is given but with 42-pound rails the load would have to be spread over two flatcars and travelling only a little faster than walking speed. Even then those light rails must have cried aloud in anguish. The boiler's safe arrival must have been an enormous relief to the superintendent. But the main drama was yet to come.

Down the icy street two teams of horses tugged the load. All went well until they reached the steep hill down Bridge Street. There the load started to run out of control, promising a serious accident to men, horses and nearby buildings. The runaways were brought under control although history has not recorded how.[1]

These were not prosperous times. Traffic along the line was light. The decision to suspend operations on the Belmont-Bessemer mine added to the gloom. The mine branch, graded ready for the track-laying, would be abandoned before it was built. The ties stacked ready for the start were sold to the C.P.R.[2]

The present state of the C.O.R. management did not go unnoticed by the editor of the Madoc newspaper. On May 10th, 1894, he observed, with no further action taken on the Bancroft extension and with the considerable grants now available, "No inducement seems to influence the lethargic Central Ontario Railway ..."[3]

Later in August he was moved to write a long editorial, the logic of which was not up to his usual standards, rapping the knuckles of those involved with either the C.O.R. or the former Belleville and North Hastings Railway.[4] But if there was little activity in new construction there was one brave trumpet blowing in the wilderness. In December the Irondale, Bancroft and Ottawa, nicknamed locally as the "I.O. & U.", financially a mendicant compared to the harrassed C.O.R., made a brave announcement. The company was applying for an extension of its line from a point in the County of Hastings to Brockville, many miles away to connect with the St. Lawrence Bridge and other lines. Struggling on its penniless way far back in the bush, the rails were still many miles away yet from Bancroft. Ottawa was not mentioned.[5]

Big news, particularly for this part of Ontario was when the Hon. Mackenzie Bowell became Prime Minister. In the New Year's Honours of 1895, Queen Victoria included him among the knighthoods. His career as prime minister was short.[6]

At the same time, hardly headline news, North Hastings Junction (for Madoc and Eldorado) was renamed Madoc Junction.

The fall of 1895, at the end of a dry summer brought a series of extensive and dangerous forest fires throughout the area. Affecting future freight revenue for the C.O.R., miles of valuable timber were destroyed. Long stretches of fencing by the right-of-way were levelled.[7] As if in compensation, out of Picton, business was better than ever. One fruit canner alone would ship twenty-six carloads that year.

One reason for the lethargy that now possessed the C.O.R. was George Collins having to get the weight of his new responsibilities, but even more difficult, he had to work under the direction of a board that knew how to rob a railroad, but nothing about running one. With Ritchie he had been working under a man who knew as much or more about operating a railroad than Collins or his predecessor. In spite of many difficulties, Collins would prove himself.

After nearly two years the Board agreed to build the extension to Bancroft. Application for renewal of federal grants was approved in April, 1896,[8] but construction had yet to start. The grants would lapse again.

The line that should have been built by the C.O.R. through the long-established village of Marmora to some of the original iron ore mines and on to the Ledyard gold mine, a distance of 9.2 miles, was now being undertaken by an independent company. The capital seems to have come from Toronto and New York.[9]

This company was chartered as the Ontario, Belmont and Northern but was not completed until 1896. At the turn of the century the company would change its name to the more appropriate Marmora Railway and Mining Company.

The O.B. & N. never owned any rolling stock. On its completion in 1896 an agreement was made with the C.O.R. to operate the line, a ten-year contract with either company having the privilege to terminate on three months notice. To all intents the line became a branch of the C.O.R.[10]

The junction was in the wilderness, 2.6 miles south of Marmora Station, a padlocked switch, the site nameless and unattended. Later the junction would be shown in the working timetables as Belmar.

The best news that year was an increase in traffic.

One Saturday night in mid-December the passenger train broke in two between Weller's Bay and Consecon. The train was only delayed twenty minutes to half an hour. Somebody had uncoupled the air hose between the cars, and the brakes had gone on automatically. Later the culprit would be prosecuted for this dangerous act. No one was hurt.[11] This episode records the fact that the automatic brake was now in use on passenger trains.

Automatic couplers, if standard on some of the big railroads on this continent, were still far from universal. A month later a Grand Trunk brakeman got his fingers caught in a link-and-pin coupler, to be left with a thumb and little finger.[12]

The following year there were many new railway schemes. A few would become reality; others after a few brave headlines in the press would never be heard of again, as had been that pattern for many years now.

One such proposal, an intriguing one, was Rathbun's declared intention to extend his line further than Bannockburn to join Booth's new east-west line from Ottawa that passed some miles north of Bancroft and from there onwards to North Bay or Sudbury — this had a strong relationship to Ritchie's now abandoned scheme. Rathbun did not, apparently, fear the C.P.R. Likely the G.T.R. now with strong leadership, and with whom he did a great deal of business, was behind him.[14]

That unfortunate step-child of the Grand Trunk, the Belleville and North Hastings, had to all intents once more ceased its operations between Madoc and Eldorado. In March a local deputation led by none other than the former prime minister, Sir Mackenzie Bowell, arrived in Montreal at the Grand Trunk headquarters to seek the help of the new general manager, Charles Melville Hays.[15]

A remarkable railroader, yet to become famous, his influence would soon be felt across Canada. His appointment had already caused a stir. Until now executive officers had always been Englishmen, now here was an American in charge. Before very long miracles happened, the Grand Trunk began to pay dividends, and, at last Canadians would be given more responsible positions. If Charles Melville Hays would fail as a strategist and a diplomat, he was a phenomenal success as a railroader. His death in the Titanic in

1912 left much unfinished business — some say this changed Canadian history; others that the course of unfortunate events was inevitable.

The deputation was well received by Hays. After explaining the Madoc-Eldorado problem one would guess they oversold their presence by suggesting a daily train to Coe Hill, still with mountains of unsold iron ore, presumably over C.O.R. rails. The C.O.R. was by now down to two trains a day, the one went as far as C.P.R. Junction, the other went on to Coe Hill. That idea was impracticable.[16]

That summer the station at C.P.R. Junction was burnt to the ground. The contents of the freight shed were saved by a train crew, but the C.O.R. agent, for it was their station, Mr. Yott, lost all his household goods, which were only partly covered by insurance.[17] No time was wasted and a new station was completed and open for business on December 2nd.[18]

What The Picton Gazette would report as the C.O.R.'s "first serious accident" happened on Saturday, July 17th, 1897. With C.O.R. luck no one was killed or even seriously injured. The wreck was to the noon train for Picton. At Niles Corners the engine ran into a defective switch. With its two coaches the train ran along the ties for 200 yards, the engine and tender then rolled over into the ditch. The baggage-smoker was left canted over at a precarious angle. The coach remained upright.

Once upon a time the delivery of the mails was a sacred trust. So they went in a hand-car to Picton. What happened to the passengers? As far as The Gazette was concerned it did not seem to matter, as no mention was made of their eventual arrival. Creditably the rails were repaired by evening, and, hauled by another locomotive the train eventually arrived in Picton at 10 p.m. The identity of the locomotive is not recorded, but she had been re-railed by the following day and hauled back to the shops for repairs.[19]

The I.B. & O. was still abuilding, slowly, headed for Bancroft. In May the employees, without warning, seized a train and other cars. Likely their pay was in arrears. This was a one-man railroad. C.J. Pusey, president and owner, happened to be away. On his return he gathered about him a magistrate and special constables. Having convinced the militants that this was not only illegal but an inconvenience to the public ". . . steam was raised and the train started off."[20]

Odds were beginning to be on the I.B. & O., the tortoise, reaching Bancroft before the onetime hare, the C.O.R. There were still these reports abroad that another company would be building into the town from the north-east. But rumours they remained.

In March, 1898, new rumours were about that the C.P.R. would buy the C.O.R. There may have been some substance to this, but with all the lawsuits going on, acquisition of the C.O.R. could only be an uncertain venture.[21]

The following month brought good news for the town of Madoc. A new company, a Canadian one, The Toronto Smelting Co. had confirmed that it would build a steel furnace in Madoc. Once more a wave of optimism hit the area, but this time tempered by caution.[22]

At the Deloro gold mine, a source of inbound freight for the C.O.R., there was the news that the manager had been relieved and another hired. This was a British company with an expensive and elaborate plant. The manager had not been producing enough gold. As his successor would discover, this was not possible.[23]

On the old Belleville and North Hastings from Eldorado to Madoc, the Grand Trunk cancelled the excursion fares on market days, and traffic dropped from 23 passengers on the train to an average of four.[24]

Traffic was busier than ever on the Picton line. From June onwards a special fruit train was running daily.[25]

Proof that air brakes had still to be installed on all the C.O.R. freight cars came in early July. T.E. Rowe, a brakeman, was applying the handbrakes, using his club, contrary to rules, to lever the brake wheel. The club broke and he fell between the moving cars to be cut in half. Railroading continued a hazardous occupation.[26]

In August, 1898, six years later, the new board of the C.O.R., made up its mind to build the Bancroft extension. George Collins must have finally convinced them that it was expand or die. The board would spend nothing on new equipment, locomotives were badly needed as well as passenger coaches and flatcars. But he had stood firm on keeping the track and road bed in shape. Proof lay in the few accidents.

That the company was in earnest was

evident. Engineer Evans was at the proposed junction point in mid-August with a survey gang running a line of stakes northward. The junction would be situated seven miles east of Coe Hill at Ormsby (formerly Rathbun) and would become known as Ormsby Junction.[27]

There were great hopes in Hastings that construction would start that year but Stevenson Burke and company were not investing heavily, if at all. Construction was also delayed because of a hold-up over the federal subsidy.

Not until June 15th, 1899 did Collins write to Cleveland saying that they expected to open tenders for the construction of the line. There was also the problem of buying the needed rail as cheaply as possible.

One of the three contracts was awarded to Robert Weddell of Trenton.

Nobody was rolling 56 pound rail any more. Collins was under the impression that the government would not pay the subsidy if second-hand rail was used. Sixty pound rail was now the lightest being manufactured. For axle loads it made a 2¼% difference, but there was no advantage as most of the line was already laid with 56 pound rail.

An offer of some 58 pound rail from the Intercolonial Railway in the Maritimes, complete with fastenings and square nuts, all in good condition, was a bargain. A concerned Collins' request to the Board to purchase five or ten miles of this to replace worn 42 pound rail on the Picton line would have to wait another year, and then only to be allowed a lesser quantity.

Not until early August, 1899, was the first sod turned for the line to Bancroft. A decade had passed since Ritchie had first proposed the extension.

Since the Burke regime had taken over much had been going on in the law courts. He and his associates had not been able to sell the railway, Ritchie and his lawyers having kept ahead of them by injunctions, "foiling" their villainies.

The world of law courts, the suits and countersuits, and injunctions were remote from the operations of the railway, though their influence was great. Then there were the people involved.

Filed away among the 1890's correspondence in the Ritchie papers, but as was often the case, undated, is a typed extract from the Toronto *Mail*. The report revealed J.B. McMullen was under a bribery charge standing before a Grand Jury regarding a city printing contract. "After making certain statements under oath ... J.B. McMullen was admonished by an outside party familiar with the transactions that perjurers were sent to the penitentiary; whereupon he went back before the Grand Jury and again, under oath, stated that in his previous testimony he had made a mistake or two. Still another member of this notorious family, D.Y. McMullen, was indicted for perjury and fraud against the United States while occupying the position of gauger." (An exciseman.)

This extract continues with an account of the McMullens' newspaper days in Chicago before they became involved with the railway. By coincidence this story was confirmed when the Chicago Daily News published its own obituary in 1978. To quote from the Toronto Mail again: "Their disposition to lie and steal is so constitutional that they even stole the despatches of a superior concern, the penny sheet called 'The News.'" The latter devised a shrewd dodge. It constructed a fictitious despatch announcing an insurrection in a Servian town and reported an excited procession by the people carrying banners bearing the sign[28] "Er us siht la etsll iws nel lum cmeht."[29] The bait took. The next edition of "The News" contained the entire despatch, including the strange device, which to be interpreted needs only to be read backwards: "The McMullens will steal this sure." This was followed by further, even more detrimental statements concerning other McMullen activities in Toronto, that would, if untrue, have given them the opportunity to enrich themselves considerably through libel actions.[30]

Ritchie becomes more credible when he accuses them of fraud when he had bought 180 C.O.R. bonds from them but never received delivery. This was in addition to the coupons, past due when the big bond issue was sold, which instead of cancelling they had cashed in. Later they would have the effrontery to register the bonds in their own names, both bonds and coupons becoming additional debts to the railway, which Ritchie personally had to make good. Heaping insult upon fraud was Ritchie losing the law case against them.[31]

This case was a greater disaster than it seemed. In the United States in Ritchie's suit against Burke and Payne, the McMullen decision was introduced in the court as a precedence. It was accepted. And the decision went against Ritchie. Ritchie would appeal to a superior court, but that took time. But that was not all, the case was further tied up by technicalities concerning the jurisdiction of the appeal court.[32]

Ritchie had a fresh tactic: gain some fresh evidence, re-open the original McMullen case in Canada, then start the whole legal process all over again in the United States.

There was one McMullen that Ritchie trusted, H.C. McMullen, with whom he would occasionally correspond.[33]

The McMullens, as Ritchie had discovered earlier, had been financed by one C.S. Wilson of Picton. He believed they had usually acted under his direction. He considered including this individual in the new McMullen suit, then decided not to do so.[34]

Whatever the villainies of the McMullens, they were small-time compared to Stevenson Burke. He was the mastermind. Once he and his followers had dispossessed Ritchie of all his holdings, mines in the Sudbury area, as well as the C.O.R., they were ready to sell the whole empire without a flicker of sympathy or generosity for Ritchie. They plainly anticipated his leaving the battlefield, broken and destitute.

Their first move was to put the railway up for sale without bothering to inform his solicitors. Ritchie was ready for that. He obtained the first of a series of injunctions to prevent the sale for he still had those bonds in his name at the Bank of Ottawa. As John Bell, that authority on railway law, was able to quote from an earlier court ruling (April, 1882), "In Canada we have no general law authorizing any Court to foreclose the franchise of a Railway Company to whom the franchise is given, can without special legislation use or exercise that franchise. It is only where statutes are passed for a given case that anything of that sort is done." There followed further details regarding the rights of bondholders.[35]

The number of lawsuits pending would multiply, some lasted with their appeals for years, and on both sides of the border. To describe them or even list them would only become confusing. For example, looking ahead, by 1898 Ritchie was involved in no less than ten different law cases. Over the years he would lose, lose, and lose

again.[36] What remains is to give some of the background, the more important developments, and new enemies as they appeared on the battlefield.

Where and how Ritchie found the money for all this costly litigation is not known, of this he makes no mention, though he was constantly being pressed for payment by various U.S. banks. It sickened him that Burke and Payne paid for their legal costs from the C.O.R. funds that could ill be spared, at that from sources in which he had personally invested three-quarters of its capital. Prior to their takeover he had never accepted his fees and had paid all his own expenses. The group took every cent that they could.

If Ritchie had only himself to blame it is hard not to sympathize with him. The takeover of the C.O.R. upset him far more than the loss of his more valuable Sudbury holdings. Incidentally, he was not allowed access to the books of any of these companies. Throughout the rest of his life he would write many briefs, often repetitive, for his lawyers, in effect supervising their legal presentations in court. A quotation he frequently repeated with variations was, "Fraud vitiates any transaction."[37]

In May, 1893, Ritchie gave notice to George Collins, manager of the C.O.R. that Payne and Burke were trying to register in their own names a large number of the bonds belonging to him.[38] But there is no further correspondence on this matter in the file. But register them they did, Payne registered his in March, 1894. Earlier the McMullens had led the way having registered their less significant number. The total value of Ritchie's bonds, including those of the Canadian Copper and Anglo-American Iron Companies (but none of the various stocks) totalled at face value $3-million.

There had also appeared on the scene the representative of one of the bondholders. He had a military title and was soon under the influence of Burke or Payne. As Ritchie saw him, "Butterworth never had any official position as Major, General, or anything else. The parading of these military titles by the plaintiff is a weak effort to magnify Butterworth's importance." This was not gossip but a statement that Ritchie directed his attorney to bring to the attention of a particular U.S. court.[39]

In March, 1894, Ritchie lost an important case in the Supreme Court (presumably of Ontario) against the Toronto General Trust[40] which held various bonds and coupons (some of which had earlier been spirited away by the McMullens). The following year Ritchie would open another case against the Trust Company.

Another enemy arrived about this time in the person of T.G. Blackstock of the Toronto law firm of Beatty, Blackstock and Co. He would in time bring an even greater complication to these happenings. Hired by Burke and Co., it was not long before he became a director of the C.O.R. His tasks were to hasten their cases through the courts as well as to act as their attorney.[41] Next he was charged with buying up all the C.O.R. bonds he could get his hands on. Once Burke and his associates got the remaining bonds they would put the railway into receivership. The stockholders would have no rights. Then they could sell the railway and collect a lot more money than they had ever lent Ritchie.

While this was going on Ritchie had some satisfaction with the news that the bondholders of the Hocking Valley were bringing suit against Burke.[42] Later he would have the further pleasure of watching the great J.P. Morgan boot Burke out of his control of the Toledo line.

There was another holder of Ritchie's bonds, Cornell, also a resident of Ohio. He had been a passive follower of Burke. The bonds had been lodged with him under similar circumstances. This lack of agreement, as with the others, had been a doubtful advantage for Ritchie, so far.

Cornell died in 1892 and under circumstances that did not help any of the contending parties. In keeping with these events, he left the world under unusual circumstances.

His will, later proved to be a forgery, left a large sum of money to his male nurse if he died while under his care. The male nurse turned out to be an unemployed private detective. The three trustees of the estate included the man who had drawn up the will. The other two died not long after. Baird, who had drawn up the will, was still alive in 1902 and had yet to give up custody of the bonds.[43] MacLaren had died in 1893; his interests were administered by his estate.[44]

Senator Payne followed Cornell, dying in September, 1896. Charles W. Bingham, his son-in-law, was his executor. He purchased the C.O.R. bonds from the estate to bring a new name into the legal battles.[45] Though active in those issues he did not seem to have had much iron in his temperament.

With the C.O.R. board busy with the Bancroft extension, it is time to return to railroading.

Chapter Twelve

The long delayed extension to Bancroft was completed in the year 1900. The line was not built to Ritchie's standards, but to the minimum demanded by the two governments to qualify for the payment of subsidies. As it turned out parts of the line were below that standard. The rail was second-hand, 56-pound with some 58-pound and some heavier.[1] Much of it was of C.P.R. origin, as well as the Government-owned Intercolonial. On the main lines, with traffic making increasing demand for higher capacity trains and heavier locomotives to haul them, light rail was fast becoming obsolete. As a result such second-hand rail was both cheap and plentiful.

George Collins had been concerned that the two governments would not pay the subsidies if second-hand rail was used. While the contract stipulated no other specification than 56-pound rail, worn rails could weigh less, if only fractionally. Anyway unofficial approval must have been obtained.

That September a government engineer, not on an acceptance inspection, remarked that the several patterns of rail (although mostly of the same weight, cross-sections varied considerably) should be sorted out as the fish plates, that joined the rails, did not fit well. Also some rail ends were badly worn or were broken. After much relaying by the contractor, excepting for ordinary attrition, those same rails remain there yet. The inspector also remarked that many of the ties were too small, and where there was ballast, it was sand.[2] The locomotive engineers would need to be cautious as well as skillful. But this was rough, rocky country with occasional sandy ridges, similar to the last few miles into Coe Hill. Not easy country for building railways.

Ormsby Jct. winter '78-79. Looking north. Left to Coe Hill, right to Bancroft. The building is the shed for Section "5".
Photo, David Hanes

Detlor formerly L'Amable (No longer standing.)   Photo, Herman Snider

Circumstances and personalities rather than fate had decided that the unsubsidized Trenton to Coe Hill line should be built to the highest standards, while Picton to Trenton and Ormsby Junction to Bancroft had, and would receive, some of the highest subsidies among contemporary railway projects. Whatever the standards Burke would have preferred, minimum federal standards had to be maintained. As completed the line had no curves sharper than eight degrees and the maximum gradient was 1.55 percent.

Evans, the civil engineer, a Trenton resident, who had until recently been self-employed working for the C.O.R. as a consultant, now joined the staff. His hobby, entomology had brought him some fame for a large collection of insects.

Progress through the construction season had been good with the usual goal of completion before freeze-up. Grading had started early in May. Labour had been scarce.[3] Before long the contractor had a strike to contend with. They refused to give way, and the majority having struck on Saturday returned to work Monday.[4]

By July 24th, the Ontario Government's engineer had completed his interim inspection of the line to report that 18 miles had been completed over which the railway was already carrying southbound freight such as ore, cedar posts, pulpwood and tan bark.[5] The contractor had told him they expected to have the line completed in six weeks, grading having been completed one and a half miles past Bancroft, half a mile short of the point the C.O.R. was to meet the I.B. & O.[6]

In August Robert Weddell of Trenton, the contractor, told the press that he had the rails laid to the end of the line, two miles north of Bancroft.[7] At this time he was completing the only two bridges of any size, and these were of comparatively modest dimensions. Both were steel, the first a 30-foot span at milepost 5.5 (from Ormsby Junction), the second a 60-foot span near L'Amable at milepost 23.[8]

At this stage Ormsby Junction, Carlow Road and L'Amable seem to have been the stations, additional to the Bancroft terminus. There were five 5,000-foot passing tracks as well as several sidings. Not in any engineering report — this line passed through some of the most beautiful of Ontario scenery.

George Collins was able to confirm Robert

Weddell's statement by travelling by train all the way to Bancroft on August 16th.[9] The line would not be ready for passenger traffic until November 1st, so Collins had informed the Minister of Railways, requesting the official inspection of the line prior to that date. All of which happened as anticipated.[10]

The first train ran on November 1st; the timetable appeared on the 5th. The south-bound train left at 6:15 a.m. and returned from Trenton at 6:30 p.m.[11]

Collins could not yet apply for the subsidies as the station buildings had yet to be completed. There was also a delay caused by an argument over a grade not in accordance with the official profile. This would be changed to suit the government, but not the contractor, Robert

Weddell, who had already had to do much additional work.

Other interests than the Board's and the contractor's were anxiously awaiting these payments — Molson's Bank, and various suppliers. Another argument would follow, a subsidy was requested for 21 miles, but it was only 20 miles to Bancroft! This would be settled a year later by applying the amount to another extension of which more will be heard.[12]

While everything seemed secure for all the disbursements from both governments, just a matter of waiting for the acceptance of the line by the government, and a few details to be put right, there happened one of those dramatic interventions that were part of the life of the C.O.R., though it came to nothing.

North of Detlor. Good rock ballast here. Not far from the long down-grade into Bancroft.

Photo, Author

Ritchie does not appear to have visited the line since he was deposed from the presidency, at least there is no record in the press of his having done so. But the Bancroft extension was something he could not stay away from. He was in Bancroft in June, and again in July.[13] To the press he would only speak of his interest in the mining prospects along the new line. But his letter dated September 6th, 1900 to Collingwood Schreiber,

Deputy Minister and Chief Engineer of the Department of Railways and Canals, a considerable figure in his own right, was another matter altogether.[14]

Inevitably he touched briefly on his own position, legally and morally, and the extent of his investment in the C.O.R., then requested that the line be inspected for its entire length. This gained him nothing but the resulting inspection report was a valuable record for posterity. It must also have disturbed Stevenson Burke and company though if only for a short time.

His second request was that no money (from the subsidies) be paid to the assignee until the litigation then pending in the courts be disposed of. This the government could not do; at best this would have been highly controversial legally, the contractors and the suppliers would have had precedence in these claims. Likely he expected this, if nothing else it kept his case before the government.

His first request, started: "The physical condition of the railway is in a bad and dangerous condition for the running of passenger trains. . . . I also request that you have a careful inspection of the whole line between Picton and Coe Hill and Bancroft as to its physical condition and fitness for the running of passenger and freight trains over it as well as to the condition of its rolling stock." He finished by saying that his purpose was to protect the public and, as far as possible, the rightful owners.

An inspecting engineer from the government was travelling over the C.O.R. within a week, H.A.F. Macleod.[15] His report is the only contemporary description of the Central Ontario Railway, and it was from his report that other particulars of the railway are available.

Macleod was thorough, but he was also more tolerant than strict. Most of his travelling was made by train, stopping from time to time at his request. From Coe Hill to Bancroft and back he had to make his journey by hand-car, 58 miles in all. He probably had a companion, but even so, that was a lot of pumping.

On the line south of Coe Hill there is much of interest noted in this report. Some excerpts: the 42-lb. rails, thirty miles of them, from Picton to Trenton were still there, marked 'Cammell Sheffield Toughened Steel, 5 mo. 1879 C.F.' These rails "are in very good order . . . with good sound ties, and well ballasted." His only criticisms here were "a good many loose bolts between 7th and 11th miles" plus a few single bolts. Both the Chief Engineer (Evans) and the Road Foreman said that it was excellent steel. (The generally held rating of British steel rails of that period was that it was 15% to 20% stronger).

Another item was the information that the pile trestle across Consecon Lake had been shortened with fill from 1,000-feet to 40-feet, sufficient space for the run-off from the lake and for a steel span.

North from Trenton to Coe Hill was in "very good order." The only exception, the condition of the ties for the last five miles into Coe Hill. At Coe Hill, Macleod recorded, was a twin to the unusual turntable at Picton, closed in with masonry walls. There was also a single stall engine shed. A mile of siding led to the idle iron mines.

Not described before, was the exception to the fine engineering of the Trenton to Coe Hill line, the grades over the last few miles into that terminus. It would seem that after the failure of the mines the company had not the will or the means to complete the necessary earth fills between the rock formations. As a result, "There are short pitches from 4 feet to 500 feet long and the grade ranges from 4% to 5%." (1 in 25 to 1 in 20). This is pretty steep and would require some impetus for the train to make it over this roller coaster. Fortunately the grades faced northbound and the trains would be hauling mostly empties. In time these hollows were filled up though a fairly stiff gradient still remained.

Macleod found all the locomotives in very good repair, except one that was in the shops for overhaul, as were the passenger and freight equipment that he encountered. From the point of view of maintenance generally he considered the C.O.R. was well-managed. After that he prudently hedged his bets by saying the line was safe from Picton to Gilmour at speeds not exceeding 30 miles an hour, and from Gilmour to Coe Hill at no more than 20 m.p.h. There was another reservation that the train crews did not need to be told, that care should be taken descending those steep gradients out of Coe Hill. On a cold winter night, with only handbrakes on many of the cars, it was slippery going from car to car and the railroaders had a rough time. In the light of later events, including Collins' own reports to the Board, there was a lot of whitewash in this document.

For Ritchie, sick and embittered, this must have been more than he could bear, on top of having to watch his extension completed on his beloved line by others and his enemies at that.

The Bancroft extension had its effects on neighbouring railways.

First the remarkable I.B. & O. which Colonel Stevens describes in his book as the love child of its owner C.J. Pusey. Sadly this line had come to a halt three miles short of its planned connection with the C.O.R. It should have been there first.[16] This enterprise, and its owner had suffered a mortal blow the previous year. It would seem for lack of the right political connections the necessary subsidy to complete the line to York River was turned down by parliament. The gallant Pusey died the same year. Not for years would the last three miles be completed. Oddly enough that is all that remains today.

The now completed east to west line from Ottawa to Parry Sound (on Lake Huron's Georgian Bay) the Ottawa, Arnprior and Parry Sound, at its nearest point was but 40 miles north of Bancroft. As to be expected there was pressure on the C.O.R. management to extend the line north to join the Canada Atlantic. The C.O.R. Board, expand or die, or maybe to eventually sell the line at a profit, and no doubt spurred on by

George Collins, with surprising promptness had applied for such an extension. That tiresome extra mile granted in subsidies would go towards this extension. These new subsidies for some 40 miles had been approved quickly in 1900. The start of construction would be slower.

The new railway across the north was a more important connection than it first seems. To all intents it was the property of J.R. Booth, the Ottawa Valley lumber king. But this line was only part of his Canada Atlantic Railway which ran from Ottawa to connect with the Grand Trunk main line at Coteau Junction. The Grand Trunk having no line into Ottawa ran a joint service between Ottawa and Montreal with the Canada Atlantic. The Booth line continued past Coteau Junction, south-easterly, to provide a short cut to the trunk lines running to the United States. All had been shrewdly planned.

BANCROFT 1900
Waiting for the first train into town.

Waiting for first train into Bancroft 1900.   *Photo, Earl Hawley*

York River Junction where the I. B. & O. finally joined the C.O.R.

Photo, Author

Bancroft Station 1977. Station is on west side.

Photo, Author

ROBT. WEDDELL

Robert Weddell, around 1911-12.   *"Evolution of Trenton"*

No matter how you fix it you can't disguise a boxcar. Bancroft 1977
Photo, Author

This new northern line of Booth's (which would soon change its name to that of the parent line) not only opened up new timber lands, but provided a new route for shipping western wheat via the lakes. Operationally it suffered from some heavy grades. In 1904 the Grand Trunk bought the railway; Hays just had to have a line into Canada's capital. The price was $14-million. Booth did much better out of the deal than the Grand Trunk.[17]

As one might guess, certain rumours would appear frequently in the local newspapers over the next few years. The first, that the Canada Atlantic would buy the C.O.R. then, when it became Grand Trunk, that corporation was reported as once more about to purchase the railway. The C.P.R. would also have its turn again. These reports or rumours would continue over the next five years. As has been noted earlier, the potential legal liabilities of such a purchase continued to outweigh the strategic value of the C.O.R. and its modest profits.

As for those two enemies battling over the line, Ritchie had won some pyrrhic victories in confounding Burke. For himself he had won nothing. Ritchie was beginning to suffer painfully from rheumatism and Burke's health was said to be none too good; a reason given for his infrequent visits to the line. This was becoming literally a battle to the death. Both contenders would hang in a while yet.

* * *

Over the past few years, the economy had been climbing out of a bad slump. The pick-up in business was reflected in C.O.R. profits. While the new line being built meant extra tonnage, as more mines opened up the railway was busier in proportion to its size than many other lines.

George Collins and his fellow railroaders shouldered a heavy burden during 1900 while the locomotives and equipment saw hard service. There is no record of the C.O.R. renting additional locomotives but adding to the difficulties locomotive No. 11 was sent to Sudbury to work for the Canadian Copper Co. for several months. For this the C.O.R. received $1200.00. Passenger cars were hired for excursions. Foreign freight cars could be used on the line on a per diem basis, but that cost money.

Three of Collins' letters to Cleveland remain in the Ontario Archives. The first, dated No-vember 16th, 1899, requests permission to sell two old Prince Edward County boxcars to Gilmours, $300 for the pair. Gilmours would use them around their several miles of line between plants and mill. He considered the price "as much or possibly more than they were worth." This money would be applied to new equipment. The answers have not survived.

The second letter dated July 18, 1900 was written after a rush of excursion traffic on the 12th of July. Eight coaches had been available, five rented from the Grand Trunk. This had not been nearly enough to meet the C.O.R. requirements. In former years any number had always been available from the bigger system. Instead "a large proportion of the crowd" had to be carried in boxcars. Something that by this time was almost unheard of. Accordingly Collins recommended that with the Bancroft extension about to be completed the Board should buy a couple of secondhand coaches.

On November 21, 1900, Collins wrote in some desperation that the combined baggage and mail car had pulled "a draw bar and attachments" on the Coe Hill run. All hands had to work through the night as the railway had no replacement. He urged that a new car be purchased. This request was granted and a car was ordered from the Crossen Co. of Cobourg; with delivery to be made in five weeks and payment to be made in installments.

The timber business had been brisk that year. Spring days saw logs and finished lumber stacked along the right-of-way waiting shipment.[18] By June the Gilmour Company had two full-time gangs loading lumber on to the flatcars.[19]

A new departure this year with labour short was floating the logs in the spring drive to the nearest point on the line, then, loading them on flatcars.[20] This was likely Rathbun's idea; he would also build the flatcars.

Rathbun had many men in the woods over the previous winter. His principal shipping ports were, Bannockburn, Coe Hill and Marmora.[21] He also had a big sawmill under construction at Marmora. The timber from this mill would be the first southbound freight over the new line.[22]

The Anglo-American Iron Company, one of Ritchie's companies from which he had been ousted, was now in the lumber business as well. With two camps of 50 men and 15 jobbers, a small operation compared to Rathbun's, they were shipping hardwood logs, cedar telegraph poles, ties, etc.[23] Much of that winter's production would be used by the C.O.R. for their new line; the rest would be shipped north over the C.P.R. to Sudbury.

George Collins visited Montreal in April, 1900 to attend the Canadian Freight Agents annual meeting and give an address. The Montreal Gazette gave this close to a column. Allowing that timber and mining was the C.O.R.'s principal source of revenue Collins pointed out that dairy products were becoming an important source of revenue that had grown 20% over the past year. North Hastings' cheese was becoming famous in Great Britain.

Other points he made were that when the line was extended to the Canada Atlantic Railway, the C.O.R. would provide a shortcut for grain shipments. This could mean heavy tonnage. The Bancroft area, a sportsman's paradise, had a high potential in tourist traffic with hunters and fishermen.

More detailed in the presentation was his description of the mining industry along the railway. A lesser boom than the one that built the railway but promising.

The new station at L'Amable was to become an important mining centre. At the Deloro mine, near Marmora Station, the gold mine there financed by British capital, would soon have no less than forty big mechanical stamps working to reduce the gold-bearing rock. (They would stamp in vain.) Another mine in the vicinity, the Consolidated Company, would soon be shipping their unattractive product, arsenic.

George Collins ended his speech: "... President J. Stevenson of the Central Ontario Railway Company has been a prime spirit in the development of Sudbury's wondrous nickel wealth ..."[24] Whatever the Judge may or may not have done, this was clearly not among his achievements. Ritchie, if he read this, would not be amused.

Concurrently in the world outside, in the South African war Mafeking was still under siege. The current rumour, causing great concern, was that Baden-Powell had been killed.[25]

Among mining developments along the C.O.R., William Coe's son Arthur was now operating, apparently with some success, a hematite mine. Employing 25 men they were shipping on average two and a half carloads a day — between 60 and 65 tons.[26]

No. 9 waits at the underpass. Soon after it was constructed to exchange passengers and express with the Grand Trunk.

Courtesy, Roy Cornish, Trenton, Ont.

L'Amable Station (No longer standing.) *Photo, Herman Snider*

At Malone the Dufferin mine had been shipping magnetic ore in unrecorded quantities for over a year.[27]

As far as tonnage was concerned, the best mining customer was the speculator A.J. Longnecker who had purchased at an extremely low price the mountain of sulphurous ore estimated at 25,000 to 30,000 tons at Coe Hill. He was shipping two cars of ore a day to a smelter in Hamilton. This was magnetic ore, about 3% sulphur. By April he had shipped 3,000 tons.[28]

A Kingston syndicate was about to open a gold mine near Gilmour, that was in July.[29] That was the essence of Collins' address.

Mines were always being opened with much fanfare. When they closed it was often ignored by the local press, leaving an impression of more mines being operated than there really were.

The Marmora Mining and Railway Company seemed to be on the verge of prosperity. The company was also threatening to build a line direct to the C.P.R. In August, George Collins visited that line in company with two of Rathbun's executives. Rathbun had purchased a controlling interest in these iron mines, and he now controlled this small railway as well.

The decision was made to extend the sidings and the "wye".[30] Marmora Village would have been feeling less the elderly Cinderella.

There were several well-patronized passenger excursions that year. This had become a useful source of revenue. One such special was to the fall fair in Picton and hauled seven cars from the north to Trenton where eight more coaches were added.[31] Other excursions, seldom recorded, meant only one extra coach on a regular train.

In December, 1900 the Gilmour Company sharply reduced its operations. The company, so it was reported, was reorganizing. The process "was not yet fully completed."[32] In truth the company was in financial difficulties.

117

Ormsby Junction looking south 1978. Right-hand tract to Coe Hill left to Bancroft. There was a wye here.

A major change in railway operations for both the Grand Trunk and the C.O.R. at Trenton had been completed in 1900. The main purpose was to reduce the grades in and out of the Trent Valley. But also with the realization that when the Trent Canal was completed, sooner or later, the line would have to be raised sufficiently to avoid having to build a lift or swing bridge; either type would be costly to both operate and maintain as well as causing unacceptable delays to rail traffic.

These works had lifted the Grand Trunk line high enough that the C.O.R. could now pass underneath. An irritating grade crossing that had caused many delays to C.O.R. trains had gone. While under construction this overpass had been a still greater nuisance to the C.O.R.

Part of the agreement with the Grand Trunk had been that the C.O.R. should lower their tracks. The old level can still be seen on the south side of the cut. This excavation resulted in a short heavier gradient out of Trenton — an impetus gradient that could be overcome at reasonable

speed without reducing train tonnages, though the locomotive engineers did not like it. The main handicap was that it filled up quickly with snow in the winter.

There was now a sharper grade for interchange traffic between the two levels, the Grand Trunk yards remaining on the low ground. The C.O.R.'s town station continued to be their principal traffic point. Now, in November, there was talk of a two storey station over the underpass.[33]

After Macleod's glowing report one can be surprised reading Collins' letter of December 22nd to Cleveland headquarters in which (misquoting 42-lb. steel as 45-lb.) he points out that it "has been in service now for twenty-one years and is not at all adequate for the very heavy traffic which we are handling over it." Apparently two years previously two miles of track had to be relayed with new 56-lb. rail. Now on December 22nd, 1900 he was asking for authority to purchase another 200 tons of this rail for relaying on the Picton line, to be laid next year "where most needed." This would be the equivalent of two and a half miles of track. Old 42-lb. rail had already been used for sidings. More sidings would also be required.[34]

Except for the odd mile in dispute, the final subsidy payments were made to Molson's Bank in Trenton on February 6th, 1901.[35] The station buildings had all been completed for the Bancroft extension in early January. The subsidy for that last mile was paid in May.

Collins had at last got authority for some more new equipment. During the summer fifty new flatcars of higher capacity, 60,000 lbs. built to Intercolonial Railway specifications were obtained. The price was $705 net, with the C.O.R. buying and fitting the airbrake equipment in their own shops. The older flatcars still ran "barefoot", with only handbrakes. Evidently Rathbun's works turned out a good car. Collins called them "beautiful", adding that the master mechanic was "well pleased."[36]

The new 56-lb. rail also arrived that July, all 200 tons.[37]

One more pleasure to the long-suffering passengers north of Trenton, an additional new coach had been ordered that winter, a combine, smoker and express.[38] It arrived in April and an additional mixed train appeared on the Coe Hill run.[39] By May there had been a third train running out of Bancroft, "a special lumber train."[40]

This was the month of the annual meeting at Trenton. Burke did not attend. Johnson, the vice president, took the chair. It was stated the annual report (for the previous year's operations) was considered "very satisfactory." After the meeting "a thorough inspection of the line was made" by special train. Returning from Bancroft, "on some portions of the line a speed of over fifty miles an hour was developed."[41]

For two years now the railway had been remarkably free of accidents. Two unfortunates had lost their lives the year before on the extension, but these were contractors' men and not involved in the railway's operations. There had been a minor derailment or two, minor injuries among train crews, so whatever the state of the rails the C.O.R. had continued with its good safety record. This came to an end on August 3rd, 1901, a Saturday.

Train No. 5 (southbound) was running between Springbrook and Rawdon with a trainload of logs and timber when the locomotive (unidentified) jumped the tracks followed by seven of the cars. "The whole was piled up in a terrible wreck." Engineer Charles Lough of Trenton was so badly scalded he died 20 minutes after being taken out of the cab. Fireman Ernest McClennan, also badly scalded, died on the following day. The head-end brakeman, H. Sarles of Frankford, riding in the cab too, the normal custom, was also severely scalded, but was still holding on to his life. Fortunately he was the only married man in the crew.

The cause of this accident was rumoured to be spreading rails.[42] This also meant one less locomotive for Collins for the time being.

Passengers interchanging with the Grand Trunk Railway at Trenton Junction found it difficult to call this an improvement, as it was for the railway with a straight run through instead of switching in and out of the Grand Trunk station. They were left with the choice of standing out in the cold waiting for the train or climbing back up twenty-five stairs to sit peering anxiously out of the Grand Trunk waiting room.[43] For those carrying luggage which was much heavier in the past, all this did not improve public relations. In the days of the railway monopoly only when a line was in direct competition did the companies exercise much concern for their passengers.

By 1898 there had yet to be a junction with the Grand Trunk (formerly Grand Junction Railway) at Anson. That year the C.O.R. had purchased sufficient land at the site to build one. Evidently the company now believed they could gain additional traffic with such a connection. The Grand Trunk had agreed to pay half the costs. There is no record of the completion of this work; one can only assume that it had been completed by 1900.

That ever popular and much respected conductor "Paddy" Shannon, the press referred to him as "genial", had to go to a Toronto hospital in December to have his appendix removed, in the past a serious operation. He must have been more aware of the value of public relations than management was in those days. Every old-timer in Prince Edward County asked about the C.O.R. remembers 'Paddy' the conductor. He recovered from his operation to 'captain' many more trains in the years to come.[44] He was a trustee of the local Separate School Board. In politics he was described as a 'reformer'.

The Underpass in 1977. The train is "The Lakeshore" Toronto-to-Montreal. The iron ore trains were still running daily

Photo, Alan R. Capon

In Picton, the crack passenger packet, a paddler, "Alexandria" had to have two new boilers. The C.O.R. brought them into the siding on April 8. A witness to this event said this transfer down to Picton docks took two days. A lot of young people played hookey from school. The operation taking several days went off without a hitch, no doubt to the disappointment of many, who had expected a repeat performance of the "Aberdeen's" boiler.[45]

The situation of the Picton station was still far from convenient. Lake Street was blocked whenever a train was in the station. The company was now taking action to extend the line further into town to avoid this. Plans had been made to do this in 1901 but two of the landowners proved difficult and expropriation proceedings delayed further progress until the following year.[46]

The winter of 1901-1902 was a severe one. The North Hastings Review of February 13th quoting from the Toronto Star on the results of the previous week's storm commented: "The Canadian Pacific had seven plows and a rotary and two hundred extra men on the 700 miles of track in the Ontario Division, on the middle division of the Grand Trunk there were 10 plows and 400 extra men . . ."[47] The C.O.R. must have had its troubles too.

If the weather was bad the C.O.R.'s financial news was not. Business was better than ever. Marmora station now had to have an assistant agent.[48] When the annual meeting came in June at Trenton the Board expressed themselves very much pleased with the prosperity of the road. Stevenson Burke was re-elected president.[49]

Rathbun's line, the Bay of Quinte Railway, was now about to start a vigorous expansion. He had caught railway fever. The principal extension was to build into Bannockburn on the C.O.R. and then on to Marmora Village via his Marmora Railway and so to his Cordova Mine. Hardly a friendly gesture to the C.O.R., but it meant a shorter haul to his Deseronto furnaces.[50]

The Bay of Quinte Railway was also reported to have started to build a line bridging the bay from Deseronto to Picton. And that was the end of that.[51]

On the Grand Trunk rail service was no more between Madoc and Eldorado. A horse-bus now ran over that rough road between the two centres.

Grand Trunk Station, Trenton. There was an elevator at the far end of the building connecting with the C.O.R.
Courtesy, Roy Cornish, Trenton, Ont. and Peter Johnson, Scarborough, Ont.

More auspicious for Picton had been the letting of contracts by the C.O.R. that totalled $10,000 in February for a new station and freight sheds.[52]

After the new station was built an enterprising Picton man bought the old station and had it slewed around to front on Lake Street. That was its second and final move to become, as it is today, a duplex family dwelling; one side occupied by a real estate office.

Times grew better; the fall traffic in 1902 was said to be twice as great as any like period in the history of the road.[53]

The C.O.R. could always be counted on for dramatic surprises. The C.O.R. could never settle down for long to the everyday business of running a railroad.

As far as the public were concerned in the fall of 1902 the railway exceeded itself.

What the public did know was that a year and a half ago Ritchie had lost an important case against his enemies, and his hopes for getting his railway back looked as if they had gone forever.

The next big news was the advertisement that the C.O.R. would be put up for sale on behalf of Thomas G. Blackstock, lawyer and director of the company. This could have been the grand finale for Ritchie.[54]

Instead some funny things had happened on the way to the courthouse. Ritchie with new riches and a big bank loan had bought from Bingham, Payne's son-in-law, and until then a Burke follower, all the late senator's stock. Harder for Burke, but no easier for Ritchie, Blackstock was now in opposition to him, having joined forces with Robert Weddell, the contractor for the Bancroft extension. But the opposition whether divided or united could not muster enough stock to oppose Ritchie who obtained a postponement of the sale, but only for 30 days.[55]

Ritchie acted fast. With a few days to spare, two to be exact, he was once again President of the C.O.R. To quote from a telegraph he sent to Cleveland (for his bankers) dated October 14th, "We elected a new Board for the Railway yesterday and full possession will be taken on Wednesday ..."[56]

Much of what was happening in the courts was not known to the public, either at that time or later, because the contending parties agreed to private hearings before a master of the court.

Chapter Thirteen

Over the months preceding the take-over, Ritchie had suffered increasingly from rheumatism. During the worst attacks he was not able to leave his room, (usually in a hotel) for days at a time, sometimes for weeks. For one so active the frustration must have been harder to bear than the considerable pain. He was now 64, twelve years younger than his archenemy, Stevenson Burke.

Ritchie's older son, having neither the temperament nor the interest to take part in his father's affairs, had stayed home and helped there. Fortunately his younger brother, Charles Edward, was now old enough and had the abilities to be of considerable help. As one of the new directors of the C.O.R. he was learning fast. If not quite of the fibre of his father — few men were — he would soon prove invaluable and for a while indispensable.

Likely Ritchie's daughter, Clara Belle, limited by being a woman in an earlier age, would otherwise have been with him. She and her father were devoted to each other. They corresponded frequently and at length. Her father named the famous Sudbury mine after her. Clara Belle never married. It is thanks to her that his papers were preserved — but to return to the events leading up to October, 1902 ...

After years of litigation, with endless setbacks and defeats, Ritchie's campaign to victory had started using the fortune he had received from the sale of his interests in the Sudbury mining groups to the newly formed International Nickel Company of New York.[1]

His next step had been to buy out the McMullen Brothers, in effect paying them twice. He bought their bonds at face value for $183,000, this included the stocks they held in the summer of 1900.[2]

Earlier in 1901 there had been a significant change in the C.O.R. board. Burke had resigned as president. He may well have been the victim of a stroke for his handwriting had degenerated into a laboured scrawl. Bingham, Payne's son-in-law, had succeeded him. Johnston, Burke's man, continued as vice-president.

George Collins' influence with the board had been growing. After Bingham became chief executive, not forgetting the increased earnings of the railway, there was now a far more liberal policy towards long overdue capital expenditures. There had been the flatcars, the new coach, the new stations. An impressive structure would be the station at Trenton, a handsome three-storey brick structure that was under construction when Ritchie returned to the presidency. Opened in 1903, Ritchie would express himself delighted with it, even praising the old board for this initiative.

The many lawsuits and counter-suits had continued on until 1897, when a judgment against Ritchie in a United States court permitted those holding his bonds to sell them to liquidate the loans made to him. The sale price must have been low for Ritchie was still in debt to his enemies, to the extent of $750,000. From then on the fortunes of law would favour Ritchie — with reservations.

Then to another court Ritchie was able to prove that the sale of his bonds and stocks (Burke and company had bought these securities back at the sale) had been illegal as he had so long contended, the holders not having had proper title.

Not until September, 1902, did he regain title to $750,000 of these holdings, paying Bingham and Burke $600,000 as part of the settlement. By then he was borrowing heavily from a Cleveland bank. Burke and Bingham had done even better out of their Sudbury holdings.[3]

For his father-in-law's C.O.R. securities Bingham had paid the estate just $20,000 to receive somewhere around $300,000 from Ritchie, something the latter did not hesitate to point out to him.[4]

In a letter to Collins dated July 13, 1899 in the Ontario Archives, Ritchie had bought 225 shares from Burke, and 653 of the 753 bonds in Bingham's possession from Senator Payne's estate. The latter had at one time owned as many as 2670 shares of common stock. By now there were 2380 remaining, the difference had been sold to other unnamed parties. (Collins letter, Sept. 9, 1899).

When Ritchie earlier in an American court had prevented Burke and his group from foreclosing and selling the railway by obtaining an injunction, Burke had ordered Blackstock to buy up every C.O.R. bond he could lay his hands on. At that time Burke and his friends seem to have held approximately 75% of the bonds, but voting remained with the stocks so they had no choice but of obtaining all the bonds (within a small percentage) for the majority of the stocks were still in Ritchie's possession.[5]

Burke, Bingham and associates' plan was obvious, and Blackstock had followed it having failed narrowly by Ritchie obtaining a 30-day respite and regaining — only just — control of the C.O.R. Once they could put the line up for sale on short notice before others could obtain the necessary financing or board decision, they could buy the line themselves thus wiping out Ritchie and all other investors except for the bonds. These they could obtain at the reserve price.

They would then be free to sell the line, no longer encumbered by litigation, to one of the trunk lines, or to any other group at a price well below its original cost and still leave an enormous profit for Burke's syndicate.

Of the considerable number of bonds that Blackstock now held most had been obtained very recently. It is not clear whether he had also bought some of these from Burke or his friends, neither is it clear whether they were supporting Blackstock from behind the scenes or he had double-dealt them at their own game. What is known is that he had kept in his possession all the bonds he had been instructed to purchase. The three sources of his recent purchases were those held by an unknown bondholder in Hamilton; the MacLaren Estate; and, unknown to Ritchie until early October, his own bonds held as collateral against a loan by the Bank of Ottawa and registered there in his name. Blackstock's agent in these last two deals, a strange association on the face of it, was

none other than the contractor for the Bancroft extension, Robert Weddell.

According to Ritchie, and there is no reason to doubt him, he had been visited by Weddell at his Toronto hotel towards the end of September while the 30-day injunction was in force against the sale of the railway. They also met on the train to Trenton some two weeks later. Weddell may have been drinking or perhaps he believed he was making a big impression on him. He was certainly indiscreet, letting not a few cats out of the bag. These conversations contain a great deal of important information, and fortunately Ritchie recorded them in a letter. Dated October 9th, 1902, the letter was addressed to the manager of the Toronto General Trust Corporation, J.W. Langmuir. This trust company had been the agent for the railway's securities from the beginning.[6] He had also been responsible for setting the price of the bonds (the upset bid) for the sale of the railway that had been aborted.

During the hotel visit, Weddell spoke freely, even bragged, how on behalf of Blackstock he had obtained the MacLaren estate bonds by paying their confidential clerk and agent $9,000, representing 2½% on the MacLaren securities plus the same percentage on the $300,000 of bonds that Ritchie had lodged with the bank. Weddell also claimed, without being specific, that other sums were paid in this connection to other parties.

Ritchie's loan was probably overdue. If it was a 'demand loan' (which is more likely), the real value of the bonds was a good deal less than the loan, so the bank would be justified on legal grounds in selling them; except Ritchie surely should have been notified first. This bank also acted as the C.O.R. bankers in the capital, and Blackstock, who acted as the C.O.R. lawyer, closed the deal.

Ritchie was never able to recover these bonds. Yet when this transaction took place Ritchie had the means to pay the loan. Another example of his extraordinary carelessness that from time to time cost him a fortune.

The reason for doing this, so Weddell explained, referring to Burke, Bingham and their representatives, was in "... removing the opposition of those sharks as they refused to work for their health." A little earlier and more coherently he had told Ritchie, "... that Burke, and his associates, Payne and his agents and representatives were a pack of robbers and cheats, that they had attempted to rob him in the building of twenty miles of the railway ..."

"The Lion" Samuel J. Ritchie

Courtesy, Hale Farm Museum, Akron, Ohio

The situation verged on insanity, Blackstock being one of their principal representatives and he had acted as legal adviser and principal negotiator in not acceding to Weddell's high claims for extra costs for the completed contract. Indeed he remained as Burke's lawyer, after Ritchie became president again.

That was not all. Weddell had a lot more to tell Ritchie. A few days before this visit, on the previous Sunday, he had chartered a special train from the C.O.R. and taken the managers of both the Molsons Bank and the Canadian Bank of Commerce from Trenton to Bancroft to examine the railway.

After the trip, so he told Ritchie, they had offered to back him with money to purchase the railway to the extent of $800,000. It is not known if this promise had been authorized by their head offices. But that had been before the unsuccessful foreclosure sale.

All these confidences, so it turned out, were the preliminaries to an offer. He was prepared to buy all of Ritchie's bonds at the upset price "secretly" set by the Toronto General Trust. He should have known Ritchie better. They had had dealings when he influenced Trenton council to subsidize the crushing and concentration plant there for $75,000. He had been sure of its success, before Burke had cancelled it the day he had assumed the presidency, the very day on which council was to vote.

The Gilmour Company, one of the most valuable traffic sources of the railway, was another subject touched upon. Vague statements and lay-offs of employees pending re-organization had caused strong rumours that all was not well. Weddell went further, the company owed the Bank of Commerce $550,000 and Molsons Bank $300,000. The two banks had now put Weddell in charge of all the company's affairs and for this were paying him $12,000 a year.

Ritchie summed up his feelings to Langmuir, "... the value that should be placed on the affidavit made by any man who will thus openly confess such shameful acts of bribery ... [you] as the head and manager of a great corporation in which more than any other form of corporation the unreserved confidence of the entire public should be absolutely unshaken and unchallenged, whether the proceedings of the character of those recited by Mr. Weddell himself to me should be endorsed by the sale of the railway for the benefit of Mr. Weddell and his associates of like character and methods."

Ritchie ended this letter by quoting Justice Harlan of the United States Supreme Court, who had referred to those using such methods as, "Committing larceny by law."

Whether Burke had stuck Blackstock with the bonds or whether he had just kept them is not clear, but in Blackstock and Weddell, he had sown dragon's teeth that had overnight grown into anti-Ritchie warriors, no doubt giving Burke considerable pleasure.

Weddell was seemingly hoping to claim out of the proceeds of the sale of the line what he considered appropriate recompense for his contract.

Not much is known about Blackstock, but of Weddell, as a local tycoon and his involvement in the construction of the C.O.R. more is known.

Robert Weddell,[7] a Scots immigrant, was at the time the most prosperous and the most influential citizen in Trenton. He was a flamboyant character, mercurial, but to all accounts well-liked in that community.

He had made his start with a small machine shop and foundry there. Listed as a civil engineer he had considerable talent on the mechanical side. His success had come as a marine contractor and by this time he owned a fleet of dredges, tugs and scows. Custom work and maintenance on his fleet kept his machine shop and foundry, now enlarged, busy. He also undertook such contracts as bridges, municipal work, or any other general contracting that came his way. His small fleet of tugs and scows, as available, freighted coal across the lake.

A proportion of the Murray Canal contracts had been his. Nearly all such marine contracts were a government responsibility under the administration of the departments of public works of both federal and provincial governments. Traditionally, as it remains today, these are the dispensaries of political patronage. A man had to know his way around, be aware of what was required of him, and to have influential friends in the right places: otherwise — no contracts. Obviously Weddell had these qualifications.

Weddell was a strong lodge member. He also managed to find the time to be Fire Chief to the town for several years. He was generous with his money to local causes.[8]

How many railway contracts he had handled before he undertook the construction of the Bancroft extension is not known, but this was likely the biggest if not the first.

At this stage neither the board, nor George Collins, or the civil engineer had much experience in drawing up contracts of this nature or magnitude. The same might be said of Robert Weddell and his knowledge of railway contracts.

There were certainly some "holes" in this one. It is unlikely that any of the parties involved in this rhubarb wanted to become involved, anymore than Ritchie wanted to inherit this mess.

Weddell had been too long used to government bodies making up the cost on miscalculations in his tenderings. Also it was not unknown that this could be an agreed upon procedure for the right man to get the contract, on the face of it, as low bidder.

There were some basic disagreements with Weddell here. The first, according to the wording, that he should be paid directly of the government subsidies as they were paid to the C.O.R. in the form of progress payments. The management read this clause differently. This had caused problems with Molson's Bank and the Bank of Ottawa and much juggling of bank accounts to prevent Weddell placing a lien on these funds.

Weddell had also written several complaints to the Minister and Deputy Minister of Railways. However great his political influence elsewhere he got little support from this Department.[10]

There was trouble over the grades. For this he blamed Evans, the C.O.R. engineer. He had put them right but it cost money, as will be explained, for this was the biggest difficulty.[9]

The second-hand rails the C.O.R. had purchased, it seems, many from the government-owned Intercolonial Railway in the Maritimes, contributed to the trouble of mismatched joints between one pattern of rail and another, as well as broken ends. Evans in the purchases had made much of the fact that these 20-year old rails were stronger than their modern equivalents. This was true, but he had not allowed for different shapes and broken ends, beyond buying an extra 300 tons which had not been nearly enough.[11] Thereafter, George Collins did all he could, not always successfully, to avoid buying anything second-hand.

Weddell had offered to get extra rails for nothing from the government. But there is no record of his having done so — he was too angry by then. Correcting these faults in the track to meet the government inspectors' requirements before the line could be opened for passenger traffic would have been a costly item on Weddell's account. (There was also some bickering over the fencing of the right-of-way, a minor item in this wilderness. This was soon settled.)

There were various attempts to meet Weddell's claims, at first totalling an additional $85,000, and at the beginning this was negotiated by Blackstock acting on behalf of the company.[12] The first round ended after direct negotiations between Weddell and Evans with the two of them no longer on speaking terms.[13]

While Weddell's claims seem to have been excessive, he may also have bid too low. His administration and his methods could have been inefficient and costly, but he did have a case. The C.O.R. management had made their mistakes, serious ones. They should have been more aware of the real costs and, perhaps, the capability of the contractor.

Weddell claimed, and with justification, that Evans' estimates of the amounts of cut and fill were low. On top of this the government inspector had modified Evans' profiles, altogether according to Weddell doubling the amount of work involved.[14]

They finally reached a grudging settlement, as Weddell said, he had accepted them rather than resort to litigation. In doing so he claimed he had made a considerable sacrifice.[15] Then, not long after the documents had been signed, the C.O.R. management trickily presented him with a bill for the extensive use of a locomotive and cars, plus accumulated charges for freight hauled on his account, totalling $9,325.70. Weddell was very angry. He swore he would rather lose all his dredges and tugs than let them get away with it. He also immediately lodged a counter-claim totalling $10,749.15.[16] Whatever the rights and wrongs, it was a poor way for the C.O.R. to do business.

Weddell now hated the railway to the point of obsession, no matter who owned it. His supporting of the moves to have the C.O.R. put up for sale must have stemmed from the hope that his counter-claim would be recognized by the court. Had the sale been permitted by the court it is questionable whether Blackstock would have encouraged such a payment when to all intents this would have come out of his own pocket.

Weddell had also got his friend Campbell, the Manager of Molson's Bank into trouble. Weddell's expressions of anger were sufficiently convincing that the manager wrote an emotional letter to Cleveland, labelled as "impertinent" by one of Blackstock's law partners who was of the opinion that the unfortunate manager would get reprimanded for writing it. All this arose from Campbell declaring his intention of paying Weddell out of the subsidy payments deposited in the C.O.R. account. Blackstock's partner was of the opinion that the bank would have to pay the cost of any legal proceedings that might arise (but didn't).[17]

Weddell's lawyers in this battle were none other than Ritchie's Barwick, Aylesworth and Wright of Toronto. As Blackstock himself wrote to Cleveland with pious concern expressed in as choice a piece of double-talk as they could have expected for their money, "we think it was unfortunate that Mr. Weddell fell into Mr. Aylesworth's hands, because while he has the highest opinion of your Board and feels that you desire to deal fairly with him, yet there is no doubt that Mr. Aylesworth [who had acted for Ritchie] had to some extent poisoned his mind and had him take the step to stop the funds in the Bank." The letter is dated January 28th. No year was shown, but it was 1901.[18]

President Ritchie would be more sanguine now over whom he could trust. So much so, that when the court appointed a receiver, the road to all intents being bankrupt, George Collins was selected. Collins was undoubtedly the best qualified person under the circumstances. One of Ritchie's early acts, because of his association with the previous board, was to urge the court to dismiss him. Fortunately this appeal failed and Collins would before long become Ritchie's most trusted advisor and, in time, a close friend. They shared a common purpose, the well-being of the railway.

Chapter Fourteen

By April, 1903, Ritchie was being attacked on two fronts. Life was back to normal. E.W. Rathbun's Bay of Quinte Railway was to be extended westwards that summer, vigorously at that, planning to connect at Bannockburn. This would leave the C.O.R. short many ton-miles on all the Rathbun traffic that had been hauled through Trenton.

From there Rathbun planned to extend his line during the following year to his Marmora Railway and Mining Company giving them a short direct route to Deseronto for his ore and timber traffic from Cordova and Marmora village.[1] The C.O.R. would lose again. The savings in freight charges for Rathbun would be enormous but whether they would justify the capital costs of his new railway only time would decide.

By now Ritchie was referring to Blackstock and Weddell as "B & W". A new battle, as ferocious as any, had begun when Blackstock gave due notice of his intention to apply for the passage of an act; it would become Bill 55, for the reorganization of the finances and indebtedness of the C.O.R. Its purpose, to transfer the voting powers from the stockholders to the bondholders. The possession of Ritchie's Bank of Ottawa bonds had given Blackstock the majority in bonds that he did not hold in stocks. The amount Ritchie claimed he had invested in the railway was $4-million, while Blackstock (and presumably Weddell) had paid for their stocks and bonds only $260,000; so Ritchie wrote in a letter to the Minister of Railways on April 7th.[2]

Bill 55 had a short life. As somebody noted tersely on the file sheet in the Department, "Thrown out of the Railway Committee of H. of C. on 5th May, 1903."[3] As a result, later in September, some funds held in escrow at the Bank of Toronto were ordered handed over to the railway after the Court had withdrawn the earlier order of sale of the C.O.R. The $21,000 was a useful windfall that could be applied to new equipment or to the extension.[4]

On April 30th, serious forest fires threatened Bancroft. The town escaped but not the C.O.R. with a section of the track burned out nine miles to the south of that community. Train services were, however, delayed for only a day. As insurance coverage on timber properties did not start until May 1st, Rathbun's and Gilmour's were heavy losers.[5]

Some profit for the railway came with the 12th of July celebrations (held on the 13th) at Marmora, no less than 5,000 were transported by rail to that small settlement. It is likely there has never been such a crowd at that community before or since.[6]

Ritchie, back in command again, though subject to the restraints of the receiver George Collins, (if indeed he restrained any actions) began to show that he was still his old self. By August he was applying for a renewal of the two subsidies that the Bingham Board had allowed to lapse. Each was for twenty miles, the first to Maynooth, the second to Whitney. He now asked that they should be made into a single subsidy of 40 miles, and (impossible legally) that they should be made subject to a ban on any foreclosure proceedings. The grant requested remained at $3,200 a mile. Presumably the additional $3,000 a mile subsidy of the Ontario government had not expired.[7] But this was only the beginning of great activity on his part.

Apart from his preoccupations with the C.O.R., Ritchie was also carrying on an acid correspondence with Colonel Schwab, heir apparent to his friend Carnegie, and head of the new International Nickel Company, bluntly accusing him of swindling him over the purchase of his Sudbury properties.[8]

At this time there were a number of odds and ends and some items of importance about the railway in the local newspapers. The Picton Gazette recorded, for the first time, that the local nickname for the C.O.R. was the "Susan Push", leaving the origins of this nickname a mystery.[9]

There were complaints about the mail due to poor time-keeping by the trains.

The Farnham Iron Mine was grading a spur line from L'Amable.[10]

At Trenton the new station was nearing completion.[11] The public were beginning to appreciate what an imposing building this would be.

In October the locomotive on the passenger train broke down at Bloomfield. Another locomotive was despatched to bring the train into Picton an hour and a half later.

That same month George Collins travelling over the line, while stopping at an unknown station, "... in speaking of the management, shook his head ominously."[12] It would seem he was still adjusting to Ritchie, and was tired of the everlasting lawsuits.

A nice gesture on the part of Ritchie was to appoint his former superintendent, the loyal Robert Fraser, to the Board of Directors.

By November, in Picton, the volume of freight handled was such that the Picton Gazette ambiguously reported, that it "required a daily freight to do the shunting." Indeed this had so far been a record year for both divisions of the line.[13]

Current litigation was between Ritchie, long representing his enemies, the Toronto General Trust. Their case was that Ritchie owed the entire interest on the bonds since their date of issue. His contention was that it was only due for the past six years. He had won the first judgment, now the Trust Company had appealed to a higher court. There, if the decision went against him, it could mean another attempt at foreclosure with the subsequent sale of his railway.[14]

The big day came on Monday, December 23rd, 1903 at Trenton, the grand opening of the new station and headquarters for the railway. Designed by the company's civil engineer, J.D. Evans, it was an impressive building as the illustrations show. Long gone now, it was described as being built of pressed brick with artificial stone sills and lintels, and a slate roof. With a basement and dormer window, it stood four stories high. In the front was a bay window measuring 4-foot, three inches by 26 feet. Overall measurements of the building were 88 feet by 33 feet. Central heating and electric lighting was provided. The claim was made that the building was completely fireproof.

Where the Bay of Quinte Railway crossed the C.O.R. heading westwards but got no further than an expensive concrete engine house.   *Photo, Author*

The Board now had a place to meet that was their own. Compared to its old ramshackle wooden station, the C.O.R. had added to its prestige — whatever the discomforts experienced by passengers in changing trains at Trenton Junction. The contractor was a Belleville man.[15]

The day after this event Edward Wilkes Rathbun died at the age of 61 years. Although he was second generation in the firm he had long been the driving force in its affairs. Much of the prosperity and the continuing expansion of the company had been of his making.[16] But he had over-expanded.

129

Foundations of the famous Weigh Scales. When built they were the wonder for miles around.

Photo, Author

The abandoned B. of Q. engine house with the dignity of a Grecian ruin; refuses to be swallowed up by the forest.

Photo, Author

Ritchie and Collins must have pondered on how aggressive the Rathbun heirs would prove to be. The Bay of Quinte Railway had reached Bannockburn just two weeks before Rathbun's death.[17] Crossing disdainfully at right angles over the C.O.R. track (with connecting switches), the station and engine house were to the west, pointing to Marmora. The latter is an enduring concrete structure.

There was as yet no revenue traffic over the new line for there was still a considerable amount of work to be done before the government inspector could be asked to inspect the line and pass it for traffic. For example, four steel bridges had to be built, replacing spidery trestles. And, no doubt, that official would find other matters that needed correcting. The Rathbuns may not have been particularly interested in passenger traffic, at best it would be light, but mail and express meant useful revenue. Freight was of course vital. But the immediate haste was to collect the government bonuses. The Rathbuns could thank the contractor for such speedy construction.

During the winter of 1903-4, which was a severe one, Ritchie's surveyors had been busy locating the most favourable route from Bancroft to Whitney. The plan was to start construction in March and to have 25 miles completed by the time of freeze-up. By July 21st, the track location had been completed for that distance.[18]

It had been a bad winter for the railway with the line often blocked for a day and once for a week. Enough snow that some of the mines had to close and wait for the spring thaw.[19]

A new development was the discovery of lead in good quantities, often near the surface. Several farmers had started mining this metal themselves. They fired their own homemade furnaces with hardwood from their woodlots. The finished "pigs" were left by the track for the accommodation train to load. The price of lead then was high enough for this to be profitable.[20]

Present Freight Station at Trenton. Probably built at the same time as the new C.O.R. Passenger Station. No records remain as to the construction date. C.N. has requested its closure. Express service to be from Belleville.   *Photo, Author, Feb. 1977*

The Bessemer Mine in its hey-day. The locomotive is the mystery engine, said to have been a former C.O.R. engine. She was not powerful enough to haul any worthwhile load to the main line, but she was busy enough switching cars about the mine workings and receiving loads from the Child's and Rankine Mines further east. 1906 photo. *Photo, David Hanes*

Ritchie had drawn up plans with the help of architects for a new home near Akron, Ohio. As to be expected, it was large, costly, carefully designed, and built to the highest standards. Plainly this was something long delayed by the financial difficulties he ·had experienced and so many uncertainties over nearly 20 years. This was something he felt he owed his ego but even more his family for he was seldom home. Obviously he enjoyed supervising every step of its construction judging by the amount of time he gave to every detail.[21]

In February Ritchie won an important case against Blackstock and Weddell in Toronto, when they had attempted to delay further C.O.R. expenditures. Ritchie's immediate reaction was to instruct his lawyer, Barwick, to hasten the court order, necessary under the receivership, for the purchase of the steel bridge over the York River just north of Bancroft.[22]

In that area the Irondale, Bancroft and Ottawa Railway was now up for sale. There were four prospective buyers, among them the Grand Trunk. Ritchie was not among them although the line would have been an outlet to the west, albeit a shaky one.[23]

One more scheme currently before the Railway Committee in Ottawa was a projected line from L'Amable (south of Bancroft) to Barry's Bay on the Canada Atlantic (GTR). This would use as

a beginning the 7.34 mile branch of the Bessemer (Ex Farnham) mines, then to Barry's Bay and on to Mattawa on the CPR transcontinental line. It would have been either a direct competitor or else a means of extending the C.O.R. northward unhampered by the current receivership. The promoters were two citizens of Detroit and two from Bancroft. A bill for the line was passed by Parliament.[24] The project never got further. An interesting sidelight was a proposal to electrify the line using hydro power generated locally.

More signs of Ritchie being back in the presidency was the arrival of new passenger equipment, a coach and a baggage car. Both were much admired by the public. Also reported was an order for two new locomotives from Kingston. These were badly needed with most of the motive power in bad shape.

Rails for the northern extension were now arriving and were being shipped to Bancroft.[25]

In April, 1904, Ritchie was "laid up completely" by his rheumatism.

That same month, on the 24th, Judge Stevenson Burke had a final stroke. The crippled Ritchie attended the funeral, no doubt dry-eyed. This was held in Cleveland on the 27th. He wouldn't have missed it.

On the day of Burke's death Ritchie wrote to Barwick, "Both principals and attorneys in the great conflict are getting pretty well thinned out." He listed five of the principals, which included one of the McMullen brothers; six attorneys, and another two that were now close to death: "... we shall soon have to turn our attention to writing epitaphs, instead of pleadings and briefs. When Burke's pulse stopped beating the linch pin and king bolt dropped out of the whole conspiracy, machine and outfit. Blackstock and his allies on that side and their counterparts on his side [he meant on either side of the border] were the 'pawns on Burke's chess-board'." But Ritchie was underestimating Blackstock and Weddell.[26]

After reading Burke's obituary in the Cleveland *Plain Dealer*, Ritchie wrote again on April 26th to give his more detailed assessment of the legal consequences in the changed situation. He was convinced that Burke had been behind Blackstock and Weddell in trying to force the sale of the railway. His letter ended: "It is astonishing how soon men become saints after death prevents them from being sinners. This is especially true where a subsidized press is the principal factor in the canonization of the deceased."[27]

On May 4th, Ritchie answered a personal letter he had received from Wilfrid Laurier, the prime minister, (the original, unfortunately, could not be found in the files) by a telegram. Plainly the letter was a warning of another attempt to foreclose on the railway. This was a singularly gracious act on the part of Laurier, who like others must have genuinely liked and admired Ritchie.[28]

Blackstock and Weddell, as to be expected, attended the annual meeting of the railway. The most recent had been on May 18th. Having raised no objections at the meeting when the matter was raised regarding the purchase of rails for the new extension, before long they were protesting vehemently.[29] Likely Barwick suppressed that one.

No. 6, at Picton waiting to haul back "The Old Boys Excursion".   *Courtesy, the Late Willis Metcalfe.*

133

In April, Ritchie lost his case regarding the loss of his bonds lodged at the Bank of Ottawa. This had strengthened the hands of Blackstock and Weddell. Next, as Laurier had warned, they were moving in towards victory, seeking a court injunction in which the C.O.R. was forbidden to proceed any further with the northern extension. So much for Blackstock and Weddell being pawns in Burke's game of chess! What was more they won this injunction. Construction had to cease.[30]

In the evidence presented in this last case it was revealed that C.O.R. now had $75,000 in surplus funds available to start the extension. As a minor backlash, the Picton Gazette's editor took the parochial view that the funds ought to be applied to reduce passenger and freight rates. He made no mention of where Prince Edward County would have been without the railway. He concluded with the vague threat that if they were not reduced a rival railway might build into the county.[31]

Operations on the line for 1904 were particularly good that year, though there would never be enough profit to pay the interest on the bonds. Morale among employees must have been high with all the new equipment.

By April, Rathbun's had 17,000 cords of hardwood ready for its furnaces at Deseronto. Stockpiled at Cordova, they covered five acres.[32] With the Bay of Quinte Railway not yet ready to haul it away from Bannockburn, the C.O.R. benefitted. By August, there was so much finished lumber coming from Rathbun's Bancroft mill that a special train hauled out 25 cars of lumber to catch up for the regular train.[33] Likely as not the motive power shortage had become extremely critical.

In June the new locomotives arrived, according to the newspapers, there were not two but three.[34] The third is listed as being built by the Kingston Locomotive Company, as were the other two, in 1902. Here she was arriving on the C.O.R. two years later. One can only suspect she had not found a buyer and Ritchie, as with some of his earlier engines, picked her up on favourable terms. She became C.O.R. No. 12. She was an innovation for the C.O.R.

Numbers 14 and 15 (there never was a Number 13 as on most lines and engine names on the C.O.R. had disappeared) were 4-4-0's, bigger than passenger-hauling predecessors, having slightly larger drive wheels, bigger boilers and cylinders. In recent years distinctions between freight and passenger duties must have often become blurred. Whatever engine was available hauled the priority train and the engineers had to make the best of its capabilities. Having been handed nothing but worn-out engines for so long the locomotive and workshop crews rejoiced. The mail, express and the passengers would benefit by more timely arrivals.

No. 12 was a different matter. For hauling freight with more grip on the rails the "Mogul" or 2-6-0 had been the first step from the "American Standard", as the 4-4-0 was known. Ritchie had been conservative in this. The type had long been in use on the Grand Trunk, who had hundreds of these engines, and would continue ordering them after they were generally considered to be obsolete. Ritchie by a bargain purchase had progressed.

Number 12, while her cylinders were no bigger than the other two newcomers, had an extra set of driving wheels which were smaller, by six inches. With a bigger boiler, she was by far the most powerful locomotive on the line. She was appreciated by management concerned with getting more tonnage over the line. (See Appendix for details.)

In September there were more reports of two possible purchasers of the C.O.R. This time there was evidence that their interest was more than casual. The first was an unknown group of American Financiers who toured the line by special train.[35]

A week later came the news that the CPR was, again, interested. A party of company officials also toured the system. The Madoc editor, ever hopeful, but more cautious, commented: "In the near future this road may be a branch of the CPR. We will ask them to build through the village. Is this like naming a child before it is born?" The answer would be "Yes!"[36] Plainly nobody wanted to buy into endless litigation.

Gloomy possibilities for Trentonians as the year's end approached was a government announcement that the Trent Canal might avoid the Trent River in its last miles entering the lake through Port Hope, some miles to the west.[37] As things turned out the canal would eventually be built through Trenton.

Not until September was the final track work for the Picton station completed. Standing trains would no longer block Lake Street.[38]

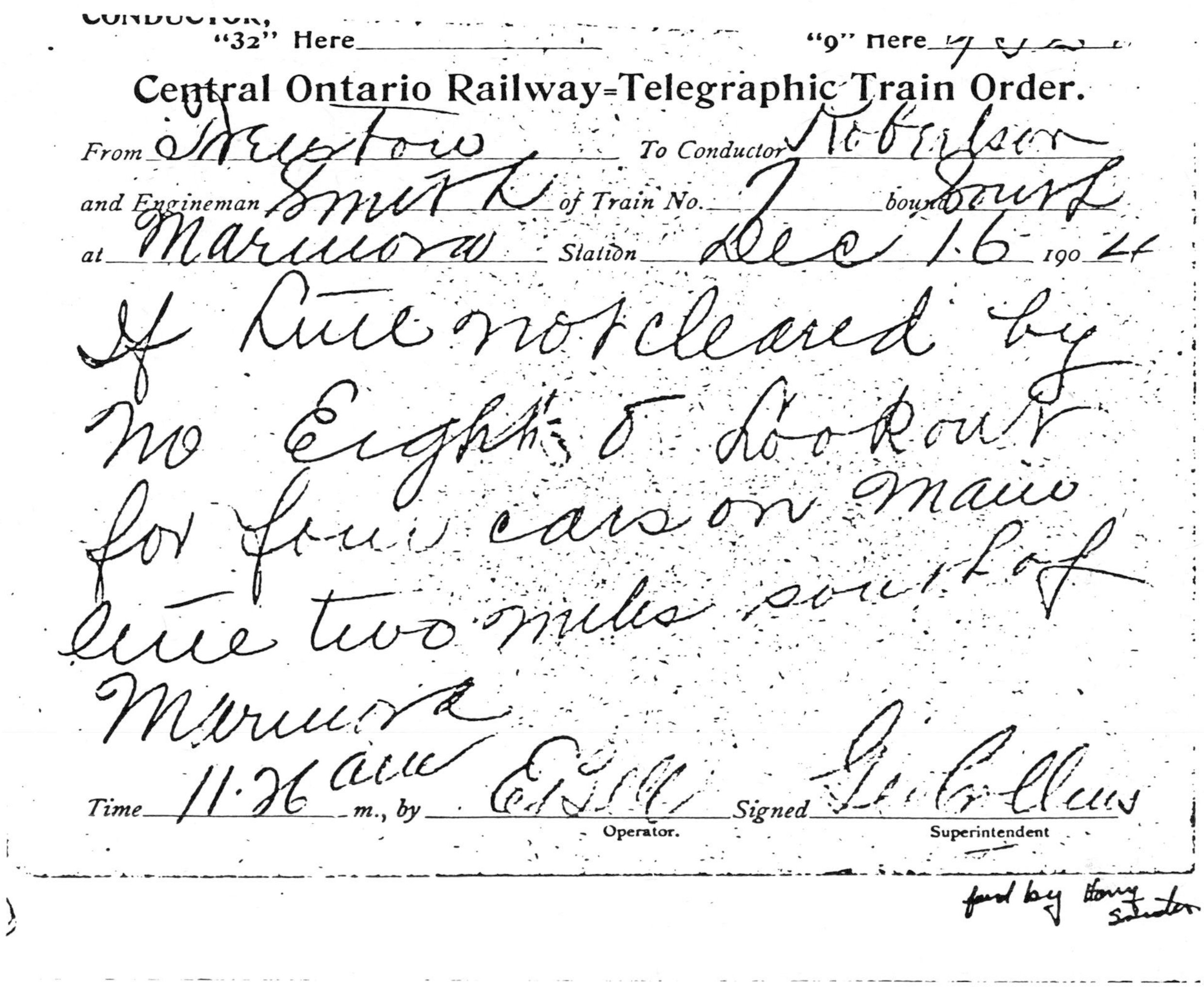

Central Ontario Railway=Telegraphic Train Order.

From _Kingston_____ To Conductor _Robertson_____

and Engineman _Smith___ of Train No. _7___ bound _South_

at _Marmora___ Station _Dec 16_ 190 _4_

If line not cleared by
No Eight to Look out
for four cars on main
line two miles south of
Marmora

Time _11.36 a.m_ m., by _Ed Sill_ Signed _Jno Collins_

Operator.   Superintendent

fwd by Harry Snider

Train Order, Dated Dec. 16, 1904

Courtesy, Herman Snider

Rivalry between the steamboats and the C.O.R. was still strong. That fall the steamer "Ella Ross" was offering a round trip excursion from Picton to Belleville and back for 75¢ to attend an evening concert there. On the same day the railway was offering Pictonians the chance to attend Bancroft Fair for $1.50 return. The railway excursion was marginally better value.[39]

For all the improved earnings and new equipment, the year 1904 did not end cheerfully for the C.O.R. The injunction continued in force, just as Ritchie had feared when he had tried to get the subsidies tied in against such a happening. For both the C.O.R. and those communities it would serve, a whole year had been lost.

The winter of 1904-5 proved to be one of the worst for many years. Let W.P. Niles of Wellington, son of S.P. Niles, (still holding his father's ten shares in the railway) speak of it, in a letter he wrote to George Collins: "During the five days I was detained at Belleville, I felt at times like criticizing your management, but after coming down on the first train through, I saw the difficulties you had to encounter, and really wondered how you got through at all. Nearly all the way from Trenton to Picton the line was more like a canal than a Railway. In some places the drifts are fully twenty feet high from the level of the track, in fact, I am told the snow was nearly to the wires on the telegraph line at Clarke's cut.

"The cuts at Hillier and on Clarke's farm, near Wellington, must have been almost impregnable . . .

"During my twenty-five years experience on the Road I never, but once, saw such drifts of snow as you were obliged to overcome, and I trust you will not be bothered again this season."[40]

George Collins forwarded this letter to Ritchie. His reply was not so much about the snow but a revelation of his belief in the humanities. ". . . Such a snow storm is phenomenal, and the men engaged in combating it must have suffered much, and I desire that you should use your own judgment and discretion in paying them liberally for all the time they were engaged in such hardship. In all cases I only think of the men who faithfully work and patiently suffer, and never of any loss which the Railway may sustain. It should always be the policy of the Company to be faithful to the management and employees who are faithful to the Company. No personal interest of my own shall ever be served at the expense of departing from

this policy . . . I long for spring as a prisoner longs for his freedom. I do not mean to overlook or to forget the great credit to which you are personally entitled to in overcoming these severe difficulties. Whatever of thanks I can convey to you I here tender to you."[41]

Also not recorded in these letters were the exceptionally low temperatures in February. Also that the snow blockade was worse up north, Bancroft being isolated for nine days.

The Bay of Quinte Railway had a further problem near Tweed when a snow plow and two engines derailed. The plow was badly damaged. Only the mail clerk was hurt.[42]

In March Ritchie was again laid up with rheumatism, a state that only seemed to increase his determination. In late April came the surprising announcement that in spite of the injunction the C.O.R. would build the extension. Meanwhile, just to add to the difficulties, both federal and provincial subsidies had expired. Nonetheless, Collins felt sufficiently confident that he forecast at least ten miles of line would be built that year.[43]

It seems the Ontario government subsidy was passed by that legislature without any delays, but the federal house brought an unexpected hold-up. Through some misunderstanding the bill for the renewal was not ready for the House when the Commons recessed for the summer. This meant delaying the work, which would only be started within the financial means of the C.O.R. which included being able to borrow against the Ontario subsidy of $3,000 a mile.[44]

By mid-July the contractors, Little and Colbertson were advertising for thirty teams at Bancroft and a start had been made.[45]

In August, a court authorized Collins as Receiver to spend $25,000 "at his own discretion." This must have been a great help, but, as the newspaper concluded ominously, "The new line will go with the rest of the road at the sale ordered by the court."[46]

There seemed to be no limit to the legal complications. Reported in the Toronto *News* on June 6th 1905 was a new suit on behalf of the railway against some of the bondholders and directors. "The claim as endorsed on the writ is against Robt. Weddell, T.G. Blackstock, G.W. Brougham, the executors of the late Judge S. Burke of Cleveland, Ohio, and H.S. Johnston, to recover $55,000, alleged to have been paid to Mr.

Weddell in July 1901, by other defendants, out of the company's money in pursuance of an alleged conspiracy. The company also asks for a declaration that the bonds held by the Bank of Toronto and the Molsons Bank over the property, subject to the banks' lien for advances and for account of the advances." The suit would in all likelihood have been instigated by Ritchie. He would have been pretty sure that the company's treasury would have been filched to buy Ritchie's own bonds left as collateral with the Bank of Ottawa and obtained by Weddell under such dubious circumstances. Ritchie would lose.

In Cleveland, parallel with these events, Ritchie was now suing Stevenson Burke's estate. "Mrs. Burke has been guilty in this conspiracy as well." On April 23rd, he remarked in a later letter that she was to receive $2,000,000 under an unsigned will.[47]

The junction for Bessemer started south of Detlor. The line did not run far before it hit these fearsome grades down to the wooden trestle over Egan Creek. This shot is looking towards the main line. Winter '77-78.   *Photo, David Hanes*

Another case in June against Blackstock and Weddell resulted in a humiliating loss for Ritchie. An appeal that had ended with the Privy Council in which he had sometime earlier sought the dismissal of the Receiver, Collins, and so get direct control of the funds, was lost. Ritchie had now sought legal authority that the considerable costs of the case from the Chancellor of the bankruptcy court, that these costs should be undertaken by the C.O.R. Blackstock and Weddell were well represented for the court ruled in their favour. Ritchie also had to pay costs.[48]

To Colonel S.S. Lazier of Belleville, a lawyer with whom he developed a close friendship, Ritchie later complained of Barwick's handling of the many cases they had represented for him, that he "concentrated on abstract legal questions and technicalities and ignored the all-determining questions of bribery and perjury."[49]

In the north business had been good for the railway since spring. There had been an enormous accumulation of every kind of forestry product over the winter. The C.O.R. had all the traffic it could manage.[50]

Ritchie and Collins were now working well together with the C.O.R., their common interest, and both being honest men, there was much progress. Telephones, a great advance, were just being installed in all stations.[51] At Bannockburn, a weigh scale was installed on a side track. This expensive machine, with the considerable capacity of 300,000 pounds, was both modern and efficient. "A train of cars can be weighed, the weight stamped on a printed card, and the number of the car put on without stopping the train." The ground is flat by the scales and many an overloaded car had the surplus dumped on the ground. Such accumulations were loaded into an empty car by the shipper at a later date. Each car had to be uncoupled to be weighed. This gave the station agent considerable trouble. When he wasn't looking, the train crews in a hurry to get home would fail to do this, leaving him with a list of inaccurate weights. In 1956 or 1957, the scales were moved to some busier location on the Canadian National Railways. The concrete foundations remain.[52]

The same year, accepting the inevitable, the C.O.R. moved their station northwards to be closer to the Bay of Quinte crossing for the easier interchange of passengers, mail, and express.[53]

Early August brought the judgment from

the Privy Council that the bondholders had the right to sell the railway. This it would seem was the final blow for Ritchie. But nothing happened, and then, it would be, as could always be counted upon with the C.O.R., the unexpected.[54] Even the editor of the North Hastings Review resisted conjecture. By October 5th, all he had to report was that the first five miles had been graded and that the bridge gang had arrived.[55] This was far short of Collins' spring forecast.

By late summer and fall, traffic was even busier between Picton and Trenton. A record crop of tomatoes, a bountiful supply of other vegetables and apples had the C.O.R. anticipating that they would have a thousand cars of canned goods to haul away. The only worry of the canners was whether they could obtain enough cans.[56]

With this growth of traffic it was decided to recruit a trainmaster. C.A. Hoag, the Grand Trunk's Trenton station agent, was pleased to accept the appointment.[57]

There was still no news of the final foreclosure of the railway. Something, it seemed, was going on behind the scenes. On October 31st, dateline Kingston, came what the North Hastings Review editor called: "A Railway Rumor that has Great Interest for Madocers." The Grand Trunk was about to buy the C.O.R. General Manager

McGuigan had just been over the line. The connection to Whitney, when finished, would give the G.T.R. a much shorter route to Ottawa. The editor did not point out that this route was still much longer than the C.P.R.'s and much money would be required before the C.O.R., and particularly the Canada Atlantic with its heavy grades, would be suitable for heavy main line traffic, largely long freight trains with heavy locomotives. But it would save 73 miles to the capital city. If this came about the C.P.R. would still have the easier route and be closer by 42 miles.

On November 9th a further report was printed as to the Grand Trunk's intent in a despatch from Montreal and this seemed to confirm the rumour.[58]

Negotiations may have been underway but on November 16th the Trenton *Advocate* said, "We are in a position to say on the most reliable authority that the rumour has no foundation — in fact, that in truth, there's nothing to it."[59]

All of which had been a useful screen for both Ritchie and his enemies Blackstock and Weddell. A great deal was going on, in great secrecy, and the principal negotiators represented a railway that had never before been mentioned in those endless reports and rumours.

The B. of Q.'s roadbed from the east has not been able to resist natural growth. The tracks are for a section car.   *Photo, Author*

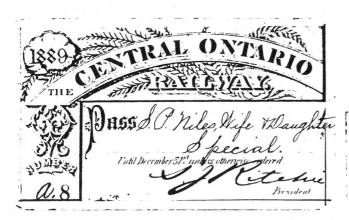

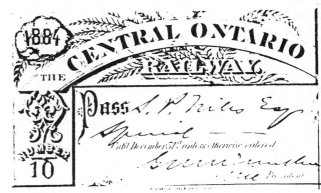

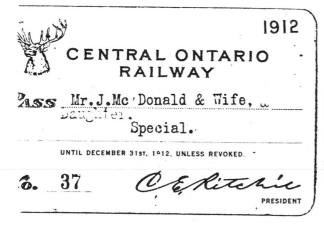

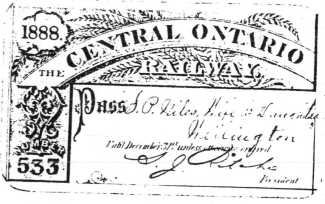

Various Passes

Chapter Fifteen

So far the only trunk line railway that had not been mentioned was the Canadian Northern Railway, the line promoted and controlled by those two remarkable entrepreneurs, William Mackenzie and Donald Mann.

Former contractors to the Canadian Pacific Railway, owning 848 miles of prairie track in 1896, they owned, by 1905, in the company's name, 1,876.4 miles of track. They had with invincible purpose planned a transcontinental railway from tidewater on the St. Lawrence to Vancouver in British Columbia. As yet they did not own a single mile of line in British Columbia or in Quebec. In this year they had built only a fifth of their final mileage but at the rate of construction these figures changed quickly. Their final mileage by 1917 was 9,433.4.

Earlier the Grand Trunk, through its subsidiary the Grand Trunk Pacific, had similar ambitions. There were great differences between the two in style and methods. The G.T.P., under Charles M. Hays, was building first-class lines with minimum grades and curvature. Bridges and plants were built of steel, brick or concrete.

The Canadian Northern line was the opposite, holding to minimum expenditures even to many secondhand locomotives and equipment and wooden structures. When the traffic came this would provide the funds for those higher standards.

The Canadian Northern, or Mackenzie and Mann, deserve to be remembered for great railway enterprise, a magnificent adventure, a railway from coast-to-coast, built on a shoestring even if vast sums of public money made this possible.

As to be expected, the CPR, GTR, and the Canadian Northern Railway, all became bitter rivals. This reached down to every level of employee. But the history of the transcontinental railways is only of concern here as it affected eastern Ontario and the Central Ontario Railway in particular.

In 1905, when the Grand Trunk, once again, showed interest in buying the C.O.R., it is possible they had hoped to forestall the Canadian Northern, but were too late. An undated, unsigned document, even unaddressed, in Ritchie's files is obviously, from its content, written by him, probably in the summer of 1905, and could only have been addressed to Mackenzie or Mann.[1]

Sometime previously the two partners had bought a block of 525 bonds from Blackstock and Weddell and at the high price of 70¢ on the dollar. Here Ritchie pointed out that if the Supreme Court upheld the Court of Appeal they would have had to pay only 14¢ on the dollar.

Apparently this was all that Blackstock and Weddell had paid the Bank of Ottawa for Ritchie's block of bonds, and giving some idea how much Blackstock was making out of the deal. In the meantime Ritchie had lost that case.

Of course Blackstock and Weddell held many more bonds but here is the reason the foreclosure proceedings ceased abruptly.

Other items of correspondence with Mackenzie and Mann, mostly with Mann, were frank and to the point as could be expected of Ritchie. They appreciated Ritchie and, as future events would demonstrate, they would show great confidence in him.

Quoting from the rest of his letter, "... Now, to make a long story short, I will agree to the cancellation of all the Bonds, coupons and judgments against the Railway, and the dismissal and cancellation of all the foreclosure proceedings against the railway, and a new issue of 4% Bonds made upon the whole line built and to be built, and to be guaranteed, principal and interest, by the Canadian Northern Railway. This issue may be made for a less amount if you wish, but in any case the line is to be completed to Whitney on the Canada Atlantic Railway, and the Railway is to refund me $10,000 of the money which I have expended on account of the litigation in connection with these foreclosure proceedings, and in the contest as to the ownership of these bonds, the Railway is also to pay Barwick, Aylesworth, Wright and Moss any and all charges which they may have against the Railway or myself in connection with any of this litigation and any and all other costs and charges which may now exist or grow out of this litigation, and to save me safe and harmless on account of such charges, no matter of what nature, kind or description. You choose to buy a law-suit, and this offer gives you a chance to fight it out with the parties from whom you purchased it. Some other provisions in the Memorandum given to Mr. Mann, will have to receive consideration in connection with this offer. I am to give you sufficient of my stock to give you full control of the Railway in connection with what you get from Blackstock."

The New Trenton Station; north end.

Ritchie was now buying up more mining claims in the Sudbury area. "As proposed by Mr. Mann, and as stated in one of the items originally submitted to him, it must be part of any deal between us that lines of railway shall be constructed by you which shall connect the Mines of the Nickel Copper Company with your Main lines of railway and working the Mines on a large scale. It is further agreed that in the purchase of this property, you shall have the right to take 40% of the whole property on exactly the same terms on which Ritchie shall purchase the whole of it."

"The terms will give you $970,000 of the new issue of Bonds. The $100,000 of cash on hand, from which to pay all claims which Blackstock and Weddell, as owners of 806 bonds, and the claim of $67,000 on the 300 Bonds purchased from the Bank of Ottawa, and $6,000 on the 225 Bonds claimed by Burke's executors, and the unpaid amounts yet due to Barwick etc., or any other claims growing out of the litigation, either against the Railway or Ritchie, and $400,000 of the new issue, and $250,000 of bonuses with which to complete the line from Bancroft to Whitney. Mr. Collins states that it will not be necessary to issue any bonds for the completion of the line from Bancroft to Whitney; that the earnings of the Road, together with Bonuses, will be sufficient to build the extension. One half of this $400,000 would be sufficient to pay the interest upon the full Bond issue while the extension is being completed. No Bonds were issued for the completion of the 21 miles of this Railway from Ormsby Junction to Bancroft, and I fully believe Mr. Collins' statement is entirely correct. This 40 miles of extension would certainly be completed within 18 months, as the work is now under progress."

The New Trenton Station; south end.

There followed various financial alternatives open to Mackenzie and Mann.

Why did those two shrewd men, Mackenzie and Mann, buy into the C.O.R.? This would involve buying out Blackstock and Weddell as well as Ritchie's interests, no easy undertaking. Ritchie did not want to give up the line but welcomed Mackenzie and Mann as junior partners. Mackenzie and Mann must have wanted the line badly.

They had a good use for the northern section of the line for it would be a valuable source of traffic to a new main line. Also important, as they now controlled the Irondale, Bancroft and Ottawa Railway, ownership of the C.O.R. by a competitor would have left that railway in an even more precarious position. The busy southern section, Trenton to Picton, would be an asset on all counts.

From a traffic point of view the C.O.R. operating profits were not enough to pay fixed charges. But when the northern extension was completed to the Canada Atlantic (GTR) line, and the possibilities of new mining strikes there was cause for optimism.

The other factor was better management. The profits could have been a lot higher if the railway had not been shackled by the Burke regime, then severely handicapped by the machinations of Blackstock and Weddell. Both parties having played that unoriginal railway game of robber barons.

The need to acquire the C.O.R. for Mackenzie and Mann lay in the station and yards at Trenton, for their planned main line from Toronto to Montreal, via Ottawa. Until this was completed the traffic base for a transcontinental railway was missing. Preferably the route should be along the heavily populated shore of Lake Ontario.

These two master strategists, with their need to practice economy, and with time vital, they preferred to buy up existing lines and ingeniously fit them into their plans. The purchase of Rathbun's Bay of Quinte line had also started in secrecy. The city of Kingston might have to be missed from their new main line for a shorter route from Toronto to Ottawa.

The C.O.R. fitted into this plan with their magnificent new station in the centre of Trenton, adequate yards, access to docks, and some real estate that allowed for future expansion and room for a good right-of-way to the west. The completed line would be so close to the Grand Trunk line in many places west of Trenton as to look like a third track of that company. The long abandoned roadbed can still be seen from Toronto-bound trains.

On July 5th, Barwick, Ritchie's Toronto lawyer passed away. On July 25th, with understandably less grief to him, Blackstock died, who having made much money yet had built nothing. Ritchie would still have his heir to deal with.

Weddell joined forces with the latter. He would make no further claims on his contract for fifteen years. Then, just before the close of the First World War, after the Dominion Government had taken over a bankrupt Canadian Northern Railway, he took the opportunity to present his claim once more. He was advised to go to law by the Department. He did not press that matter further.[2] He died not long after, his son carrying on the business.

Captain Walter Bowen of Trenton, retired master mariner and Commodore of the Hall Line, knew Robert Weddell for many years. At one time his father owned a freighter in partnership with him. He remembers Robert Weddell as seldom being clear of financial difficulties but found him a likeable man.

Henry Black of Kingston, retired marine engineer with many years experience in the dredging business remembers the son, Robert G. Weddell, bidding on a big dredging contract in Goderich harbour in the mid-twenties when no other company would touch it. He had badly underestimated the amount of rock and went bankrupt. He was sold up. The craft that had no bidders were beached on the shore east of the mouth of the Trent. Some of the remains are there yet.

* * *

Behind the scenes negotiations by the Canadian Northern Railway would last for some time. A year later Ritchie summed up his feelings and his intentions succinctly in a letter to J.J. Warren of the Trust and Guarantee Company of Toronto, Mackenzie and Mann's agent, who were involved in the negotiations, "... I have now been connected with this railway from its birth and do not propose to sever my connection until I make it the best railway property in the country for its length ..."[3]

* * *

The section gang stop to have their picture taken in front of the new building.

Courtesy, Roy Cornish, Trenton, Ont.

The Marmora *Herald* started off the year 1905 with a plaintive cry that the C.O.R. should route their mainline through their community.[4] Branch line status with dilapidated track was not good enough for that long established settlement that had recently, by incorporation, grown from a village to a town. The branch, however, belonged to the Rathbun's, not the C.O.R., who only leased it.

The editor, inspired by this new importance of the community, if only nominal, wanted real growth — and why not? In the same column he had another complaint, "that the chief drawback to Marmora is the lack of unity of the people and pride in the town."

On February 1st, between CPR Junction (later Bonarlaw) and Marmora Station, the C.O.R.

suffered a head-on collision between two freight trains. No one was hurt, the crews of both jumped in time. As usual the locomotives were not identified but "the engine on the southbound train was badly wrecked. The operator at the Junction was held responsible. He had orders to hold the Coe Hill train but neglected to do so."[5] Like as not the operator did not wait around to collect his pay. The locomotives were repaired and returned to service.

Construction work had been comparatively easy that winter. As was observed in the press on March 1st, on the same date a year previously, a nine-day snow blockade had halted the trains. Now there was hardly enough snow for sleighs.

The same month the contract for the construction of the last seven miles to Maynooth was given to William Gibson of Toronto.[6] Other progress was the installation of the 100-foot girder bridge over York River, the heaviest engineering on the extension. Earlier Ritchie had been frustrated by Blackstock and Weddell blocking the order with the bridge company. Sited 3.8 miles north of Bancroft, its absence had hampered construction and added considerably to the costs. Another Ritchie initiative had been the purchase of a big steam shovel for $6,500. Collins had insisted on a new machine.

Whatever the state of Ritchie's rheumatism, that March he travelled all the way from Akron to see for himself the work on the extension. He was also able to observe some 35,000 telegraph poles along the northern extension ready to be shipped. It could be the start of another good traffic year.

Ritchie told the local press that in the Bancroft area he was convinced there were some of the most remarkable deposits of red, blue and grey granite in the world, as well as white marble, sodalite and other beautiful building and finishing stone.[7]

A few months later, Ritchie, with his son handling the business details, purchased the land to start marble and granite quarries. By early winter a five-mile spur had been built. This, in the Ritchie style, was not a small operation. It included two 30-ton derricks, a powerhouse, special machinery and sturdy buildings, with a finishing mill to come. The larger of the marble deposits was only a mile from Bancroft, though it would require a two-mile spur. As Ritchie pointed out their nearest competition was across the border in Vermont. The Marmora Herald described the operation as "mammoth."[8]

In early April, 1906, the Toronto Daily Star thought the rumour that Mackenzie and Mann had bought the C.O.R. seemed to be well founded. Because of the litigation and because the line was in the hands of a receiver the price was reasonable. This report seemed to be based on the knowledge that Mackenzie and Mann had bought a large number of shares on the Toronto Stock Exchange.[9] In truth, the partners were a long way from completing the deal.

An indication that the Rathbun empire was declining was an offer to sell to Ritchie all their northern timber lands, a large proportion being situated along the C.O.R. This included water power rights at Bancroft and Baptiste Lake.[10]

That they had given up the idea of extending the Bay of Quinte line from Bannockburn to Marmora Village became evident when Rathbun's offered the Marmora Railway and Mining Company to Ritchie for $35,000. This included an additional five miles of track they had built earlier.[11]

Ritchie could not afford this bargain. He was running short of money himself and was currently seeking a loan for $100,000. That summer he told Collins that a desperate effort would have to be made to finish the line into Maynooth that year, "even if it cost more than we intended."[12]

Another event among neighbouring railways was the resurrection of Madoc's long standing grievance against the Belleville and North Hastings Railway, and its successor the Grand Trunk, who had each, in turn, abandoned the Madoc to Eldorado section.

Having contributed $30,000 to the line and received only a few years service the community was not going to let this be forgotten. An indignation meeting was held in June. The City of Belleville was also interested enough to send an official representative.[13]

Sir Mackenzie Bowell, now safely seated in the Senate, no longer worried about elections, on or about July 12th gave full voice to this matter, making no mention of his original involvement in this unfortunate line. The extension had at first been fairly busy with traffic from a hematite mine, but when that traffic fell off it had been the end of sufficient revenue traffic. The Dominion Government had also subsidized its construction. He did not know whether the rails had been taken up. Unfortunately there was no law compelling the Grand Trunk to continue service (as would have been the case in later years).

He described how he had headed a deputation to wait on Charles Hays, the General Manager of the Grand Trunk, to no avail. What had not been known to the public, a local group had at that time been prepared to take over this notorious seven miles of track, repair it, and operate it independently. There had even been strong talk of seizing the line. (They would, however, soon have gone broke.) A senior senator was duly impressed by Bowell's comments and promised to see that this matter was put before the Minister of Railways.[14]

Meanwhile the citizens of Madoc continued to ride the stage coach to the C.O.R.'s Eldorado station. Ritchie and Collins would have been indifferent. There was no reason why they should short-haul themselves.

The C.O.R. annual meeting was held in Trenton in mid-May. It was reported that traffic was increasing by "leaps and bounds." New equipment and rolling stock would be purchased.

By mid-August a handsome new coach and the first ten of a twenty boxcar order arrived from Cobourg. Also ordered were ten convertible ballast cars. Barged in from Kingston there arrived another locomotive, No. 16. Identical in her dimensions to Nos. 14 and 15, she was likely a stock design, another light "American Standard" and plainly intended for passenger service. Her cost was $14,500. Without the coach, but including the steam shovel, Ritchie had bought $51,750 worth of equipment.[15]

On the southern section, heavier rail was being laid between Trenton and Picton, the last of the 42-pound rail had been lifted.

Picton Station. No longer used and up for sale. 1976   *Photo, Alan R. Capon*

Promising more traffic a new cannery was under construction at Wellington. The C.O.R. was building the siding.[16]

In the north there was promise of a big increase in traffic. The Mineral Range Iron Co. were building a spur from L'Amable to their mine. It would be completed by late October. This company had already secured several large contracts with U.S. steel companies including a 500,000 ton contract (20 carloads a day) with Colonel Schwab, Carnegie's successor. The magnetite ore was unusually rich.[17]

The C.O.R. also had contracts on another 30,000 tons of ore from other mines for onward shipping to the Soo.[18]

Work on the extension was progressing well. Trains were now running to Bird's Creek, five miles; the remaining ten miles to Maynooth was expected to be completed by September.[19] The workers were newly arrived Hungarians. New 70-pound rail was being laid. The steam shovel was hard at work at the gravel pit in Bancroft, keeping two ballast trains busy.[20] The ballast along this extension was of poor quality, little more than heavy sand.

The ballast trains had their adventures. One started its day's work by running over a sheep. Further on, a heifer was encountered. Next they met a flock of geese. As the newspaper reported, "The pilot was covered with wool, hair and feathers."[21]

End of Steel, present day, of the former Belleville and North Hastings. This was the unfortunate Madoc-Eldorado

Photo, Author

147

On August 25th, at Deseronto, the Rathbun's had a disastrous fire, losing valuable buildings, plant and an enormous quantity of lumber.

The same month there were reports that Canadian Northern surveyors were laying out a line that would run north of Belleville.[22] This seems to have been a decoy to keep the CPR from discovering their real plans.

The best news the Town of Trenton had heard in a long time was the decision from the Department of Railways and Canals on February 17th, 1907, that the outlet for the Trent Canal would be along that river and through their town.[23] A close second was the announcement by the Canadian Northern that they would definitely build their Ottawa — Toronto line through Trenton. It looked as though Trenton was catching up on Belleville at long last.

Business was indeed good on the C.O.R. This year might be the best yet. In anticipation

Ritchie had already ordered four more freight locomotives from Kingston, all were ten-wheelers. These were the same dimensions as their lone sister, Number 12, except they carried 30 pounds more boiler pressure and accordingly, were more powerful, but smaller in size than average for this classification.

The engines would not be ready until January, 1908. Collins, in December, had written to Ritchie that he had arranged to pay half the money down. They would need $50,000 to tide them over, "We have never yet made default on any contract with loco, or car builders and I dislike very much making exception in this case."[24]

Back in April Collins had written to Ritchie of another financial problem. He was buying a house in Trenton for $4,500. He was getting married. He wrote expressing the problems of others down the centuries, "I haven't the slightest idea how I will ever pay for it," adding, "but I am trusting in you and providence to see me through."[25]

Second Bloomfield Station. A fine brick and concrete structure to Ritchie standards — but with outdoor plumbing. No longer standing.

Photo, Charles Fraleigh

148

Ritchie was now following up an acquisition even closer to his heart than his beloved mansion. This was the purchase of a business car. This one was to be called "Bancroft." What had happened to the old one is not known. It may have just become too old to use or may have been converted into a coach or a baggage car.

In May Collins was in Montreal to speed up delivery of the car from the Grand Trunk from whom it was being purchased. This was a surplus G.T.R. business car. As Collins wrote to Ritchie, "I find the car has been in their shop several days and they are giving it a thorough overhaul. They have fixed up the trucks and platforms and put a new cover on the roof, they are varnishing it inside and also painting and giving it 3 coats of varnish. I counted 12 men working on it but it takes time for varnish to dry and the Superintendent informed me that the very best he could do was to have the car on Tuesday, 21st. inst. [May] — of course he could slight the work and rush it through faster, but I did not feel like telling him to do this."[26]

There was a new source for yet more traffic on the northern line that spring. From Marmora Station a spur line would be built to the Deloro Mining and Reduction Co. which expected to be in full production shortly, but this would be delayed.

The first train of the year over Rathbun's Marmora Mining and Smelting line was a special freight on May 2nd.

Towards more efficient operations the railway in March started running "special" freights in both directions throughout the system. (In official terminology they would be "extras.") The passenger trains, heroically referred to as "expresses" were now running on time. Years of public complaint were at last being heard. The shortage of locomotives had probably been the main reason for the delays.

April and May, 1907, brought some unusually severe snow storms. The derailment of a train in the April storm delayed the mail for several hours. The May storm was the heaviest in years but there were no mishaps on the C.O.R. There was, however, a tragic accident that month not related to the snow storm.

The Bancroft train broke in two near Millbridge. The rest of the train, due to failure of the air brakes, followed the locomotive and whatever cars were still attached. The fireman, Hennessy by name, was on top of the tender moving coal forwards when this happened. The engineer backed up to re-couple his train. The fireman must have fallen off when the train came together again with a heavy shock. The truck of one of the cars ran over both of his legs. He was brought to Marmora Station where a doctor was waiting, but Hennessy died not long afterwards.[27]

On May 24th, another accident, this time on the Picton line, with no casualties. The morning passenger train, not far from town, pulling five coachloads of passengers on a holiday trip derailed near J.P. Thorn's barn. The rear coaches bumped along the line's ties "until the train was stopped, to the manifest fear of the passengers." None of the coaches overturned.

The passengers from the derailed cars, though shaken had to walk the rest of the way to Picton. The distance was not far.[28]

Less than a month later, on June 20th, there was another accident, this time to a construction train "up north," and again with no injuries or loss of life. A car loaded with spikes broke loose and ran wild for some six miles. It finally crashed into one of the newer locomotives, No. 16, "smashing it rather badly." The engine crew saw the runaway coming and, to use old railroad language, "joined the birds," in time.[29]

Chapter Sixteen

Each extension of the C.O.R. had a character of its own, both geographically and socially. Somewhere north of Bannockburn is the beginning of the Precambrian shield though there is no sharp boundary.

Bancroft, soon to become the most important town north of Trenton on the line, was also a point on the watershed. Rivers now ran northwards, north-east to be exact, eventually emptying into the Ottawa River.

Before the railway came L'Amable had been the bigger of the two communities. Both were on that colonization trail bravely called the Hastings Road which had been the dubious but only means of communication with the rest of the world. It is difficult to appreciate now the enormous advantages the railway brought to this isolated area of ox-wagons and extensive hills, without the advantages of the lakes and rivers in the country immediately to the west. Benefits brought by the C.O.R. are little appreciated today in this age of highways. Even then in no time at all there were strong complaints if the train was late with the mail.

Though L'Amable is still very much alive its decline was due to a deep gorge opening on to the nearby lake. To bridge this was far beyond the resources of the railway so the line had to detour some distance to the east, due to a deep gorge opening on to the nearby lake. L'Amable station had to be built some three miles from that settlement. In time the name was changed to Detlor after a local family. In this area there is a strip of good farm land, so there were local benefits.

Typical of the sandy ballast used north of Bancroft.　　*Photo, Author*

Soon after completion, Maynooth Station. Ritchie had a concrete station at last. When he could, he built forever.

Photo, David Hanes

After the building of the railway the Algonquin Indians moved north.

Many years later the Ontario Government built a fine highway that will take you all the way to Whitney once on the Canada Atlantic. This same highway cuts through L'Amable over what was the best, but impossible route for the railway. The road builders were able to use long, steep hills and a shorter, lower bridge.

Bancroft, soon the trading centre and a tourist attraction (present population 2,600) was originally known as York River. One of the early mill owners, although he did not live there, was responsible for changing the name. This was none other than the old merchant adventurer whose forays into railways have already been told, Senator Billa Flint. This was his wife's maiden name, although if she ever saw the place it would have been a rare visit. He made the name change around 1878-9, by the simple means of writing to the Postmaster General. A local protest got nowhere. Such was his power.

He seems to have been forgiven for later three streets were named after the Senator and his wife: Billa, Flint and Phoebe.

Northwards the new line ran across the flatlands of a basin several miles across, surrounded by high rock hills.

If the new line ran through country where construction was a great deal easier there was the disadvantage that it was thinly populated, with a few scattered farms and some logging operations. Rathbun's had already established camps there. With the ruthless destruction of forests then prevailing in North America, already the case south of Coe Hill, Ritchie would be aware this could only be a source of traffic for a limited number of years.

For Ritchie the prime objective was to reach the Canada Atlantic line to gain the through traffic. Ritchie also had high hopes of new mineral strikes along the line. Such discoveries as were being made at the time would have disappointed him. A graphite mine would seem to have been the most profitable mineral enterprise north of Bancroft.

151

Maynooth Station in 1977, with Mr. J. Robert Burns, Area Manager, Canadian National Railways, Rideau Area.

Photo, Author

Maynooth, normally having a population of a few hundred persons, had the air of a gold rush and all the blind optimism that went with it. There was such a shortage of accommodation that the village was now surrounded with tents and improvised shacks.

Ritchie's new station was an added boost to their optimism. Not only was this substantial concrete structure the largest building there, but after Trenton's, it was the biggest on the line. One would suspect that it was planned for it to be the divisional point when construction to the Canada Atlantic Railway had been completed.

True, it was nearly a mile from the town, and at the bottom of a steep hill in the Papineau valley, but that was the fault of Maynooth's founders for having sited on a hilltop.

If without any distinctive architectural style, the building has a certain sturdy grandeur. Such a permanent structure was the kind of station Ritchie would have built all along the line had he

continued as president, (and had he the money). The station stands there to this day, empty.

The top floor was taken up with the spacious quarters for the agent and his family. The main floor not only contained the agent's office, waiting room, etc., but a restaurant as well. This would become the kitchen and living room for the agent. This was unusual on branch lines. Ritchie still had memories of the CPR's main line station at Sudbury that had no such facilities. Express was handled in a wooden annex on the south side of the station.

A most important part of the character of this section of the line was the people; hardy pioneers, even more so than those to the south. The environment had, of course, much to do with this, not only in the survival of the fittest aspect. Isolated, their main transportation routes had not been by rivers, but by ox-teams along sandy cart tracks.

In Trenton and Prince Edward County, the

northerners were often held to be ignorant and superstitious people. It was the price of isolation. But they were and still are self-reliant, friendly and generous people, in spite of an almost perpetual lack of prosperity. They possessed their own sophistications, the skills of living in the wilderness that rivalled that of the Indian. They also produced such sterling patriarchs as that magnificently named lumber-mill operator Darius King Card.[1]

North of Maynooth grading of the next extension had already started. Ritchie was plainly determined to make up for those lost years. Here logging operations had been on a small scale. Many great pines had been floated down the Papineau River, in spite of severe obstacles, and northwards to the Ottawa River.

As for the engineering details of the new extension there is not much to be said compared to earlier sections for it was built for the greater part through easier country and to minimum government standards, compared to the Coe Hill line. The higher costs were largely due to speeding up of construction and the court-ordered delay in the construction of the bridge at York River. Certainly the standards were not as high as Ritchie would have liked but they were all, or more, than he could afford. At least the rail was new.

The worthy John D. Evans had estimated the cost of the line from Bancroft to Whitney, 42 miles, at $773,445 or $18,414 a mile. By February, $217,286 had been spent. The largest single item, the York River bridge, cost $8,612.[2]

South end of Maynooth Station 1977

Photo, Author

153

This dilapidation is a rarity nowadays, the body of an all wood boxcar (except iron stays, bolts & straps). It served as a bunkhouse for train crews.

Photo, Author

In March, Evans had to write to the Deputy Minister of Railways to state that he had "inadvertently" omitted the cost of ties in his estimates. This totalled 3,000 ties (hemlock or cedar) per mile at 40¢ apiece. This meant $1,200 a mile or $50,400 for the 42 miles.[3] (An interesting comparison, though these ties were not treated, is that second-hand ties sell nowadays in Toronto for $8 to $11 each, fetch-and-carry.)

The Government Chief Civil Engineer, M.J. Butler, after visiting the line, and learning of the company's financial state and that a bond issue had not yet been approved, wrote to the department: "I wish you would do all you possibly can to hurry the payment to the Company, as they are badly in need of money."[4] A cheque for $31,840 followed not long after, on July 24th.

Although Ed. Ritchie had been vice-president for some time now, George Collins, not Ritchie Sr., handled all the correspondence with Ottawa. This was both a measure of confidence by Ritchie as well as a sign of his failing health.

On August 26th, Collins was requesting the Department to arrange for the final inspection of the line to Maynooth so that it could be opened for all traffic and the subsidies could be paid.[5] On September 20th he was requesting an extra subsidy payment on account of construction costs being in excess of the estimated figures.[6]

The same M.J. Butler found this claim excessive. The line was, however, two miles longer than the original survey. For the final additional subsidy, including the extra two miles, he recommended a figure of $1,627.66 per mile for the original 40 miles.[7] This amount seems to have been accepted. The subsidy payments were made in November, totalling $45,026.

On October 19th, E.V. Johnson, the government engineer, inspected the new line accompanied by Ritchie who would have returned from the dead to do this. No doubt they rode proudly in his business car "Bancroft."

The line was officially opened on November

7th, 1907, without, it seems, any ceremony.

That October there had been good news for his friends, Mackenzie and Mann of the Canadian Northern. Thomas Shaughnessy, President of the CPR, made it known that the CPR would not be building their new Toronto line along the shores of Lake Ontario for the present, not until times got better. This put the Canadian Northern Railway in undisputed second place to the Grand Trunk and a better than head start in building up traffic.

This fetching structure might have once been the summer house in a Victorian Garden. But not so! It was the base of the water tower. When the tank was condemned a resourceful section foreman roofed it over for an extra storage shed.   *Photo, Author*

For those seeking the re-opening of the Madoc-Eldorado section of the old Belleville and North Hastings Railway, the news was not encouraging. Charles M. Hays, head of the Grand Trunk, gave his price for repairing the line (the rails were still in place) as $49,000.[8]

There was worse news for the C.O.R. Just when the iron ore traffic was growing considerably in volume, the United States Government imposed a duty of $7.00 a ton on all imported iron ore. The Blairton mine closed immediately for a period of 28 days. The mine owners then offered to lease the property to Ritchie.[9] He had more immediate demands on his financial resources.

All through 1907, Ritchie's numerous law cases had continued. Now he faced the heirs and executors of the various estates. Nothing decisive seems to have been settled. Blackstock's heirs, no longer able to seize the railway, were now pressing him to "pay his indebtedness" on the bonds from the date of issue. How much profit did they want?

Reference has been made to Ritchie's plan for a new bond issue. In January, through the C.O.R.'s lawyers, permission was sought to increase the capital stock from the present nominal figure of $750,000 to $4,090,000. It was also proposed that all outstanding bonds be surrendered and a new bond issue of $1,200,000 take their place. Stock was to be issued in lieu of overdue interest. The brief noted that the road had been earning a substantial profit, but the bondholders had allowed their money to be invested into the extension of the road. It would seem that Mackenzie and Mann, not yet in full control, supported the plan.[10]

The government, understandably shy from all the C.O.R.'s legal problems, would be over a year mulling over their proposal. Ritchie, short of money, now must have become greatly frustrated, no doubt so were his bankers. Nothing new for either party.

Chapter Seventeen

Without originality, this chapter could be called "Winter's Tale." February and March of 1908 brought some of the worst weather in the railway's history.[1] Ritchie was extremely ill at the time so George Collins went to some trouble to keep him informed, leaving for posterity an interesting first-hand account of the responsibilities of running a railroad in the early years of this century.

"This has been the worst storm we have had here in about 3 years," he wrote in his first letter dated February 1st, "about 18 inches having fallen during night and day. We have had to run the snow plow all over the road and expect to make two trips to Picton. The train got from Coe Hill through alright and is returning but we were obliged to cancel the train to Maynooth entirely."

Two days later he wrote again, "... We have had a terrific time here on Saturday and Sunday but managed to get the track all opened up by Sunday night so that all the trains are running today. The snow plow, however, is still moving and we are unable to handle but little freight as all side tracks are still blocked. The Grand Trunk had a very hard time of it east of Belleville."

Four days later, February 7th, he reported that the C.O.R. was open but that they had not received any freight from either the G.T.R. or the C.P.R. for three days. He continued, "The trouble with us now is that the snow is getting so very deep through the yards that we have no place to put it and we cannot get it out of the cuts. If the weather should moderate and keep clear for a couple of days we will soon be alright again."

"We have been fortunate in not having an accident or a breakdown of any kind for which we are thankful."

Nearly a fortnight later, one would assume the weather had improved as Collins had hoped and accumulations of snow had been removed at considerable cost by brigades of shovellers, then another storm blew in. Collins wired Ritchie on the 20th, "Not blocked but several trains stalled." Worse news was to follow two days later. "... [a] rather unfortunate accident this a.m., however was not attended with very serious results. The snow plow with special engine and flanger running from Trenton to Picton which left Trenton about 5 a.m. was derailed about 2 miles north of Wellington. The plow struck a heavy bank of snow on one side of the track, the other rail being practically clear which crowded it off. It turned completely around and fell on its side practically clear of the track. The plow was rather badly damaged and the engine, flanger and caboose were all scraped along the side but not seriously injured. The accident happened about 6 o'clock and we had the line all clear by 11 a.m. We simply shoved the plow clear to allow trains to pass and will go down to get it tomorrow. We have been obliged to run this plow every day this week since the 18th in order to keep the line open.

"Fortunately we have everything clear today and the weather is fine with prospects of milder weather tomorrow."

The milder weather did not last long. Two days later he wrote, "We had another terrific storm here last night; a heavy fall of wet snow accompanied by a gale of wind which has practically filled all the cuts again. The train from Coe Hill got through this morning but the Bancroft train (northbound) only reached Frankford and had to return. The morning train to Picton we had to cancel but expect to run the afternoon train. We fitted up a steel plow for one of the engines and we are making an effort to clear the line with it.

"I am negotiating with the Russell Snow Plow Co. of Ridgeway, Pa. for a new Model, up-to-date snow plow which would cost us $2,500 delivered here and I think I will try and get it at once for it is hard to tell how much more snow we may have before spring. I trust this meets with your approval."

On March 6th, they had yet to receive the new snow plow, with the only means of clearing snow the make-shift blade on the locomotive, a flanger and manpower, and the news was discouraging. "We are still having our troubles here on account of the bad weather. We had a terrific storm of snow and sleet last Sunday afternoon which very nearly put us out of business Monday. We were obliged to cancel several trains but had the line well opened by Monday night. Tuesday, Wednesday and Thursday were nice and mild and we were able to get pretty well caught up with our work. We have had another very bad storm this afternoon, in fact we are in worse shape at this writing, 5 p.m., than we have been at anytime this winter.

"At five o'clock this afternoon we had five trains stalled in the snow at one time. There was considerable snow fell about noon with a regular blizzard from the south east which has turned to rain. The afternoon train for Picton was stalled at the Canal for an hour and a half but finally got through and is now on its way back, the Maynooth train on the way down stalled at Brinklow and a freight train following was stalled at L'Amable. An up freight train was stalled north of Marmora and the afternoon train for Coe Hill was stalled hard and fast at Anson. We are practically helpless and to give them any assistance until the storm is over, but I am in hopes that they will work their way out and get through alright.

"We have any quantity of business offering which we are almost unable to handle on account of the condition of the track. Our engines are also getting very bad on account of the continual pounding through the snow. I am in hopes, however, that this will be the last."

It was. Collins' letter of March 16th stated, "The weather has been nice for the past week and business has been fully up to the average."

Ledyard's Gold Mine on the Marmora Mining and Smelting Rly.

Topley Photo, Public Archives of Canada

THE
CENTRAL ONTARIO RAILWAY

TIME TABLE No. 26

EASTERN STANDARD TIME.   TAKING EFFECT TUESDAY, SEPT. 17TH, 1907.

No. 10 Pass.	No. 8 Mxd.	No. 6 Pass.	No. 4 Pass.	No. 2 Pass.	STATIONS	Miles	No. 1 Pass.	No. 3 Pass.	No. 5 Mxd.	No. 7 Pass.	No. 9 Pass.
P.M.	P.M.	A.M.	P.M.	A.M.	Dep. Ar.		A.M.	P.M.	A.M.	P.M.	P.M.
7 15			3 30	9 00	.. Picton	.07	8 30	1 15			7 00
7 25			3 40	9 10	Bloomfield..	4.22	8 15	1 05			6 50
f7 30			f3 45	f 9 15	Hallowell..	7.59	f8 10	f 1 00			f6 45
7 40			3 55	9 25	Wellington .	10.97	8 00	12 50			6 35
f7 50			f4 05	f 9 35	Niles' Corners	14.90	f7 50	f12 40			f6 25
f7 53			f4 08	f 9 38	.. Hillier ..	16.55	f7 45	f12 30			f6 20
8 05			4 20	9 50	..Consecon..	21.32	7 35	12 20			6 10
f8 15			f4 30	f10 00	Weller's Bay	25.64	f7 25	f12 10			f6 00
f8 20			f4 32	f10 02	....Canal....	27.02	f7 20	f12 05			f5 55
8 30	12 45	6 15	4 45	10 15	...Trenton...	30.60	7 15	12 00	10 35	5 05	5 50
8 40	1 00	6 25	4 55	10 25	Trenton Jct	32.17	7 00	11 50	10 25	4 55	5 40
P.M.	1 20	6 40	P.M.	A.M.	..Frankford..	38.50	A.M.	A.M.	10 10	4 40	P.M.
	1 40	6 55			..Anson Jct..	46.02			9 50	4 25	
	f1 55	f 7 10			...Rawdon...	50.45			f9 35	f 4 15	
	f2 05	f 7 18			.Springbrook.	53.41			f9 20	f 4 10	
	2 20	7 25			C.P.Ry. Jct.	55.61			9 10	4 05	
	2 40	7 40			..Marmora..	61.09			8 45	3 45	
	f3 00	f 7 55			...Malone...	67.03			f8 25	f 3 30	
	3 15	8 10			..Eldorado...	71.25			8 10	3 15	
	3 30	8 25			Bannockburn	76.25			7 55	3 05	
	3 50	8 40			Millbridge..	80.67			7 30	2 50	
	4 20	9 05			..Gilmour...	90.31			7 00	2 25	
	f4 35	f 9 15			...St. Ola...	93.20			f6 50	f 2 15	
	4 55	9 25			Ormsby Jct	96.94			6 35	2 05	
	f5 10				...Ormsby...	99.45			f6 25		
	5 30				..Coe Hill..	104.15			6 10		
	P.M.	f 9 30			..Brinklow..	98.51			A.M.	f 1 58	
		f 9 50			...Turiff...	105.17				f 1 40	
		10 05			L'Amable..	109.44				1 25	
		f10 15			...Bronson..	112.77				f 1 10	
		10 30			..Bancroft...	116.52				1 00	
		10 45			.Bird's Creek.	120.32				12 50	
		f11 05			.. Hybla ...	126.36				f12 30	
		11 25			.Maynooth..	132.30				12 10	
	A.M.				Ar. Dep.					P.M.	

(Left and right margins marked: SATURDAYS ONLY)

Trains Nos. 9 and 10 run on SATURDAYS ONLY. All other Trains run daily (Sundays excepted).

f Flag Stations, trains stop only when passengers at or for.

GEO. COLLINS,
Manager.

USEFUL INFORMATION

STATION TICKET OFFICES are open for the sale of tickets thirty minutes before departure of trains and passengers are requested to purchase tickets before entering cars.

ROUND TRIP TICKETS, first class, valid one month from date of issue, are for sale at reduced fares between stations on the Central Ontario Railway. They are not transferable, and are not good to stop over at any intermediate station unless so stated on ticket.

MILEAGE TICKETS, at low rate, can be purchased at all stations. Commercial Travellers' tickets on sale and Travellers' samples checked through from principal stations on this line to all points on the Grand Trunk and Canadian Pacific Railways.

COUPON TICKETS to all points on the Continent can be procured from principal Central Ontario Railway agents.

CHILDREN under five years of age, when accompanied, will be carried free; children between five and twelve years will be carried at half fare. All twelve years and over must pay adult fare.

LOST TICKETS. Railway companies are not responsible for lost tickets. All possible precaution should be taken to prevent their loss. Upon purchasing tickets passengers should make a memorandum of the "Destination," "By what Railway issued," "Form Number," "Consecutive Number," "Place and date of Sale," also of the consecutive numbers of their baggage checks. This will aid in their recovery if lost or stolen.

PERSONAL BAGGAGE consisting of wearing apparel to the extent of 150 lbs. in weight will be checked on each adult passage ticket and 75 lbs. on each child's half ticket. Personal baggage exceeding these free allowances will be charged for. No piece of baggage weighing more than 250 lbs. will be checked. All baggage should be addressed.

Passengers paying for excess baggage will receive an excess baggage check which must be delivered to agent when baggage is claimed.

It is unlawful to carry dangerous articles such as matches, gunpowder, etc., in baggage.

BAGGAGE FOR FLAG STATIONS or stations where agents are not on duty must be claimed at baggage car door immediately on arrival, otherwise it will be carried to next station where agent is on duty and held for further orders.

FARES CANNOT BE ADJUSTED BY CONDUCTORS. In the event of a disagreement with a Conductor relative to tickets required, privileges allowed, etc., passengers should pay the Conductor, take his receipt and refer the case to the Manager for adjustment. The Conductor is governed by rules he cannot change.

GENERAL OFFICE, TRENTON, ONT.
OFFICIALS

S. J. RITCHIE, President	J. D. ROWE, Treasurer
C. E. RITCHIE, Vice-President	J. D. EVANS, Chief Engineer
GEO. COLLINS, Manager	G. A. HOAG, Superintendent

The Best Fishing and Hunting Resorts in Canada are found along this line of Railway.

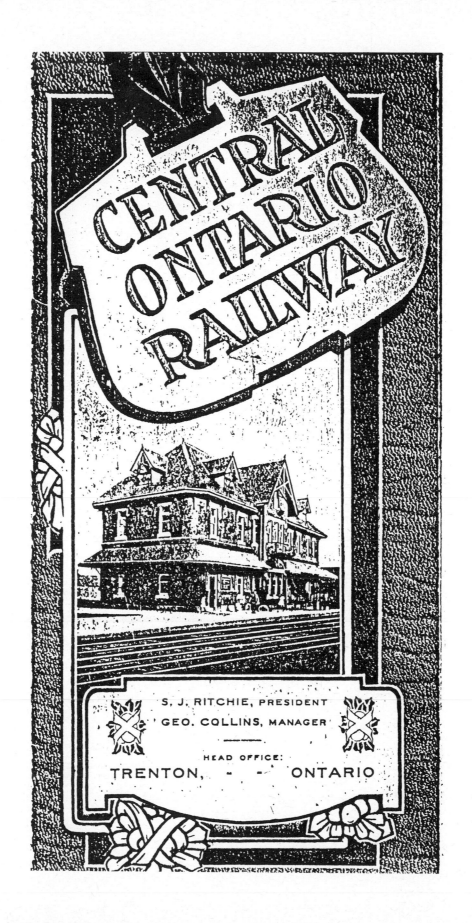

CENTRAL ONTARIO RAILWAY

S. J. RITCHIE, PRESIDENT
GEO. COLLINS, MANAGER

HEAD OFFICE:
TRENTON, - - ONTARIO

Chapter Eighteen

The year 1908, after the setbacks from the weather of the earlier months, promised to be one of vigorous expansion. There were also hopeful signs of government authorizing the big capital increase. Ritchie was determined to continue construction against all odds, for they would still have to sell these bonds and stocks, though this lack of capital had slowed construction of the line north of Maynooth.

Collins was busy in January and February negotiating with the Town of Trenton to find space for "larger and better Roundhouse Accommodation for locomotives, also machine and other shops." He suggested to the Mayor that while the present shops were outside the town limits, the new shops, which would cost $40,000, would employ at least double the number of men. They could be located in Trenton at a site known as the ballast pit lots, while a large freight shed would be constructed on the site of a skating rink.

Collins requested that with the increased business being brought to the town that the present by-law assessing the company on a valuation of $19,250 be increased to only $20,000 and that this remain in force for 25 years. The town agreed to $30,000, but this would include any other new company building such as a cement works or a marble crusher.[1]

Mackenzie and Mann holding a considerable number of COR bonds and determined to buy control of the line would need space for enlarged divisional facilities, in the town. Also a small, independent and not-too-rich railway would be far more likely to get a better deal. But that is supposition.

On February 15th, Collins, in the middle of his snow problems, wrote to Ritchie saying that he had managed to get a loan of $20,000 from the Bank of Montreal. This it seems, was quite an achievement. He was now able to pay off all outstanding accounts including Rathbun's — but not the bill for the new locomotives.[2]

That September William Harty, owner of the Kingston Locomotive Works, wrote, "you will not accuse us of having been importunate in dunning you for payment of the engines delivered to your company last January. Owing to the heavy outlays entailed upon us by the enlargements and improvements of our Works, we are beginning to feel somewhat embarrassed by the long delay in your settling for our engines.

"May I request you will take the best steps possible to place us in funds for at least two additional engines at an early date, and oblige."[3]

George Collins must have been truly embarrassed.

The annual meeting was held on May 20th. Among those present sat a new director, S.S. Lazier, a successful Belleville lawyer and a close friend of Ritchie. Some interesting items were reported.

In equipment the company now owned 16 locomotives, seven passenger cars, four baggage cars, 11 stock, 181 flat (40 had been added since the last meeting) and 10 ballast cars. Not included in this listing was the business car "Bancroft", unless it was considered as passenger equipment. Two new vans (cabooses) had been purchased. The snow plow was not mentioned.

On the extension northwards from Maynooth, grading was almost finished for the eight miles to Lake St. Peter. Two miles of track had been laid. Altogether since the previous meeting the company had received $76,840 in federal grants and $43,500 from the Province of Ontario. Earnings at $138,690.27 were by $36,000 the highest in history.

The bond issue had been approved at last for Ritchie reported $2.2 million of 6% bonds, and of that the issue $1.2 million had now been made.

Fixed interest for the company was $60,000. Preferred stock had been increased to $1,336,000, common to $2,004,000.[4]

The total represented a good deal less than the original investment, which was still no guarantee of dividends. Earlier Blackstock and Weddell had given their assent, but Mackenzie and Mann now had the say in that quarter.

Ritchie was of the opinion that the present economic depression was over. He was correct. During the previous year 2,600 carloads of ballast had been used and 30,000 ties had been replaced.[5] More than available funds really permitted, Ritchie was working with all despatch to bring the C.O.R. up to his own high standards. Harty of the Kingston Locomotive Works, even if he did not realize it, was helping to finance some of the work.

Ritchie described relations with the present trustees as pleasant and satisfactory.

Along the line prospects looked good for 1908. Ritchie commented in a letter that the Bessemer Mine, having been purchased by a syndicate, would reopen that spring.

In February Collins wrote to Ritchie that, "our friend Mr. Kirkaard of Deloro Mines, near Marmora Station, had booked space to ship by express 80,000 ounces of silver, worth $200,000, to England. This would be their first shipment of any consequence and a source of considerable revenue to the railway." This was also the mine that was to produce arsenic in quantity,[6] but not until May would regular shipments of that unpleasant chemical of many uses be made.

Swing Bridge Trent Canal   *Photo, Author*

New sawmills were being built beyond Lake St. Peter. The Bessemer mine was now shipping five carloads of ore a day.

After a lapse of nearly thirty years, construction of the Trent Canal had started again.[7] Built too late, for low capacity canals had been overtaken by the railways. This would not affect the C.O.R. as a competitor, but 12 miles of the canal, more or less, ran in the vicinity of the line and would provide considerable freight traffic during its construction.

The new canal brought only one physical change to the railway. It was to that most costly single engineering work, the Trent River bridge at Glen Ross which had to be shortened. Between the island and the north bank a swing bridge would be substituted over new locks.

The swing bridge was installed by the government at no cost to the railway beyond some dislocation of traffic. It was second hand and where it came from is not remembered. The bridge is so well balanced that it can be moved by one man, though the bridge tender, Ezra Scott, a CNR employee, found it easier and quicker to open and close it with his own small tractor. A minor engineering feature is that the rails at each end lift to fall into slots that match the track, compared to the usual sliding, locking system.

Ritchie's progress in rehabilitating the line, ably carried out by George Collins, was paying off, particularly in the southern section. By August, over the previous twelve months, the railway had shipped out 1,100 carloads of canned goods and 300,000 bushels of apples. There were also big shipments of lake fish. Additionally, Picton station had sold more tickets to Toronto (at Trenton they naturally booked on the Grand Trunk) than all the other C.O.R. stations combined.[8]

What of a more grandiose future for the railway? Early in the year T.M. Kirkwood, a new director (he was absent from the annual meeting), had written Ritchie a letter full of imaginative ideas. This must have pleased the adventurous Ritchie. The theme, if the ultimate purpose was to sell the railway, was that they should buy the Irondale, Bancroft and Ottawa Railway and extend the line to Midland, a port on Georgian Bay, some 50 miles to the west, providing a through route for grain shipments from the West, via steamer. He said nothing of the costs of making that unfortunate line fit to carry heavier traffic.[9]

Something of the I.B. & O.'s reputation is illustrated by the local tale of the lady rushing to the station near Bancroft as the train slowly pulled out. Running along the platform she called out to the station agent, "Do you think I can make it?" To which he is supposed to have answered, "Lady, if you keep up that speed better watch out you don't pass them!"[10]

The rest of Kirkwood's plan envisaged considerable barge traffic, if not from Picton, then from South Bay which had deeper water in its approaches. This would mean a revival of the original route planned in 1852. He also suggested running a car ferry that could take loaded cars across Lake Ontario by what would be a shorter route from several points. He considered the Lehigh Valley, the New York, Ontario and Western, or the great Pennsylvania Railroad as likely purchasers of such a route.[11]

Even for Ritchie, the plunger, the odds on the enormous capital costs involved in such a gamble could not be considered. Nonetheless he still planned to extend his line to North Bay to join with the CPR and the new Ontario Government railway running northwards.[12]

In his personal life Ritchie still kept in touch with Henry C. McMullen of Picton, indeed their letters were cordial. The latter was running for the Liberal party that year, but lost. McMullen in a letter dated July 28th, wrote, "... I am very thankful for your expressions of confidence in my integrity, as well as my impartiality," and ended his letter, "I hope you are more comfortable than when I saw you, and I will ask you to remember me to Mrs. Ritchie and the members of your family."[13] On top of those ferocious attacks of rheumatism, Ritchie was now further handicapped by diabetes.

Thomas G. Shaughnessy, President of the Canadian Pacific Railway, still found time to continue a friendly correspondence with Ritchie. Whatever their differences of opinion in the past this great man plainly held Ritchie in high esteem.

While Ritchie was always willing to talk about selling his railroad, when offers came in it was a different matter. At least he would first finish building it and have the system in first class shape. One such example was when the Hon. J.M. Gibson, who may have been acting on behalf of either the Canadian Pacific or the Grand Trunk enquired about such a sale, Ritchie wrote back, "I am not surprised that having unloaded on me that tired old Coe Hill stock, you now feel inclined to purchase this railway. The property is not for sale ..."[14]

His great mansion had been completed by now but there were still details of the furnishings and grounds to be settled. He continued to supervise all these matters, mostly by mail. Somehow he managed to continue his travels if on a reduced scale. But for Ritchie 1908 was a bad year indeed.

The big marble quarry on 700 acres of property at Bancroft, a hasty venture with little or no prior testing of the product before the huge plant and machinery had been bought and installed, turned out to be a disaster. Not far from a total loss for himself and others who may have bought an interest.

Not long after production had started, which had included shipping a seven-ton block with considerable publicity, it was discovered that the rock contained, of all things for Ritchie, a high percentage of iron ore. Exposed to moisture rusty stains from the ore ran over the cut face and stained the porous stone. At the same time the ore dissolved and the fabric of the rock was loosened. At least so it was reported. Further quarrying was tried, but in vain. There was nothing else to do but close down the venture and sell the plant and equipment for what it could bring. The final "amen" for Ritchie was when the mile and a half of rail siding was torn up. In August, Senator Sir Mackenzie Bowell, out of curiosity, came to view the remains.[15]

The following year it was discovered that the expert Ritchie had hired to cut the marble had done so the wrong way, as it were, against the grain. When this was discovered the modern machinery and the spur line had been dismantled. In spite of this fair quantities of marble were quarried by individuals from time to time. New quarries, more accessible, were opened between Bancroft and L'Amable. Here a short spur was built by the railway and a shelter for passengers was provided. This flag stop was shown in the timetables as Bronson.

When any of his bigger enterprises failed Ritchie searched energetically for another venture to recoup his losses. When the iron ore mines failed in 1885 he had bought up copper strikes at Sudbury. After they had failed, because of high nickel content, he had successfully turned to promoting and mining that metal. But for the

Central Ontario Railway he could have been fabulously wealthy by now. Somehow it seems he would not have had it otherwise. He had one more big venture at hand. This time it was not in Canada but back in his own country in the State of Virginia.

In the years before he had first invested in Canada, when he was still manufacturing horse carriages, he had bought some 50,000 acres of coal and timber lands in that state. He had for a time paid the taxes regularly, the last time several years before when he had mailed a cheque to the local officials. Typically Ritchie since then had never verified the extent of his tax bill. Now the local authorities were claiming that the cheque had never been received. Meanwhile the land had been sold for sums so small that this smelled of skulduggery. The land had now been built across by several railroads buying their right-of-way from squatters and others. Ritchie had no choice but to go to court, something he had earlier plainly enjoyed, but one can only wonder if by now it pleased him at all.[16] Whatever his feelings his spirit had not weakened.

Concurrently he was also suing Colonel Schwab and his International Nickel associates for half-a-million dollars, claiming misrepresentation and fraud in their purchase of his nickel interests.[17]

There followed in early August what must have been the biggest blow of all the setbacks Ritchie had received in his unique life. The Privy Council of Great Britain, then Canada's ultimate legal authority, gave judgment in favour of the bondholders (primarily Blackstock and Weddell) against the stockholders (primarily Ritchie). Ritchie also had to pay all legal costs. To quote from a clipping from an unnamed and unsympathetic Canadian newspaper, "the 'defeated' Ritchie, ... in his endeavours to deprive others of their lawful rights ending in his own discomfiture and defeat. As soon as details can be arranged the line will be sold to the highest bidder. Blackstock and Weddell vindicated."[18] In reality the case meant little by now Mackenzie and Mann having bought control of those interests — fortunately for Ritchie.

There had been fresh rumours that the Grand Trunk would buy the line. If this was their purpose it could only be to keep out the Canadian Northern.

If Ritchie had awful problems this year the C.O.R. was much better off, once the winter was past. The worst accident, a minor one was a boxcar derailment near Bancroft in July. The wrecker had rushed there from Trenton and the crew had worked all night replacing 140 ties, then spiking down the rails. The trains were running again by morning. There remained another kind of mess to clean up, the car had been loaded with flour and sugar.[19]

That same month George Collins was under pressure from Picton groups to run a night train, primarily for mail and the Toronto newspapers. The day train was so often late. Earlier he had recommended this proposal to Ritchie who disagreed, claiming the potential revenues would be far short of the cost to the company.

Collins was convincing enough. He gave the figures of the train arrivals in Picton. Then with equal detail matching the late arrivals of the Grand Trunk trains in Trenton. Furthermore if this train was instituted the train crew would have to work from 6 a.m. to 9 p.m., and no one crew could do this. With the revenue involved an extra crew could not be justified.[20]

A complaint that Ritchie had listened to was that of the citizens of Marmora Village who lived on the leased branch line, as to the state of the track. There was also self-interest here. Derailments were becoming frequent. The line would be brought up to better standards. That fall he promised that the service, if traffic justified it, would be increased to three trains a week.[21]

When fall came the woods, with no rain for weeks, were burning fiercely along the northern lines.

*　*　*

While the fires were blazing along the Central Ontario Railway, many miles away in Charleston, Virginia, Samuel Ritchie was working hard on the briefs for his lawsuit to regain title to his coal and timber lands. Early on a Saturday morning, 19th September, 1908, he was found dead in his hotel bedroom. His body could no longer meet the demands of the spirit.

His seventieth birthday would have been the following month. But considering the pressures and uncertainties he had lived under, he had a long life.

Only the night before he had telegraphed home that his work would require him to remain a while longer.[22]

Among his last thoughts may have been that his work on the C.O.R. had not been completed; neither the extension to Whitney, nor the rehabilitation of the railway's plant and equipment to his own high standards.

Once so well-known in industry, transportation and politics on both sides of the border, he is a forgotten man today, even along his "own" railway. With his death passed much of the corporate personality of this unusual railway.

Over the months that followed there was little news as to the future of the line. His son Charles E. (Ed.) Ritchie succeeded him as president. The almost irreplaceable George Collins continued as general manager.

In March came the last, final newspaper report that the Grand Trunk was going to buy the C.O.R.[23] How much truth there was in this is hard to tell. It was too late. Had Grand Trunk bought the line earlier the Canadian Northern's plans would have been seriously curtailed.

Meanwhile his son Charles Ritchie had completed the final negotiations with Mackenzie and Mann. On April 5th, 1909, the public was informed of this. The immediate assumption locally was that the C.O.R. would now disappear as such to become just another branch line of the Canadian Northern. Instead the Canadian Northern announced not long after that, for the present, the C.O.R. would remain a separate company. Young Ritchie would remain as president and Collins as general manager.

There were several reasons for this. The company was an efficient operation under Collins. The biggest reason as T.D. Regehr, in his history of the Canadian Northern, points out that wages on the non-union C.O.R. were lower.[24]

In the final settlement Colonel Stevens states that the stock and bondholders received a total of $3,340,000. Out of this the Ritchies had received $1,200,000.[25] While this was a large amount to have paid, all things considered, though a great deal less than Ritchie had put into the line, most of the balance would have been paid to Blackstock and Weddell. They had invested next to nothing and had seriously hampered construction, but they had the law on their side.

In December, 1909, Mackenzie and Mann purchased the Marmora Railway and Mining Company for $100,000. This line would be left to keep its own identity for many years.[26] The famous first president of the Canadian National Railways, Sir Henry Thornton, sat at its annual meeting in 1923 as president of this diminutive line,[27] that had never owned a locomotive or revenue equipment.

The short line from L'Amable to the Bessemer Mine, once the starting point for a projected rival to the C.O.R., would be purchased by Mackenzie and Mann in 1915. Approximately $100,000 was paid.[28]

A fair guess is that once Ritchie's estate was settled his family would be fortunate to receive any balance. He always seemed to have huge loans at various banks, often past the limit of his equity. There were enormous legal fees piling up, even $1,200,000 could soon disappear under such heavy liabilities. But guessing is a risky business for Ritchie left his widow, two sons, and his daughter a fortune, more than double that of his archenemy, Judge Burke, with his estate of $2,000,000. He had also been fortunate in that his younger son had proved to be an able manager.

While the extension had been completed as far as Lake St. Peter (24 miles from Bancroft) by February, 1909[29] the regular passenger train still ran only as far as Maynooth.

Earlier the company had to apply for an extension of the federal subsidy, with the program lagging so far behind.[30] This was granted in December of that year. Samuel J. Ritchie had died with 32 miles of his railway still to be completed.

The year 1909 was a poor one, as far as profit was concerned, down 17 per cent from the previous years. But the gross was down only .8%. Generally the C.O.R. had been written off as an unprofitable line, handicapped by endless litigation.[31]

But what is hard to assess over these past years is what the true earning capability of the line really was; amounts of the company's earnings being paid out directly for construction costs of the northern extension and litigation costs during the Burke regime.

The future of the line was now in the hands of Mackenzie and Mann, who would also have to pay the bond interest.

* * *

Bessemer Branch. Bridge over Egan Creek looking towards mine.　　　*Photo, David Hanes*

167

The year 1909, even if much was happening in secrecy, was quiet along the line; no accidents and few incidents. The C.O.R.'s safety record was better than ever. Unfortunately, it was a poor traffic year, the gross being down 35 per cent.

The best that could be found as dramatic event of the year, seems to have been, "an exciting time at Eldorado Station concerning the Coe Hill train." The local newspaper reported: "It appears that a man named West Fox had an altercation with Conductor Vandervoort and as the train was moving into the station Fox shoved the conductor off the train. Fortunately the conductor was not injured and in the mix up that followed gave Fox considerably the worst of it. Fox retaliated afterwards by throwing stones and breaking some windows. Chief Glass of Trenton went to Eldorado on Wednesday to arrest him."[32]

While traffic was down this year there were no changes to the timetables. Picton had its regular service, normally a coach and a baggage car, three times daily. North of Trenton there was almost a suburban service, a short run to and from Frankford. Coe Hill had a daily mixed train; Maynooth was at the end of the regular passenger train service. On a ton-mile basis the Picton line remained the busiest. The small number of extra freights marked the drop in car loadings.

With operations of the line now well established north of Trenton, some description of these is timely.

How extensive the custom was elsewhere of using train agents is not known, but on the C.O.R. this had been successful. By this means a large number of flag stops and sidings could still receive the same service as a manned station. The train agents rode the mixed trains and the way freights leaving empty cars as requested. When loaded, and ready to be hauled away, the train agent was there to complete the bills of lading and other business. They also handled the lesser number of inbound loads.[33]

Passengers boarding at flag stops paid their fares to the conductor. As a group, conductors were honest men, proud of their prestigious calling. Unfortunately there was the occasional exception who could not resist the temptation to pocket the money. One such was caught within a couple of years off his pension. He was fired. There was genuine sorrow among his fellows but little sympathy.[34]

The ruling gradient northbound was the climb to Ormsby Junction, and beyond, to either Coe Hill or Bancroft. The switch was kept open for the main line to the north. If the engine was in good shape, had a fast start, a good fireman, a dry rail, plenty of steam and the train not overloaded, it was easy. North-bound trains were generally light in any case. Otherwise it was double the hill. This meant backing down, leaving half the cars at the bottom and taking the train up in two sections.[35] For the engineer and fireman it could mean, deserved or not, an excess of criticism ranging from their own conductor, the crews of trains they had delayed, to reprimands from the despatchers in Bancroft and Trenton, or from George Collins himself.

For Coe Hill trains it was worse. The head end brakeman had to drop from the labouring engine and make like a greyhound for the switch and throw it before the train got there. If he failed, for it was easy enough to stumble or be slowed down by snow, the engineer had to back all the way down and start again. This time it was the locomotive crew that cursed the brakeman.[36] There is no record of anyone throwing the switch under the locomotive but Murphy's Law makes it likely this must have happened.

The civil engineer that surveyed the line in the Burke regime must have had small understanding of railway operations to have located the junction here. In any case Evans would have approved the site. No more than a hundred yards to the summit on the already existing Coe Hill line, siting the junction another hundred yards or so further, this operating headache need never have existed. Apart from individual frustrations there were the costs over the years in man-hours and fuel.

Southbound from Maynooth, the direction of loaded trains, the ruling grade was just past Turrif (approximately 12 miles south of Bancroft) and the worst of the two. It was known to the railroaders as "The Nobs." At the foot of the grade was Nobs Siding, built as a refuge for trains doubling the hill — by no means a rare event.[37]

The Bessemer Mine's railway was worked by the C.O.R., like the Marmora line, though in this case apparently not under lease. The junction was around a mile and a half south of L'Amable (Detlor) and if the despatcher had new orders for the train at the junction it often meant the agent there had some walking to do.[38]

The Bessemer Mine had two locomotives;

one was a small, ancient American type. It is reported as having been a former C.O.R. locomotive. If so this must have been bought fourth or fifth hand from the Gilmour Lumber Co. An old photograph in the possession of David Hanes of L'Amable, skillfully enlarged, suggests this. The other possible candidate is locomotive (No. 3) sold by the C.O.R. in 1891, purchaser unknown. This is a mystery that remains to be solved. The other Bessemer locomotive was an ancient dinky (two axles).

What the picture does prove is that she was not powerful enough to haul anything approaching an economic load to the main line. Instead she confined her labours to shifting cars about the mine — except at one time she is said to have brought those that lived near the mine on round trips to Bancroft and back. They were courageous folk!

The unusual feature of this line were the two roller-coaster grades of fearsome steepness down and up Egans Creek, not far from the main line. The more cautious crewmen did their best to avoid this run. After the I.B. & O. became part of C.O.R. operations, this became part of their duties, alternating with the freight train north of Bancroft.[39] It might also have been based on the logic that any man who could work trains on the I.B. & O. would find the Bessemer line no worse.

The line is said to have been laid with light steel. Possibly some of the 42-lb. rail from the Picton line was used. In later years it was definitely 56-lb. steel, the same as many miles on the C.O.R., but like the Bessemer engine, it may have been very second-hand indeed, for much of the time money was scarce. Track maintenance was said to have been minimal. But these were only additional factors to the main hazard. The trip down to Egan's Creek and the wooden trestle at the bottom was one to remember.

The Child's and Rankine Mines shared a common crusher. The Child's was situated on the side of a hill. This little "Dinky", origin unknown did the work. This is also an interesting social group. 1908 photo.   *Photo, David Hanes*

The Child's Loco again, but a more complete view.   *Photo, David Hanes*

The earliest photographs show the ore being loaded into gondolas instead of the short, standard ore cars. This could be to give a better distribution of the weight. There is no record of how heavily they were allowed to be loaded. But in later years, when more powerful locomotives were available, four loaded cars was the limit. Even with this it meant a wild ride down grade to rush the hill or the locomotive would stall. This grade was known as "Gobbler's Nob."[40]

The names Gobbler's Nob and Nobs Siding have no common origin. Nobs Siding was named after a local settler who farmed nearby. Gobbler's Nob came from the shape of this odd hill, it resembled a turkey's head and neck.[41]

Mr. Herman Snider of L'Amable, for many years the station agent there, remembers taking this ride with his young son. The occasion was many years after the mine had closed, the year 1939. (The line was still in use carrying the output of two sawmills.) Four ore cars were being shipped out for some special analysis.

The engineer, named Grant, had a reputation as a runner. Sitting in the van the run downgrade was exciting enough, but when they hit the trestle Herman thought the whole train had left the track. After a lifetime of railroading this still remains his most frightening experience.[42] There are no records of any serious accidents here.

As mentioned earlier the mining company complained bitterly of the 50¢ a ton rate the C.O.R. charged them. This seems to have contributed to the short life of the mine. However, for the C.O.R., this must have been a costly operation with only 160 to 180-ton payload.

There were also two other mines situated in close proximity and about two and a half miles past the Bessemer, the Rankine and Child's. The first was eventually worked out. But both the Bessemer and Child's are said to contain large reserves.

These two mines possessed another locomotive, a "dinky" not only small but incredibly ancient. She was kept busy bunting cars across to a common crusher.[43]

Other individually owned locomotives were at Gilmour's in Trenton and the Deloro Mining and Smelting Company. These belonging to Gilmour remain an unknown number. A dinky, like the one at the Rankine mine, was seen several times working there around the turn of the century. It is likely there were others.

The Deloro Mine also had a dinky, but a large and modern machine. Here the company operated its own tracks and yards, picking up and leaving cars on the C.O.R. siding at the north end of Marmora Station.[44]

Chapter Nineteen

Mackenzie and Mann having far greater financial resources, were able to proceed with long delayed developments on and around the C.O.R. in 1910. As they now owned the Irondale, Bancroft and Ottawa Railway a high priority would be given to the many needs of this line, particularly after having already given notice of their intentions to fulfill that railway's original charter.

The first and obvious move was to extend the track to the C.O.R. line. For the northerners this would be the event of the year. The I.B. & O. was now leased to the C.O.R. for five years. Its accounts would be kept separately.

Following this George Collins was appointed general manager of both lines.[1] After the three-mile gap was closed, 51.9 miles would be added to the system, plus whatever mileage was completed that year on the northern extension. In all the C.O.R. would grow during 1910 from 149 miles to nearly 210 miles.

The costly task was also begun to upgrade the railway, to catch up with the neglected maintenance. The original construction of the line had been poor and derailments were routine, so much so that these were frequently not reported in the local press unless someone was seriously injured or killed, or there were some unusual circumstances.

On the I. B. & O. sub-division. Bob Clarke. The famous Frank Askey and George Thomson, train agent. Date unknown.

Photo, Earl Hawley

Bob Colling, telegraph operator. W. A. Ward, Supt. I. B. & O. sub-division and George Thomson, train agent
— not wearing his uniform on this day.

Photo, Earl Hawley

The railway did not possess a great deal of equipment: three ancient old "Kettles", one of which had been the only locomotive owned by a former broad-gauge railway rebuilt to standard gauge.[2] Another was leased. Two were ready for scrapping and another needed heavy repairs. Once the lines were connected George Collins would not allow any of these engines over 'his' line until, if not scrapped, they had been completely overhauled.[3]

Passengers, mail and express, as well as freight were carried by mixed trains. Indeed regular freights were not scheduled for the railway did not own a van (caboose). In freight cars all the company owned were 28 flats and two boxcars.[4]

There was an extremely heavy grade, 3.6% at Baptiste Hill, nine miles from Bancroft. Pulling anything but a light train meant doubling, even trebling the hill. The line abounded in sharp curves. Passengers could only take life as it came; with the railway's reputation they likely could not expect otherwise.[5]

Fatal accidents were rare. One reason was that speed was restricted to 15 miles an hour. Consequently, derailed equipment tended to remain upright. The other reason was the enormous skill the railroaders acquired from such operating difficulties. Three examples of the kinds of mishaps that could happen are described. These took place in 1911, when the line was still being brought up to C.O.R. standards.

In February the Bancroft Times reported that the I. B. & O. train had stalled on Saturday at Gooderham, 34 miles away, "Another locomotive breakdown ... Another engine was despatched to bring the train in. But it was Sunday before she reached Bancroft at 2 o'clock." The reporter omitting to state whether this was in the morning or afternoon.[6]

On a Friday night in late September, the coach left the train and headed for the woods. In the process a 100 yards of track were torn up. With a minimum of delay the passengers, and presumably the mail, were put into an empty ore car and "the run to Bancroft was made without further mishap."[7]

In early December five freight cars derailed.

It was thought the rails had spread, if so it could have been caused by rotten ties. This time only the engine was left mobile. So the passengers, about twenty in number, rode the rest of the way in the locomotive. On the small locomotive the fireman must have had problems.[8]

Returning to 1910, before the two lines had been connected after a delay of twenty years. The local speculation was that this would come about on July 1st as the ballast train had already been observed working on the new section. Whatever the delays this did not take place until Monday, September 12th, when the first revenue train whistled into Bancroft Station.[9]

Taken in Canadian Northern Days; an unknown locomotive draws into Union Depot.

Photo, David Hanes

As was customary along the C.O.R. there was no official ceremony, but a big crowd appeared to welcome the train and greet the officials and crew members.[10]

The arrival of the train brought with it exciting prospects for the community as a railway centre, especially when (and if) the Ottawa line was built. One is also reminded that although the station and tracks still stand today, there are no more trains. But this is how the editor of the Bancroft Times, seventy years ago, expressed the feelings of the community, "Bancroft. Change cars for Kinmount, Junction, Fenelon Falls, and points east. Listen to that now. We are getting to be some pumpkins as a railway centre." Further on he happily referred to the depot, it became local custom, as "Union Station."[11]

To add to his optimism an engine house was

already under construction. A turntable was already there.

With the new train service over the I.B. & O., in spite of the slow speeds, Toronto could now be reached the same day. Happier still were the passengers who no longer had to transfer to the stage at Mud River for the slow, jolting trip to Bancroft. Happiest of all were the commercial travellers with their big sample trunks.

Back in April, a month after George Collins had taken over, Hutchinson, superintendent of the I. B. & O., resigned. No reason was given, nothing is known of his ability or character, but if only for

running the line he deserved a hero's farewell. R.H. Derbyshire of the C.O.R. succeeded him.[12] I. B. & O., personnel became part of the C.O.R. operating over both lines.

The C.O.R. also inherited a staunch character, well-known around for many years, Fred Askey, brakeman and unofficial wrecking-boss. Unfortunately he had little formal education and was too nervous to take the official examination for conductor. His friends believed otherwise, but could not persuade him to try. He then had to suffer for many years working under younger men whose knowledge and talents were inevitably less.

The last remaining track of what was once The Irondale, Bancroft and Ottawa. The structure is a Domtar chip-board mill. When it closed down in 1975 this was the end of traffic south to Marmora. 1977 Photo. *Photo, Author*

Abandoned roadbed near Wallace.   *Photo, Author*

His abilities in rerailing cars were quite remarkable. With speed and judgment he could fasten the chains to such a car from the locomotive, and work them back to the line and back on the tracks, all without further damage and with great speed. Over the years he must have saved the I.B. & O. a lot of money.[13]

The only mishap on the Bessemer grade took place during a winter of the late twenties when the snow plow derailed half-way up the hill to the main line. Fortunately Fred Askey was one of the train crew. He soon had the chains hooked on and with the help of the locomotive and the gradient soon had the plow back on the rails.

Another oddity of the grade was that the rails constantly expanded in hot weather but never contracted as much when the temperature cooled. Likely this was because of the weight of the rails on the slope. As a result the rails used to kink. The lesser ones the train crew used to beat down on their way in; the worse ones the section crew had to cut. Over the years these stretched-out rails must have become thinner and lighter than their original weight.

These two items were learnt from Mr. Stanley Maxwell, retired engineer of Marmora, who ran into the Messemer Mine area for many years.

The line would always be known in the area as the I.B. & O., though its legal name would be changed four times before its life ended in 1960.

The winter of 1909-10 was an in-between one, though more severe than that of the previous year. On January 27th the southbound train from Maynooth became stuck in a drift a few miles short of Bancroft. Under certain conditions along this sandy stretch a mixture of sand and snow could fill the few cuts. Packed hard this was difficult to clear. The train finally reached Bancroft 24 hours later. A tough experience for the train crew and passengers. Of this the editor of the Marmora Herald, 60 miles to the south, commented piously, "Another reason for being thankful we didn't live in the northern wilds."[14]

In February, during another snow storm, the railway's difficulties were increased when, at the height of the blizzard, the plow was derailed at Bancroft. North to Maynooth the line remained blocked for several days.[15]

Other operating mishaps that year were few in number. Only one had to be reported to the Railway Commissioners. This was in June when a brakeman was killed in Trenton yards. Nobody saw the accident happen when the man was crushed between two freight cars.[16]

Another accident, that might have been more serious, but for good fortune and quick thinking, took place on February 9th on the Picton to Trenton train, a mile east of Bloomfield. At the throttle was George Neun, who more than a quarter century earlier had been fireman of the first train into Picton. What happened was that with a shattering crash the side rod broke with one end flailing the cab. He managed to stop the train quickly. Often a fractured rod killed the engineer, even piercing the boiler so that the escaping steam prevented the surviving fireman or engineer from stopping the train. George Neun was lucky, receiving only a slight foot injury. So was the C.O.R., although it took four hours to clear the track.[17]

Another accident that did not show in the government reports was in July, a head-on collision between handcars, a pathos-bathos affair. The Coe Hill section foreman had two handcars, one old, one new. One afternoon Patrick Finnegan lent the old one to a young man who wanted to go to Ormsby on business one Saturday.

Later that evening, after dark, Finnegan, his wife and family set off for Ormsby. At the bottom of a dip, going fast, he was abruptly reminded that his other car was around. Neither party carried a light. Patrick sailed through the air for some fifteen feet to land on his head. He received a severe cut and a shaking up. Off again, on again! His unfortunate wife, sitting on the front, had one foot badly crushed. As the paper's editor concluded laconically, she was taken to hospital on Monday morning.[18]

Abandoned roadbed, near the final end of steel.   *Photo, Author*

Like many of the mining enterprises along the C.O.R. the graphite mine was bigger than is generally realized. An interesting item was that the mine products were shipped to the C.O.R. at Maynooth by wagon train hauled by a steam tractor.

Photo, David Hanes

In May a special train of the Bay of Quinte railway, arrived via Bannockburn, bringing E.W. Rathbun to Bancroft. His visit brought bad news for the community, his mill there would be closed down. From then on the logs would be shipped directly to Deseronto,[19] via Bannockburn. The C.O.R. benefitted by the bigger loads.

A work program was announced that March from Canadian Northern headquarters in Toronto. A new steel bridge was to be built over Beaver Creek, near St. Ola. This was the stream where a comparatively big dam was opened to flush the logs down those sluggish waters. The original structure must have taken a lot of punishment. The new bridge would be completed early that summer.

Back in January there had been the annual complaints from Marmora about the lack of service on the branch. In March the Canadian Northern announced the line would be ballasted (probably for the first time) and a tri-weekly mixed train service would be inaugurated.[20]

The owner and editor of the Marmora Herald, who had long campaigned for this, as well as for the expansion of that community, received a final visit from the bailiff that spring, a poor reward. And that was the end of the newspaper.[21]

A month later that admirable editor, and officer of the militia, Lt. Colonel J.R. Orr, his health declining, sold his North Hastings Review. The purchaser was the local high school principal[22] who would not be successful, although the newspaper survived. Sadly Orr had not long to live. But he deserves to be remembered as a great journalist among weekly newspapers.

Work had started early that year on the northern extension. Back again was the contractor's engineer in charge, Mr. Wallace,[23] well thought of by the local people. Construction had now become difficult. The area consisted of hills of solid rock, swamps and lakes.

By the end of October the track extended 34 miles from Bancroft. Thirty miles of this was finished. Two miles had yet to be ballasted, using the same light gravel, or coarse sand. For the last four miles 75 per cent of the permanent roadbed remained to be completed. Telegraph poles had been erected to the end of the track. There was now only a ten mile gap between the end of steel and Whitney.[24] Samuel Ritchie's goal could be reached in another year.

The parent Canadian Northern was close to its peak in rapid expansion, and in nearly every province. Their most important line under construction was the lakeshore main line, eastwards from Toronto. This spring the company had announced that instead of building this year as far as Trenton, they would reach Belleville. Forty miles of the line had already been graded, the work being carried out from fifteen different points. The equipment and supplies grudgingly delivered by the Grand Trunk often but a few steps from their own busy line.

On April 19th, the first spike was driven joining the Central Ontario Railway to the Canadian Northern. But this had more significance as a corporate event than in operations. It was an isolated spur built for the convenience of construction, providing delivery of ties and poles from the north.

The Canadian Northern was moving fast. Purchase of additional land to that already owned by the C.O.R. was almost complete. A new roundhouse was under construction. Canadian Northern officials were now occupying offices in Trenton Station though they were only interested in the construction of their new main line.[25]

What was appreciated by C.O.R. employees, at all levels, was the press release from Toronto headquarters that all the smaller lines recently acquired would receive the benefit of Canadian Northern's standard equipment in locomotives and cars. The C.O.R. engines, though none of them was second-hand, were light power, even the newer locomotives compared to what the rails could carry. Most of the engines were now old and just about worn out.

The end of steel on the Central Ontario Railway extension at the beginning of 1911 was now 148.2 miles from Picton, or 117.6 from Trenton, and 41.7 from Bancroft. More important, the line was now only eight miles from Whitney, (joined) at a point that joined the old Hastings Colonization Road. A year's work could easily complete the line. But no additional track would ever be laid.

Construction would continue this year but with reduced crews. A deep cut was blasted through the next rocky hill, the spoil being used to provide fill across a creek; it would never receive any rails.[26]

Most of the construction gang spent the summer finishing off the track and roadbed to mile 41.7 bringing the line up to government standards to qualify for the subsidies. After the inspecting engineer had approved the work on this final section the company would receive payment at year's end,[27] subject to certain small holdbacks.

It was the intent to finish the line when more important work was completed as requests for subsidy renewals would be made and approved by government up until 1914.[28] As this would be the final terminus of the C.O.R. it deserves some attention.

The location had quickly become known as Wallace after the enterprising engineer-in-charge for the contractors. Nowadays few people in the region have ever heard of the place, let alone the man.

When the railway arrived there were some ten or so farms. All were occupied by pioneer settlers who had cleared the land themselves, finding a good proportion of fertile land among the rocky hills, lakes and streams. There remained a considerable expanse of woodland and plenty of game.[29]

This was a Roman Catholic community, as devout as they were resourceful. They had built their own small church; behind it was the cemetery on the side of the hill.

A shallow ravine ran across the front of the church shared by the rails with the rough roadway. South on the other side of the railway is the Lavalley farmhouse. That summer a wye was added.

Nearby was the big, two storey, boarding house. At capacity around 150 immigrant labourers lived here. After that the numbers dwindled.[30] Running this establishment with a firm hand was a Mrs. Duval. Paddy Birkett was the cook.[31] The structure itself was constructed of rough lumber from the nearby forests. As with nearly all such temporary camps there were no foundations, so nothing is left to show it once existed.

Wallace had opened a general store here as a sideline. Both the labourers and the settlers found it convenient. The owner found it profitable. Managing the store was John Keogh who came from a well-known family at the other end of the line, Prince Edward County.[32]

The farmers found the railway a great benefit when the freight service started in April. They could now get good prices for a winter's logging. Cars were left at the wye on a short siding for loading.[33]

Before long, one F. Walsh built a small lumber mill half a mile south. Two miles further on the McCrae Lumber Co. built a bigger mill.[34]

The freight trains used to lay over for an hour before returning; the train crews becoming accepted as part-time members of the community.

South, 4.4 miles from Wallace, was McConnell's, but no more than a name in the working timetable.

The only station north of Maynooth was Lake St. Peter, a half-way house, 7.9 miles from Wallace and 8 miles from Maynooth. Here a siding was provided.

This was the northernmost station on the system, although it never officially served any passengers. Later, in the 1970's, when the line was lifted southwards, this point became the end of steel, the station long gone. Afterwards a washout took out a trestle and a short length of track a hundred yards back, leaving, so to speak, a double end of steel. And so it remained in 1979. When further track is lifted remains to be seen.

Present day Wallace has only two farms. When the McCrae Mill closed, so did the line back to Lake St. Peter. The number of farms around Wallace grew fewer.

The Lavalley farm still stands, well kept. Joseph Lavalley is now over seventy years of age. Though in good health he is less active. Across from the farm, over the abandoned roadbed with the ties rotting under a heavy growth of alders, is the foundation of the former church. To the left is a more recent structure, a community hall no longer used.

The graveyard is not neglected. But one's eye is caught and held by a tall, slender, white cross rising as high, perhaps, as the church once stood. It is freshly painted. A memorial of the community — but also, if unintentionally, to the work of many who spoke no English, no French, and who worked hard to build a strange, cold country. A memorial, moreover, for a railway and another foreigner, Samuel Ritchie, and his brave dreams that would never be realized.

There is an odd postscript. In the early twenties the Dennis Lumber Co. built a logging road south from Whitney. Whether the company hoped to sell its rough and ready roadbed to the Canadian National Railways, who by then owned all the common carriers in the area is not known. But the line ended up within 800 yards of the C.O.R.'s trackless rock cut and fill.[35] When the lumber company had cleared out the woods the tracks were lifted. Quiet descended again over the rocks, the waters, and the tree stumps.

The Grand Trunk management, no doubt in the person of Charles M. Hays, seem to have wanted the connection with their line at Whitney more than Mackenzie and Mann. Frustrated by what amounted to the end of construction past Wallace the Grand Trunk sent out a survey crew in April, 1911, to select yet another route between Barry's Bay and the I.B. & O.,[36] presumably at York River junction.

This may have been a bluff. Although the I.B. & O. could carry traffic to Kinmount Junction and Grand Trunk rails, the bluffing theory is more probable. The 3.64% grade plus the curves and light rail of that line could never have handled anything approaching heavy traffic. What was already handled was a costly enough operation.

Whatever the purposes of the Grand Trunk they were lost at sea when Hays was drowned in the sinking of the Titanic in the following year on April 14th, 1912.

With each passing year there were changes along the C.O.R. In February William Weddell appeared up north. He had bought the Bessemer Mine,[37] likely on speculation, for he sold it the following year to Canada Iron Mines, a Toronto syndicate.

More positive news was the opening of the Canadian Talc Company's mine near Eldorado. It was reported in February that the C.O.R. would build a spur line into their operations.[38]

That same month the graphite mine was opened, and the flag stop between Maynooth and Hybla followed. This was a rich deposit and would bring considerable traffic to the railway. Graphite, as the Bancroft Times pointed out, was used in more than pencils, it was used for gunpowder, crucibles, steel and in the manufacture of electric lights.[39]

In the spring the Toronto syndicate bought

the Blairton mine at the end of the Marmora branch. It had been closed for many years. They followed this up by purchasing a site on part of the former Gilmour property in Trenton and would soon start building a concentrator plant to process the iron ores from the Hastings mines[40] — shades of one of Ritchie's biggest defeats.

In May there was a disastrous forest fire round Lake St. Peter that brought heavy losses to the Rathbun Co. In the settlement five homes were destroyed as well as the C.O.R. station.[41] The railway would lose more than the cost of the station in carloadings.

Operations that year were without fatalities. There were three mishaps, all took part in the third month, and all were within a few miles of each other, just south of Bancroft. There was variety though.

The first was no more than a minor mishap. Two miles south of L'Amable, a Grand Trunk boxcar jumped the tracks. Two hours later the crew had the car on the rails and the train was on its way again.[42]

A few days later the locomotive of a southbound freight broke down near Turrif. The train finally reached Trenton some 12 hours late.[43]

The third accident, more serious, was when the passenger train ran into an open switch at the marble quarry near Bancroft. The engine and a flatcar landed in a swamp, but the baggage car and the coach remained upright. Even the crew of the locomotive escaped injury. Whether the open switch was the fault of a careless brakeman or the section gang was not revealed. The wrecking crew had several days work recovering the locomotive.[44]

If the accident gremlins working this section of track disliked railroads, at least they were humane.

While the C.O.R. was busy that year, Trenton was busier than it had ever been before, beyond the dreams of earlier civic optimism. These were also boom times for Canada.

Although freight services had started some weeks earlier, the big event of this year was the arrival of the first passenger train from Toronto.

The town, although it had other industries, had not been prosperous since Gilmours had closed down their operations. The Canadian Northern Railway had yet to be completed to Ottawa. The freight yard, south-west of the town was under construction. The bridge across the Trent would be completed in November. East and west, grading and track-laying crews were busy. The building of the C.P.R.'s lakeshore line was now a certainty. The future looked even brighter.

"Old Boys" Special heading for Picton. It has just passed Bloomfield. Picture taken around 1910.

Photo, Homer Talcot

No. 12, at the gravel pit north of Bancroft. One would guess the engineer is identifiable by the oil can while the fireman looks out of the engineer's window.

Photo, Western Reserve Historical Society

J.D. Evans, C.E., was chief engineer of the Central Ontario Railway and a much respected citizen of Trenton. Interested in entomology he maintained a valuable collection of insects at "Springbank" his fine residence. Elected president of the Entomological Society of Ontario he held various offices in that Society.

George Collins, General Manager and a Director of the Central Ontario Railway, attained his chief post through ability, sound business judgment and years of railroad experience, having held various positions with the railway. Mr. Collins was born in Ameliasburg and educated in the Trenton schools. His wife was the former Miss Annie Snook.

The bottom of the Bessemer grade as it is today. The old roadbed can be seen in the distance climbing up through the woods.

Photo, David Hanes

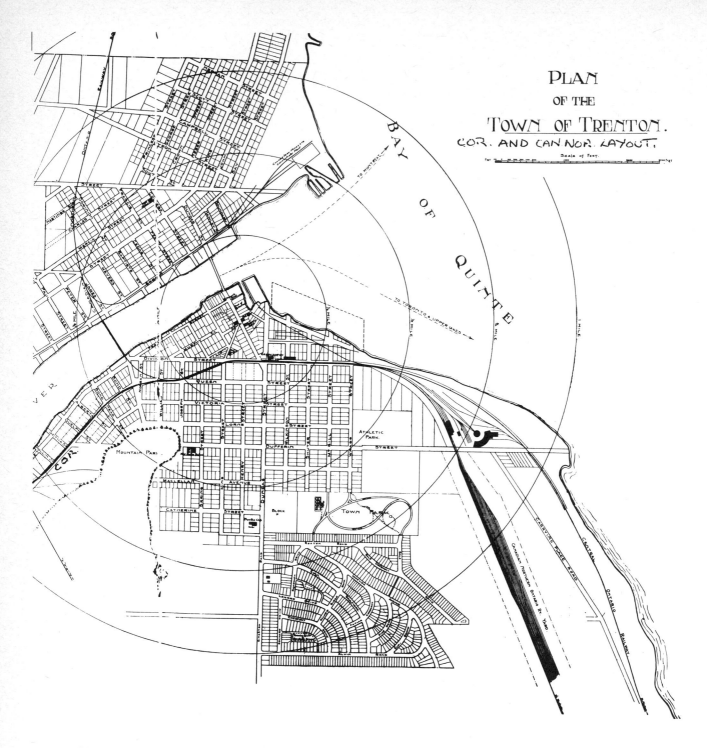

Map of Central Ontario and Canadian Northern facilities at Trenton. 1912

From "Evolution of Trenton"

Head-end of first through train from Toronto. Locomotive is Canadian Northern No. 229 making the C.O.R. engines look puny. 1914.

Photo, Western Reserve Historical Society

G.A. Hoag, a citizen of value to the community, was born in Walters Falls.County of Grey, May 31, 1866. He later moved to Cardinal and then to Kingston in 1877. Associated with the Grand Trunk Railway until 1905 in the capacities of telegraph operator, agent and yard master, he resigned from the Grand Trunk to become Train Master of the Central Ontario Railway, finally holding office of the superintendency for several years. Mr. Hoag, active in the Methodist church, was also president of the Young Men's Christian Association and a member of the Public Library Board. A sportsman, he valued honourable conduct in the games at all times.

Trenton Station after the first Canadian Northern Passenger Train's arrival from Toronto.

Hastings County Museum

Premier Roblin of Manitoba visits the family home in Prince Edward County. The private car is newly varnished. The braces across the station roof were copper sheathed. The skylights over each of the fourteen doors were stained glass with the C.O.R. monogram. (See Illustration)

The headquarters offices of the C.O.R. above the station had become crowded with Canadian Northern officials.

Along the C.O.R. there was uncertainty and much speculation, particularly as to when the title would be changed to Canadian Northern.

There was little sentiment among the employees. With the Canadian Northern paying union wages this was to be expected. But there was also some unease. The final takeover could also mean transfers. Station agents knew they would be the first to be moved. Section gangs knew they would be the last, for nobody could know better the strengths and weaknesses of the track of their own sections.

In September 1911 the Canadian Northern "formally took over the C.O.R." This meant C.E. Ritchie was in town, and there was a special to carry Canadian Northern officials over the system.

There followed some changes. At the station the Canadian Express signs came down and Canadian Northern Express signs went up.[45] There were some modest adjustments in train schedules. Otherwise it remained the Central Ontario Railway with George Collins as general manager, and C.E. Ritchie as president. Accounts continued to be carried separately.

Shippers along the line believed they could only get better service from the bigger corporation. Trentonians were delighted to see the monopoly of the Grand Trunk about to be ended.

The public also had expectations. In an age that enjoyed passenger service they were convinced the railway could bring them more punctual trains (and mail), and better passenger equipment. Some of C.O.R. coaches were, by now, decidedly ancient, even if well maintained.

For the C.O.R. this would be the best year yet in both traffic and profits. The present Canadian Northern was at the height of its extraordinary expansion with its western lines yet to penetrate the Rockies, the Montreal tunnel still to be bored, and the Toronto to Ottawa line nearing completion. London bankers were willing to lend huge sums to those two adventurous partners — provided the bonds were guaranteed by the federal government. The future could not have looked better.

In the C. O. R. Yards at Trenton

Chapter Twenty

George McMullen, long absent from the railway scene, was back as the promoter of one of two projected radial railways in Prince Edward County. He proposed to build the long projected line to South Bay, but with additions. Eventually it would be a feeder to the C.O.R.

Radial railways were popular at this time, but with the automobile age not far off those that were built would have short lives. The majority would be electrified becoming long distance street railways with freight services in varying proportions or with none at all.

In September, 1911, McMullen held a meeting at Cherry Valley Town Hall. This meeting was followed by a second in Milford. The residents of the two communities showed considerable interest, to the extent that there were a number of offers to buy stock. The general sentiment was that the line must be owned by County people.[1] But what had George McMullen been up to over these past years? Could he at least partly finance such a line by now?

George McMullen had become even more prolific an inventor. As with many who follow this uncertain calling, some of his ideas had been successful, others had not. When he had needed capital for some bigger project, a trip to the United States usually seems to have been successful. Local backers had become scarce.

One particular invention that appears to have been profitable was a process for making paper out of sugar cane pulp. The giant United Fruit Corporation had backed him in this. A success that 'might have been' was pioneering the reduction of liquid milk into powder. The experiment had been carried out in his Picton home; the entire household becoming involved for many months. Once this had been a success, without bothering to patent the process, he moved on to some other idea that had caught his attention.

His centre of operations was Beaver Meadow, five miles from Picton. This was an extraordinary agricultural-industrial complex of several hundred acres. He employed as many as forty men and extensive buildings were erected. The number of ideas that flowed from his undoubtedly brilliant mind ranged from growing ginseng to celery, from new explosives to a monster cannon that had no takers. At this time he was developing a new process for creosoting railway ties.

Over the years in this continuous creative fever he used up more money than he made. The answer to the question posed earlier was that he did not have sufficient funds to finance a radial line.

In the background, it seems, was "Banker" Wilson, his former backer when he purchased the original Prince Edward County Railway. Wilson now owned the electric power company in Picton. There was the usual power surplus in off-peak hours, plus a small margin. McMullen proposed drawing additional power from the famous Lake on the Mountain, at Glenora, though the volume of water available had not at that time been measured.

At the two meetings George McMullen was quite open. He envisaged a spur line to Beaver Meadow, and he told the meeting he expected to be shipping two hundred carloads a year. He did not say what commodity would be shipped, perhaps creosoted ties.[2] His enthusiasm made it plain that he had not lost his interest in railways.

His description of the line showed he had undertaken some careful planning. It was to start from Picton docks, as he had planned in his proposal of many years earlier. This section at that time should have proved profitable and not too costly to construct as he proposed to come to an agreement with town council to lay track along some side streets.[3]

George W. McMullen in his sixties.

Courtesy, Mrs. J. Milne

Once clear of the town, crossing the C.O.R., he would follow the old route of the original line as projected to Cherry Valley, past Milford to the head of South Bay, but no further. At Port Milford, where there was a big canning factory, a lake terminal would be built.[4]

From Port Milford a new line would be built to Black Creek, and from there back to Picton, to complete the radial. At least part of the line would be surveyed and agreements made for purchasing of the right-of-way.

Another radial was envisaged through Bloomfield and Wellington villages, south via West Point and back to Picton. These communities are all shown on the map of the other more ambitious scheme.[5]

The role of these lines as can be envisaged by their routes was to provide the equivalent of pickup trucks and buses. These lines would have had to struggle for their existence long before the advent of paved roads.

For George McMullen progress was slow. The years 1912 and 1913 were years of recession following the boom, particularly in the capital market. Once it became painfully real after the First World War had started that the boys would not be home for Christmas that was the end of the scheme and many like it.

The other proposed system of radial lines, bigger and more ambitious, probably contributed as much as anything to McMullen's failure to make further progress. No charter was ever sought for his project, neither does his proposed line appear to have been given a name.

George McMullen's home life was that of the well-to-do. Still living in the big house on Main Street, it verged on the ideal. His grandchildren recall him as a good and kind grandfather. The domestic staff also found him kind and generous. He respected them as fellow human beings. Once a month he permitted them to have the house to themselves to entertain their relatives and friends. He treated his other employees with respect, listening attentively to their ideas.

The McMullen house was well-known for the musical evenings held there. They amounted to an 'open house'. Those that could play brought their musical instruments; others were expected to sing. The only tone deaf member of the family was George himself. Unabashed, he joined the choruses in full voice, to be accepted with uncritical affection by all present. He appears to have been a humorous, dignified, easy to approach gentleman. Definitely there were two sides to George McMullen.

George McMullen died on March 23, 1915.

He died while riding a suburban train out of Chicago. Accompanied by his son Barrett, he was on his way to sell his new creosoting process at a railway convention.

As might be expected his death was unusual. He had been reading a newspaper when he came across an installment of Mark Twain's famous anti-religious writings, published posthumously. They were extremely witty. George laughed out loud. The more he read, the more he laughed, finally so heartily that he had a stroke, and died on the train — in the country he loved best.

McMullen, for better or for worse, had left his mark. He was after all the principal figure in the first major event of Canadian history after Confederation; the fall of its first parliament.

In February, 1912, the Trentonian reported that an application had been made for a charter to construct a new railway in Prince Edward County. Those signing were all men of substance in the county: G.M. Farrington and Thomas Walmsley of Picton, W.H. Gough of Bloomfield, Harry Dempsey of Albury, and W.P. Niles of Wellington. The last named was the son of S.P. Niles, who had done so much to promote the original line. He was the owner of a big seed warehouse in that town and employed a hundred men.

Earlier the editor of the Picton Gazette had warned the C.O.R. that with the high freight rates, a rival line would be built some day. Here was the rival line. Proposed initially, as part of the whole plan, was a 28-mile line from Picton via Bloomfield and Wellington to the Murray Canal. (see map) For this proposal a charter was received, dated April 6, 1912. A subsidy of $6,400 per mile was sought based on an estimated cost of $22,500 per mile. The line would run through open farmland with only a 25-foot creek to be bridged.[6]

The Trenton newspaper found the farmers to be happy over this proposal, but editorialised, "We will hope that the people applying for incorporation to the Dominion Government mean business, and it might be a fair story to suspect that one of the Trunk lines now running through Trenton and Belleville is behind the scheme."[7] Could this mean the Grand Trunk with the C.P.R. only starting construction? But the editor gave no further clues.

The new line was incorporated as the Prince Edward and Hastings Railway Company. The original map is reproduced showing the line as originally chartered. Additional lines projected are shown in dots, though only approximate routes are known.

On the same date another charter was granted for further extensions. (Approximate routes of these extensions are also shown in dots.) This is an abbreviated description of these routes: ". . . from a route at or near Trenton .., by the most feasible route to Gardenville .., then easterly via Albury, Rednersville, and Rossmore to the city of Belleville; thence north-westerly to Frankford and back to Trenton," thus completing the radial. It may have been intended the railway share the road bridge to Belleville, if this was the case, the bridge would have needed strengthening.

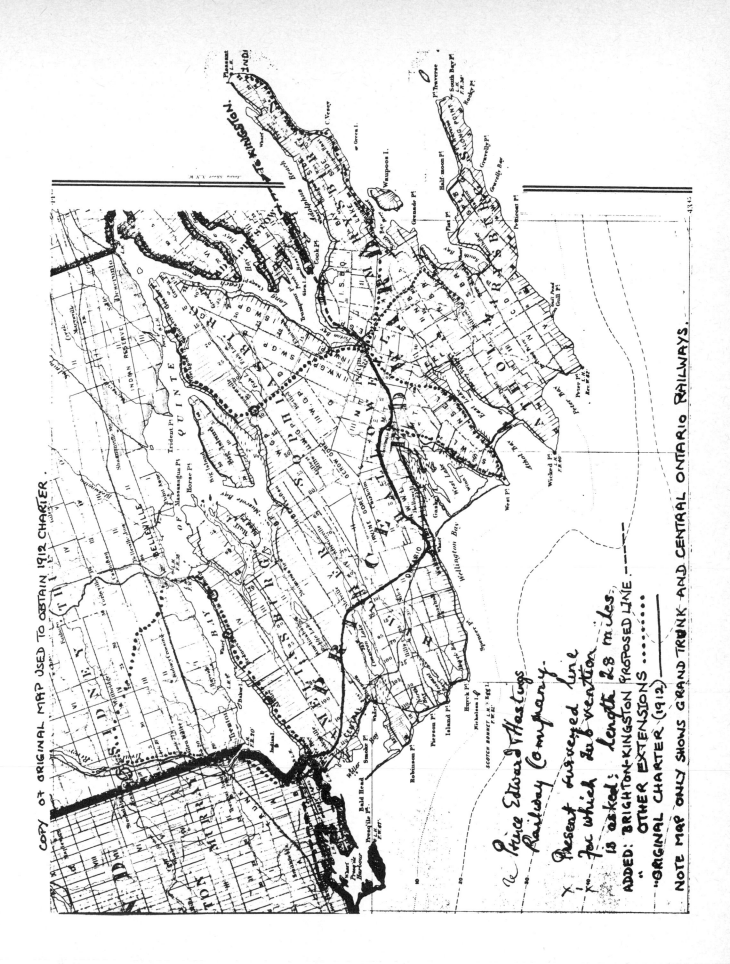

COPY OF ORIGINAL MAP USED TO OBTAIN 1912 CHARTER.

Prince Edward & Hastings Railway Company.

× ——— Present surveyed line
•———• For which Convention is asked: length 28 miles,
ADDED: BRIGHTON-KINGSTON PROPOSED LINE —————
  " OTHER EXTENSIONS ••••••••
"ORIGINAL CHARTER (1912)

NOTE MAP ONLY SHOWS GRAND TRUNK AND CENTRAL ONTARIO RAILWAYS.

Other lines were projected in this charter. One was to run from between Albury and Rednersville to join the other line "through or near" Bloomfield to form a second radial line. A non-radial branch was planned from a point "at or near Picton" north through Demorestville and Northport to Ferry Point (across the Bay of Quinte from Deseronto). A third (borrowing the plan from George McMullen) was a radial branching off from Bloomfield and West Point and back to Picton. The fourth was a branch to Black River (a half of McMullen's plan).[8] The fifth and last line was projected east to Waupoos and to Indian Point, at the eastern end of Prince Edward County. Some of these projected lines were surveyed. They would seem to have been overtaken by an even more ambitious scheme.

Undeterred by the need to raise millions of dollars, it was proposed to build a line from Brighton, west of Trenton, through to Picton, bridging the Glenora to Adolphustown ferry route and along, or near, the lakeshore to Kingston. This proposal, authorized by Dominion charter on May 28, 1914, would have been a major engineering work, particularly in crossing the Adolphus Reach. The mileage from Brighton to Kingston was estimated at 72 miles. A large proportion of the line, Brighton to Picton, would parallel the existing Canadian Northern lines. The Adolphus Reach between Glenora and Adolphustown remains to this day, a ferry crossing.[9]

Up until May, 1915, the syndicate seems to have been busy trying to raise funds, although some surveying was carried out. In this month, G. R. Hepburn, M.P. for Prince Edward County, came into this scheme as sponsor of the Bill. In the course of the hearings he was asked, "Is this railway for some large company now in existence?" His answer was "It is an independent company. The directors all reside in the County of Prince Edward." He indicated that this would be a steam railway. The Bill was duly passed.[10]

An optimist wrote to the Picton Times referring to "this long neglected historical and scenic route" anticipating that transcontinental passenger trains would pass along the line to the satisfaction of the passengers. He expressed surprise that Mackenzie and Mann should have let such an opportunity slip, but ... "Should the C.P.R. come into control of this line in the future ... it will outstrip and leave far in the shade all other transcontinental railways."[11] A demonstration, if nothing else, of positive thinking.

A possible, if dubious, clue to this was that the syndicate had obtained the charter on the chance that without laying a single rail they could sell it to the C.P.R. which had earlier been experiencing difficulty in gaining access to Belleville. The Canadian Northern had pre-empted the only practicable site remaining. This was partially sorted out by this becoming a joint station, though still owned by the Northern. For all that the Prince Edward and Hastings Railway sponsors were busy seeking a subsidy in the next session of parliament.

In May of that year a big meeting was held in Belleville city hall "to secure the building and operating of electric radial railways." There was a large group in attendance from Prince Edward County, among them W. P. Niles.[12]

This coincided with the passing, by Picton town council, of a resolution to investigate the practicability of constructing an electric railway from Belleville through Wellington and Picton to Deseronto. This project was not heard of again.

The death of the Prince Edward and Hastings Railway was informal. The pressures of war, the impracticability of such a scheme, capital funds almost impossible to obtain, ended the adventure. Maurice Clapp of Milford remembers how those involved, "met in Picton one night, quietly over a bottle." Next day the news was out that 'it was all over'.

Chapter Twenty-One

News of the 1912 rush by the Canadian Northern to complete its facilities in the Trenton area and to the east of the Ottawa line crowded the affairs of the Central Ontario Railway out of local newspapers and everyday conversation. Trentonians seemed to have forgotten this was still the headquarters of what had been 'their' railway.

As far as the public were concerned oblivion soon followed when gradually all the engines and passenger equipment were lettered "Canadian Northern" and renumbered to conform to that company's classification system. Before long the scrapping of the oldest locomotives would begin. But the C.O.R. was not deceased, her separate corporate identity remained.

By summer the new Northern roundhouse was half completed and in use. The adjoining machine shop was being equipped. The car works were opened in May. Before long all equipment repairs for the region would be handled here until additional facilities were opened near Ottawa. The C.O.R. facilities would become supplementary.

Traffic prospects for the C.O.R. looked good. Although it was short-haul traffic, two new paper mills at Frankford and Glen Miller would be good customers. Promising far greater revenues were the activities of the recently formed Canada Iron Company, now operating the mines at Blairton, Coe Hill and Bessemer. The new concentrator in Trenton, with one unit completed, was processing 350 tons of ore a day. When the plant was finished this would be increased to 1,000 tons.[1] Unfortunately the history of the Hastings iron mines would be repeated. Before long the entire operation would be closed.

The new developments were not enough to offset the effects of the economic recession. Instead C.O.R. earnings would be lower this year, not helped by a drought in the region.

The huge loans to the two new transcontinental railways, largely guaranteed by the federal government and seemingly unending, had become frightening to the London bankers. As the future would demonstrate, their caution came too late. This was competition running wild. The Northern's Mackenzie and Mann, faced with uncertain sources of new capital, were in a situation that would have reduced other men to timid caution. There was no going back on railway building in the east, but the expensive Montreal tunnel could have been delayed, and construction of the line through the Rockies to Vancouver halted, at least for the present. But with grim determination they pressed on.

With the Canadian Pacific building its own main line along the lakeshore, though the busiest route in Canada, there was no need for three main lines; one, the Grand Trunk, was double-tracked. Early in 1912 the C.P.R. had started approving tenders and the rate of construction would be breathtaking.

Trenton was becoming one of the busiest railway centres in Canada, but only until all the construction was finished. But from then on Trentonians believed, with some logic, that as the divisional point for two of the railways, Belleville would never catch up. If Trentonians could not forsee future problems, neither could Prime Minister Laurier, who had wanted to go down in history as 'the great railway builder.' He would leave a heritage of a country with more miles of rail per capita than any other country in the world, but with insufficient traffic to support them.

In April, amidst so many railway events of magnitude, Picton got into the news again when Canada's first gas-electric railcar (constructed in Schenectady, N.Y.) appeared in the town. This smart looking machine was the ancestor of today's diesel-electric locomotives, but more directly the rail-liners.

Can. Nor. Gas Electric Car No. 500. At Belleville on her first trip.

Courtesy, Roy Cornish, Trenton, Ont.

The car had arrived on an April Saturday from Toronto on its first official trip carrying both Sir William Mackenzie and Sir Donald Mann, accompanied by several senior officials and some journalists.

On the following Monday the car was turned over to the Central Ontario for a trip to Picton. It left at 2:45 p.m. carrying George Collins and a number of guests. "Spectators gathered all along the line." The journey took 45 minutes and the stop-over at Picton lasted half-an-hour. On the return journey the car overtook the regular train at Hillier. Allowing for this delay, the return journey took 38 minutes, the net time, 48.3 miles per hour.

The reporter who made the trip was "particularly impressed by the complete control of the operator over the car." On the Picton turntable, which may have been a tight fit, the car was "moved forward and backward a couple of inches with the same ease as when travelling under a high rate of speed."[2] (Technical details are given under the Motive Power Appendix.)

Later the gas-electric was to see more of the County. From Trenton it was despatched to Quebec City for the summer, carrying vacationers to Lake St. Joseph. In early fall the car returned to Trenton going into service between Napanee, Trenton and Picton.

Before long the car proved unreliable. This was partly because steam-trained technicians and engineers did not take easily to the internal combustion engine, or electric generators and motors. Also because this was an early date for these sciences. The car would depart elsewhere where the runs were shorter.

There was a rumour in the press, with or without foundation, that the Grand Trunk would be detouring through Trenton. Did this have any connection with the Prince Edward and Hastings Railway?

On January 23rd, 1913, the Canadian Northern headquarters announced that George Collins would succeed A. J. Hill as superintendent of the Trenton area. This was an important promotion for Collins. The C.O.R. was included in his new responsibilities. It was also another step towards integration of "his" old line into the Northern, which by now had 300 men on its Trenton payroll.

In February the first locomotive was brought in to the new shop for heavy repairs. Used in construction work, its condition was reported as "dilapidated." Already reclining in the shop was the unfortunate gas-electric.

The people of Prince Edward County had first welcomed the Northern's purchase of the C.O.R., with high hopes of better transportation and lower rates. By the summer of 1913, they had become angry and disillusioned. Hence their enthusiasm for the projected Prince Edward and Hastings Railway.

The Picton line, a captive one without competition, the Northern desperate for profits, had made the mistake of charging more than the traffic would bear. One by-product of this indignation was a sentimental regard for the "old C.O.R." That was something new.

Climax of their discontent came in July at a special Board of Trade meeting held in the Picton Public Library with representatives of the Farmers' Institute present. Among their grievances:

Passenger traffic: An endeavour to organize a 12th of July excursion had been turned down by the Northern because the company had no spare coaches. (No longer could the C.O.R. draw on the now rival Grand Trunk's large pool of ancient but serviceable coaches.)

Connections at Trenton disregarded the County people. In order to catch the early train to Toronto it had become necessary to stay at a hotel in Trenton for several hours; then take a cab for the two-mile journey to the Grand Trunk station. Mails were no longer affected. The meeting may not have been aware of it but it was a quicker journey from Bancroft.

Freight rates: The tariffs between Picton and Trenton had become "simply outrageous." Examples were given of the rates such as between Trenton and Niagara Falls, approximately 193 miles, a competitive route, which were lower than between Picton and Trenton, 30.6 miles.

Express shipments: This applied particularly to early fruits, important to the County economy. The "old C.O.R." — Grand Trunk combination had been far better. Now, not only were deliveries delayed, causing the fruit to spoil, but for this dubious privilege the charges were higher.

There was also another valid complaint not mentioned at the meeting. This was the length of time it took to obtain empty boxcars for loading. Under the old regime the local agent would call Trenton and the way freight would deliver them the following day. With car control moved to Toronto shippers could wait many days.[3]

At the end of the meeting those present were told that B. R. Hepburn, M.P. had already spoken to Mackenzie and Mann about their problems. He had been assured they would send a senior official down to meet with them.[4]

In August, G. H. Shaw, General Traffic Manager, came from Toronto. With him were other senior officials among them George Collins who seemed to be the junior man of the delegation. Not so long before he would have dealt with the matter himself with as much authority as Shaw, and many months earlier.

If anything was settled the newspapers did not say.

Other changes were becoming apparent, but the public still did business with the same train crews and agents at the stations.

By August the Northern was operating a passenger service as far as Napanee. The main line was built with 90 lb. rail, a big jump from the Prince Edward County's 42 lb. rail of 1879. Today 90 lb. rail is, of course, considered light.

The Canadian Pacific was catching up fast. Their high level bridge over the Trent would be completed that fall, looking down on the Northern's drawbridge, which, when the canal was finished could be an inconvenience. Their station would be closer to the town than the Grand Trunk's. By October, the C.P.R. line would be complete except for the unfinished bridge at Port Hope.

Everyday happenings and mishaps on the C.O.R. continued to retain a degree of originality and with the usual good fortune in the matter of human life.

There was Herb. Marshall of Wellington, one would assume, in a state of profound meditation when he drove his horse and rig over a level crossing oblivious to the approach of the regular train. The horse was killed. Herb was lucky.

Early one July morning while the Trenton yard engine was switching the dock sidings the engine crew managed to bunt a car over the edge onto the dredger "Dragon Rouge" (she was not of Weddell's fleet). The car all but demolished the deckhouse containing the crew's quarters. Luckily the dredger's crew were already up and about their work.

Unimportant, in the midst of all these important events, but when that well-liked conductor, 'Paddy' Shannon of the Picton run, lost the end of a finger in the door of a passenger car, he became the only senior member of a train crew for miles around with a mutilated digit not lost in a link-and-pin coupler.

Small cheques were still being received from the federal government on the balance due from the bonuses for the Wallace extension. Such a cheque, received early in 1912, reduced the amount due to less than a thousand dollars, that was until such time as work should start again.[5]

C.O.R. No. 7, Can. Nor. No. 41 built by Rogers in 1882. Scrapped in 1917. Taken at the Can. Nor./C.P.R. joint station in Belleville. The station was Can. Nor./Can. Nat. property for many years. Finally sold to C.P.R. Was a bus terminal for a short time before this handsome structure was demolished. The train would be the Picton via Trenton local. She would pick up a few freight cars on the way. Picture taken between 1912-17.

Photo, Charles Heels Collection of Lindsay, Ont.

In view of Mackenzie and Mann's troubled finances the account accompanying the cheque is of some significance. The last figure given by the company for completing the line to Whitney was $131,117.00. Deduct the round figure of $50,000.00 for bonuses based on the rate paid on the Maynooth to Wallace section, the cost to the Northern to finish the line would have been $81,117.00. Under contemporary conditions the additional traffic should have justified this comparatively small investment, especially when one considers the purchase price of the C.O.R. But they were neglecting the line in other ways.

The Northern, in spite of financial hardship generally maintained its locomotives and rolling stock well. But the C.O.R. track and roadbed was already feeling the effects of deferred maintenance. A single sentence in the working timetable of 1914, speaks for itself. "All trains must reduce speed to ten (10) miles per hour and not work steam over any bridges between Trenton and Ormsby Junction."

On January 5th, 1914, the Canadian Northern inaugurated its fast freight service between Toronto, Ottawa, Montreal and Quebec City. At the same time limited passenger service was extended to Sydenham, east of Napanee. Through passenger service was not inaugurated until July. By May the Northern finances were such that it had to seek help from the federal government to avoid bankruptcy.

On June 1st, the C.P.R. began through freight service along the shoreline. This event was observed by starting two trains simultaneously from Smiths Falls and Toronto. The Smiths Falls train was the first to arrive in Trenton, a D 10 class locomotive (a tattered sister is on display in front of Kingston City Hall.) She was hauling 65 cars. She would be the first locomotive to use the new Trenton roundhouse.[6] Several weeks afterwards a scheduled passenger service was started.

The beginning of several important changes in Northern management began in June when George A. Hoag, then superintendent of the Trenton area under George Collins, was promoted and transferred to Toronto.

A month later with the new lines in the region fully operational a reorganization was announced. The line from the outskirts of Toronto, including all the branch lines, would be known as the Ottawa Division with George Collins as Superintendent. His headquarters would remain in the C.O.R. station at Trenton. Both he and the station building had reached undreamt-of importance. J.D. Evans, civil engineer, became Chief Engineer of the new division. Two other C.O.R. officials also benefitted; C.R. Derbyshire was appointed assistant superintendent and J.D. Rowe became the Yardmaster at Trenton. This spoke well of the reputation of the Central Ontario Railway administration.[7]

1914. The end of an age and a small railroad at Picton Station. County men off to war to make a great reputation for themselves.

If all was going well for Trenton, Bancroft was less fortunate. On July 27th, a fire starting in a bakery at 6 o'clock in the evening destroyed all but a few buildings of the business district. The town would take a long time to recover.

On August 4th the Great War began. In Trenton the first signs of war came a few days later when militia guards were posted on the railway bridges.

On August 9th, a Sunday, the war came closer. Late that evening a car-cleaner at work in the Northern car tracks near the station noticed a stranger walking by. The man said he was a special detective. A little while later the car-cleaner, talking to others on duty, was told that the railway had not any such officials here.

About 9 o'clock he caught sight of the 'special detective' again. He was leaning over the running track and placing something under one of the rails. More curious than suspicious the car-cleaner called out, and walked towards him. Being armed with a revolver added to his confidence. As he approached the stranger, the man picked up a rock and, with an accuracy that a pro-ball player would have envied, smashed the globe, extinguishing the light. The car-cleaner took a pot-shot but the man escaped. So did another man hidden in the bushes nearby.

War nerves make every stranger and his movements suspicious. For hundreds of thousands of spy scares there may be only a single spy — but not this time. Under the rails was a partly wired stick of dynamite, and with a troop train due in at 11 o'clock.[8] The train at this point would have been moving at a walking speed and injuries would have been unlikely. The locomotive would have been derailed, however, the train delayed, with considerable despondency and nervousness resulting along the railways. The Great War had reached the rails of the C.O.R. and in no time at all. Was this the first serious attempt at sabotage on a Canadian railway?

The press reported in late August that the Canadian Northern had failed to market a $15-million bond issue. The flow of immigrants for the West, vital to the Northern's future, was slowing fast, soon to stop altogether.

For the C.O.R. itself, the last report of president C.E. Ritchie visiting Trenton was the year before, in September, 1913. This was as much as the Trenton newspaper mentioned. Inevitably he had become no more than a figurehead. Collins took his orders from his immediate Northern superiors. Ritchie just quietly disappeared from the railway.

The employees still felt they were C.O.R. men. Listed prominently in the Trenton newspaper each week were the contributions to the Patriotic Fund for Canadian soldiers. Of these self-organized groups collecting money the C.O.R. and the Northern remained separate.

By November the C.P.R. was claiming that their Trenton payroll was double that of the Northern. By then they were running two passenger trains a day to Toronto, and getting much of the Grand Trunk business, being nearer to the town.[9]

The only local announcement from the Canadian Northern before the end of the year, and the company had a most aggressive and progressive public relations department, was that the new Trenton coal chute had been completed.

Chapter Twenty-Two

How and when did the Central Ontario Railway Company die? Not the physical plant, for the track, equipment and buildings would outlast the parent Canadian Northern Railway for many years. Some of the freight cars would never receive Northern stencils. Operating personnel would be running the same trains, maintenance employees would continue looking after the track and bridges. The concern here is for the C.O.R.'s highly individual corporate identity, a living thing created by many people from presidents to section hands.

The C.O.R. had been fading away like those old soldiers that never die. Dreaming of hard campaigns long past, battles with weather and hazards of the rail; remembering good and bad generals, officers, and luck.

The railway's corporate soul finally faded away, a mundane death, when its operations ceased to be a separate account in the Northern's books. That was at the year's end of 1914. The corporate name disappeared with this final move, accompanied by routine legal formalities.

There were no ceremonies, but that was in character. There was little sentiment and no regrets shown by the public beyond comparing the present quality of service with that of the past. Yet the C.O.R. had brought innumerable benefits to Hastings and Prince Edward Counties. But so it was with many other lines, there is nothing new about that either.

*　*　*

Present end of steel at Lake St. Peter. In the distance the washed-out culvert.　*Photo, Author*

Second end of steel, washout.

Photo, Author

The Canadian Northern did not survive the Great War. The shore line lasted only a little longer. After the Canadian National Railways had been formed it was torn up all the way from the outskirts of Toronto to Napanee. With the abandonment of the line the need was gone for the C.O.R. station and headquarters, so that impressive building was demolished. Today the site is occupied by an A & P supermarket. But the freight shed remains, though the Canadian National Railways have recently petitioned to close this depot, L.C.L. and express service to be trucked from Belleville depot.

* * *

What is left of the former Central Ontario Railway? The track is still intact between Trenton and Lake St. Peter. The branches have gone. The year 1965 saw the ending of all train service followed by the lifting of the track between Ormsby Junction, the line to Marmora Village and Cordova, and the last remains of the Bessemer branch.

Service remained to Maynooth after the line to Wallace was closed, then this was cut back to York River and the last few miles of the former I.B. & O. which served a chipboard factory owned by Domtar, until the plant closed. Freight service was but back to Bancroft (these tracks also remain.) Finally all traffic ceased in 1975 between Marmora Station and Bancroft.

In the years following the Second World War, Bethlehem Steel returned to Hastings County after a long absence with an open pit mine that would produce enormous quantities of good grade iron ore. The ore was pelletized before shipping. The mine is situated a short distance south and west of Marmora Station.

The Canadian National laid heavy main line steel from Marmora Station to a junction near the Picton town boundaries. Here a short branch line was built eastwards to the high cliffs of Picton Bay, where storage bins were built for unloading the pellets directly into ore carriers during the shipping season.

Several years later the Lake Ontario Cement Company built its plant less than a mile to the east, close to limestone and a short extension was built, providing the cement company with the option of shipping by rail or by lake steamer.

After many years of profitable operation the Marmora pit had grown to an enormous hole in the ground and the ore was beginning to run out. In the winter of 1978, the last iron ore train ran ending the scheduled freight.

200

The rails between Trenton and Marmora soon became as rusty as those of the rest of the remaining northern lines. The cement company at Picton remained a railway-user, with sufficient traffic to justify three or four extra trains a week. Without this traffic the rest of the railway would have had to close, the remaining traffic coming nowhere close to covering operating costs.

Sometime before the iron ore trains stopped running, the last remaining station in operation, south of Trenton — Picton, was closed. In March, 1972 the building was put up for sale and became part of a new sales centre of a Picton lumber merchant.

The wye remains and some little used sidings. Except for the line to the cement plant that just about puts us back to where we started, exactly one hundred years ago.

The neighbouring lines fell faster before the paved roads. The Canada Atlantic (later Grand Trunk, then Canadian National) on which lay the settlement of Whitney, terminus-to-be of the C.O.R. lost its railway before Wallace. This line now runs only as far as Barry's Bay, another goal of rival lines that were never built.

The Ottawa and Quebec Railway (the O. & Q.), long operated under a 99-year lease as part of the Canadian Pacific's original main line to Toronto, then as an alternative route after their shore line was constructed, was, in recent years, abandoned between Tweed and Glen Tay. A limited freight service still operates to the former town, crossing the rusting C.O.R. rails at Bonar-law.

If its glory days had gone as a busy main line the stockholders of the original shares have discovered that they have a legal case in property rights against the C.P.R. As a result the O & Q has become renowned for what might be one of the most costly corporate law-suits in Canadian history.

The former Bay of Quinte line to Bannockburn died after the Second World War. The empty roadbed has been reclaimed by the forest. The massive, concrete engine shed a hundred yards to the west of the highway, its roof long fallen in, still asserts its presence. Close by are the walls of the turntable pit.

The unfortunate Belleville and North Hastings line to Madoc is still in use. How long can it survive?

* * *

Among more recent events are some that deserve mention: In June, 1972 Picton station was closed and in that same year an unusual rail excursion was organized by Alan Capon and Bill Thorley of Picton with the assistance of Frank Becker, C.N.'s area passenger sales representative. Two modern passenger coaches were added to the ore train as part of its consist for its scheduled run.

The trip was a sell-out, mostly to Prince Edward County people, among them many who had never before seen their countryside from the train. Many came from the United States, as well as from Toronto and Montreal. Among them the famous Rogers Whittaker (E.M. Frimbo) of The New Yorker and "Sandy" Worthern of Montreal, editor of Canadian Rail. The following summer a second excursion was equally successful.

Not to be forgotten was another excursion in the last years of steam, a double-header, from Belleville to Bancroft. Much of this heroic journey was filmed by a C.B.C. crew for posterity, standing on the deck of the tender. Another special train was provided through the generosity of the late Harvey J. MacFarland, well-known contractor, who paid for a train to take Picton school children to Belleville and back "to see the Queen."

As for the future? No great sums of money are needed to put the line north of Trenton back into shape. But lack of traffic closed it.

Standing on the empty track by Ormsby Junction in the fall of 1978, one heard the frequent rumble of heavy tractor-trailer units headed south loaded with lumber or cordwood. Will rising fuel costs bring traffic back to the rails? Or will the rails be torn up before that happens? There are still enormous deposits of iron ore, some of it of excellent quality and other materials may exist, perhaps, in quite large deposits. Who knows?

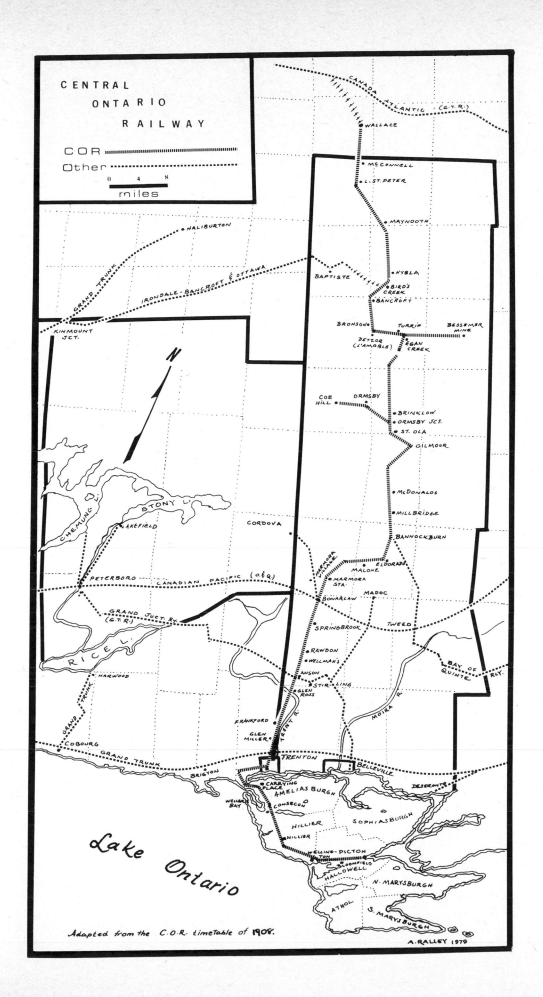

CANADA ATLANTIC (G.T.R.)

WALLACE

McCONNELL

L. ST. PETER

MAYNOOTH

HALIBURTON

IRONDALE-BANCROFT & OTTAWA

BAPTISTE

NYBLA

BIRD'S CREEK

BANCROFT

GRAND TRUNK

KINMOUNT JCT.

BRONSON

TURRIE

BESSEMER MINE

DETLOR (L'AMABLE)

EGAN CREEK

N

COE HILL

ORMSBY

BRINKLOW

ORMSBY JCT.

ST. OLA

GILMOUR

McDONALDS

MILLBRIDGE

CHEMUNG L.

STONY L.

LAKEFIELD

CORDOVA

BANNOCKBURN

PETERBORO

CANADIAN PACIFIC (O.&Q.)

MARMORA VILLAGE

ELDORADO

MALONE

MARMORA STA.

GRAND JUCT. RY. (G.T.R.)

BONARLAW

MADOC

RICE L.

SPRINGBROOK

TWEED

HARWOOD

RAWDON

WELLMAN'S

BAY OF QUINTE RLY.

ANSON

STIRLING

GLEN ROSS

MOIRA R.

FRANKFORD

TRENT R.

GLEN MILLER

GRAND TRUNK

COBOURG

GRAND TRUNK

BRIGTON

TRENTON

BELLEVILLE

CARRYING PLACE

DESERONTO

AMELIASBURGH

WELLER'S BAY

CONSECON

HILLIER

SOPHIASBURGH

HILLIER

WELLING-TON

PICTON

N. MARYSBURGH

BLOOMFIELD

HALLOWELL

Lake Ontario

ATHOL

S. MARYSBURGH

Adapted from the C.O.R. timetable of 1908.

A. RALLEY 1979

203

ABBREVIATIONS

A.B.J.	Akron Beacon Journal
B.T. .	Bancroft Times
C.N.I.	Canadian National Railways (Stevens) Vol. I
C.N.II	Canadian National Railways (Stevens) Vol. II
C.P.A.	Canadian Pacific Archives, Windsor Station, Montreal, Que.
D.H.	David Hanes, L'Amable, Ont.
D.I.	Daily Intelligencer, Belleville, Ont.
D.O.	Daily Ontario, Belleville, Ont.
H.A.	Historic Atlas, Hastings and Prince Edward Counties (Mika Publishing)
H.H.	Historic Hastings, Boyce
H.S.	Herman Snider, L'Amable, Ont.
J.L.	Joseph Lavalley, Wallace, Ont.
M.C.L.	Malcolm and Caroline Love, Waupoos, Ont.
M.H.	Marmora Herald
N.H.R.	North Hastings Review, Madoc, Ont.
O.A.	Ontario Archives, Toronto, Ont.
O.F.	C.O. "Ossie" Fuller, Bancroft, Ont.
O.I.	Ontario Intelligencer, Belleville, Ont.
P.A.C.	Public Archives of Canada, Ottawa, Ont.
P.E.	The County, R. & J. Lunn, Picton, Ont.
P.G.	Picton Gazette, Picton, Ont.
P.T.	Picton Times, Picton, Ont.
T.C.	Trenton Courier, Trenton, Ont.
W.R.H.S.	Western Reserve Historical Society, Cleveland, Ohio

REFERENCE NOTES

CHAPTER I
1 — H.A.
2 — H.A.
3 — P.G., Dec. 29, 1930
4 — P.E.
5 — M.C.L.
6 — Prov. Statute
7 — P.G., Dec. 29, 1930
8 — P.G., Dec. 29, 1930
9 — P.G., Dec. 29, 1930
10 — P.G., Mar. 5, 1914

CHAPTER II
1 — P.G., Mar, 5, 1914
2 — P.G., Mar. 5, 1914
3 — P.G., Mar. 5, 1914
4 — P.G., June 28, 1878
5 — Mar. 5, 1914 (McMullen)
6 — July 26, 1878
7 — Mar. 5, 1914 (Calnan)
8 — The County and other local sources, also W. Kaye Lamb's
9 — CPR History.
10 — P.G., Nov. 23, 1878
11 — P.G., Dec. 13, 1878

CHAPTER III
1 — O.I., Jan. 5, 1879
2 — T.C., June 5, 1879
3 — P.G., June 21, 1879
4 — T.C., June 21, 1879
5 — T.C., June 24, 1879
6 — N.H.R., Mar. 11, 1880
7 — R.W., 1977
8 — R.W., 1977
9 — P.G., Aug. 20, 1879
10 — P.G., Aug. 30, 1879
11 — O.I., Oct. 27, 1879
12 — D.O., Oct. 4, 1879
13 — D.O., Nov. 5, 1879
14 — N.H.R., Oct. 2, 1879
15 — P.T., Oct. 2, 1879
16 — D.I., Oct. 29, 1879

CHAPTER IV
1 — P.G.

CHAPTER V
1 — N.H.R., Nov. 11, 1880
2 — P.T., June 18, 1880
3 — N.H.R., Dec. 2, 1880
4 — T.C. Advert. dated May 27, 1880
5 — N.H.R., Nov. 11, 1880

6 — T.C., Feb. 11
7 — N.H.R., Feb. 10
8 — N.H.R., Feb. 10
9 — N.H.R., Feb. 10

CHAPTER VI
1 — N.H.R., Mar. 23, 1882
2 — T.C., Jan. 19, 1882
3 — T.R. & W.M., Nov. 24, 1883
4 — N.H.R., Feb. 23, 1882
5 — N.H.R., April 6, 1882
6 — N.H.R., June 1, 1882
7 — N.H.R., June 1, 1882
8 — N.H.R., June 8, 1882
9 — N.H.R., June 8, 1882
10 — Akron Beacon Journal, Sept. 19, 1908
11 — N.H.R., Feb. 1, 1883
12 — N.H.R., Mar. 15, 1883
13 — N.H.R., Mar. 22, 1883
14 — "Ontario" Belleville (NHR), Mar. 22, 1883
15 — N.H.R., July 26, 1883
16 — N.H.R., June 7, 1883
17 — N.H.R., Oct. 4, 1883
18 — N.H.R., Aug. 23, 1883
19 — N.H.R., Aug. 30, 1883
20 — N.H.R., et. seq.
21 — N.H.R., et. seq.

CHAPTER VII
1 — Courtesy C.N. Area H.Q. Belleville
2 — "Elements of Railroading" N.Y., Wiley & Sons Publishers
3 — A.K.B.
4 — C.N.
5 — C.N.R. History Vol. 1 & Stat. Hist. Can. Rlys., Ottawa.
6 — H.H.
7 — H.H.
8 — Mrs. Lloyd E. Thompson of Picton
9 — "Buster" Courtemanche of Belleville

CHAPTER VIII
1 — N.H.R., Sept. 4, 1884
2 — N.H.R., Sept. 4, 1884
3 — N.H.R., Sept. 11, 1884
4 — C.P.A. Letter 1884
5 — N.H.R., Oct. 30, 1884
6 — N.H.R., Oct. 30, 1884
7 — N.H.R., Dec. 4, 1884
8 — N.H.R., Dec. 4, 1884
9 — N.H.R., Dec. 9, 1884
10 — R.W. Interview

11 — R.W. and others. Interviews
12 — Gerard Kavanagh, and R.W. Interviews
13 — Gerard Kavanagh
14 — N.H.R., Feb. 19, 1885
15 — N.H.R., Jan. 8, 1885
16 — N.H.R., Jan 8, 1885
17 — P.A.C., 1885
18 — N.H.R., Feb. 18, 1885
19 — P.A.C., 1885
20 — N.H.R., Mar. 19, 1885
21 — N.H.R., Mar. 26, 1885
22 — N.H.R., Mar. 26, 1885
23 — C.P.A., 1885
24 — N.H.R., June 18, 1885
25 — N.H.R., Sept. 24, 1885
26 — N.H.R., June 11, 1885
27 — P.A.C., 1885
28 — N.H.R., June 25, 1885
29 — N.H.R., July 2, 1885
30 — N.H.R., July 23, 1885
31 — N.H.R., July 23, 1885
32 — C.P.A., 1885
33 — C.P.A., 1885
34 — N.H.R., Nov. 12, 1885

CHAPTER IX
1 — C.P.A., 1886
2 — N.H.R., 1886
3 — N.H.R., Apr. 8, 1886
4 — N.H.R., May 20, 1886
5 — N.H.R., Nov. 25, 1886
6 — Trentonian, Apr. 15, 1886
7 — N.H.R., May 13, 1886
8 — C.P.A., 1886
9 — C.P.A., 1886
10 — C.P.A., 1886
11 — N.H.R., May 27, 1886
12 — Napanee Express, June 3, 1886
13 — N.H.R., May 27, 1886
14 — N.H.R., July 8 and 15, 1886
15 — N.H.R., July 15, 1886
16 — N.H.R., July 15, 1886
17 — P.A.C., 1886
18 — N.H.R., Oct. 21, 1886
19 — P.A.C., 1887
20 — N.H.R., Feb. 10, 1887
21 — P.A.C., 1887
22 — P.A.C., 1887
23 — N.H.R., Mar. 10, 1887
24 — N.H.R., Mar. 10, 1887
25 — N.H.R., Mar. 17, 1887
26 — P.A.C., 1887
27 — P.A.C., 1887
28 — N.H.R., May 19, 1887
29 — N.H.R., May 19, 1887
30 — N.H.R., June 2, 1887
31 — N.H.R., June 9, 1887
32 — N.H.R., June 30, 1887
33 — N.H.R., Sept. 22, 1887
34 — N.H.R., Nov. 1, 1887
35 — N.H.R., Aug. 4, 1887
36 — N.H.R., Aug. 4, 1887
37 — N.H.R., Nov. 3, 1887
38 — N.H.R., Nov. 3, 1887
39 — N.H.R., Oct. 27, 1887
40 — N.H.R., Nov. 17, 1887

41 — N.H.R., Mar. 15, 1888
42 — N.H.R., Mar. 15, 1888
43 — N.H.R., Apr. 12, 1888
44 — P.A.C., 1888
45 — P.A.C., 1888
46 — N.H.R., Apr. 19, 1888
47 — N.H.R., Apr. 19, 1888
48 — C.P.A., 1888
49 — C.P.A., 1888
50 — N.H.R., May 24, 1888
51 — N.H.R., May 24, 1888
52 — N.H.R., June 14, 1888
53 — N.H.R., June 14, 1888
54 — N.H.R., July 19, 1888
55 — N.H.R., July 26, 1888
56 — N.H.R., Jan. 31, 1889
57 — N.H.R., Feb. 14, 1889
58 — N.H.R., Feb. 21, 1889
59 — N.H.R., Feb. 21, 1889
60 — N.H.R., May 16, 1889
61 — N.H.R., Feb. 28, 1889
62 — N.H.R., Mar. 21, 1889
63 — N.H.R., Apr. 4, 1889
64 — N.H.R., Apr. 18, 1889
65 — N.H.R., Apr. 18, 1889
66 — N.H.R., Apr. 25, 1889
67 — N.H.R., May 23, 1889
68 — N.H.R., May 30, 1889
69 — N.H.R., June 7, 1889
70 — N.H.R., June 13, 1889
71 — N.H.R., July 11, 1889
72 — N.H.R., July 11, 1889
73 — N.H.R., July 11, 1889
74 — N.H.R., July 11, 1889
75 — P.A.C., 1889
76 — W.R.H.S., 1889

CHAPTER X
1 — N.H.R., Jan. & Feb. 1890
2 — N.H.R., Jan. 16
3 — R.L. & H.S., Bulletin 53, 1940
4 — W.R.H.S.
5 — W.R.H.S. Correspondence starts Nov. 22, 1889,
      Container 4.
6 — N.H.R., Feb. 27, 1890
7 — N.H.R., March 6, 1890
8 — N.H.R., Oct. 30, 1890
9 — P.A.C., 1890
10 — N.H.R., Jan. 22, 1890
11 — N.H.R., Feb. 5, 1890
12 — P.A.C.
13 — P.A.C.
14 — N.H.R., Feb. 12, 1890
15 — N.H.R., May 21, June 25, July 2, 1890
16 — N.H.R., July 9, 1890
17 — N.H.R., Aug. 27, 1890
18 — N.H.R., Aug. 27, 1890
19 — N.H.R., Oct. 8, 1890
20 — N.H.R., Oct. 22, 1890
21 — P.A.C.
22 — W.R.H.S.
23 — P.A.C.
24 — P.A.C.
25 — Interview 1977
26 — P.A.C.

27 — N.H.R., May 7, 1890
28 — N.H.R., Feb. 19, 1890
29 — N.H.R., Sept. 3, 1890
30 — N.H.R., Oct. 22, 1890
31 — W.R.H.S., 1892
32 — W.R.H.S., 1891
33 — W.R.H.S., 1891
34 — W.R.H.S., 1891
35 — W.R.H.S., 1891
36 — W.R.H.S., 1891
37 — W.R.H.S., 1891
38 — W.R.H.S., 1891
39 — W.R.H.S., 1891
40 — W.R.H.S., 1891
41 — W.R.H.S., 1891
42 — W.R.H.S., Ritchie Letter, Mar. 13, 1893
43 — W.R.H.S., Summaries of documents, 1893
44 — W.R.H.S., Summaries of documents, 1893
45 — P.A.C., Ritchie - Bowell letter, 1893
46 — W.R.H.S.
47 — W.R.H.S., McLaren - Bell letter, 1893
48
49
50 — See Pioneer Life Bay of Quinte (Mika)

CHAPTER XI
1 — P.G., Jan. 12, 1894
2 — N.H.R., Apr. 5, 1894
3 — N.H.R., May 10, 1895
4 — N.H.R., Aug. 9, 1895
5 — N.H.R., Dec. 27, 1895
6 — N.H.R., Jan. 3, 1896
7 — N.H.R., Oct. 10, 1896
8 — P.A.C., 1896
9 — P.A.C., 1896
10 — N.H.R., Dec. 18, 1896
11 — N.H.R., July 22, 1896
12 — N.H.R., Jan. 14, 1897
13 — N.H.R., Oct. 1, 1896
14 — N.H.R., Feb. 18, 1897
15 — N.H.R., Mar. 4, 1897
16 — N.H.R., Mar. 4, 1897
17 — N.H.R., June 17, 1897
18 — N.H.R., Dec. 2, 1897
19 — N.H.R., July 22, 1897
20 — N.H.R., May 27, 1897
21 — N.H.R., Mar. 10, 1898
22 — N.H.R., Apr. 21, 1898
23 — N.H.R., Apr. 21, 1898
24 — N.H.R., June 23, 1898
25 — N.H.R., June 30, 1898
26 — N.H.R., July 7, 1898
27 — N.H.R., Aug. 18, 1898
28 — N.H.R., Aug. 17, 1899
29 — W.R.H.S.
30 — There are minor differences between these live sources.
The quotation for the 'device' is taken from the Sunday
Star, Toronto, March 5, 1978.
31 — W.R.H.S.
32 — W.R.H.S., Various documents
33 — W.R.H.S., Various documents
34 — W.R.H.S., June 17, 1900
35 — W.R.H.S., Feb. 16, 1893
36 — W.R.H.S., File 1902
37 — W.R.H.S., File 1898
38 — W.R.H.S., File 1898

39 — W.R.H.S., May 16, 1893
40 — W.R.H.S., No date
41 — W.R.H.S., March 1894
42 — W.R.H.S., Apr. 19, 1894
43 — W.R.H.S., No date 1894
44 — W.R.H.S., Various documents 1894
45 — W.R.H.S., Quoted from a resume of past events written
by Ritchie for one of his lawyers. Dated Aug. 7, 1902

CHAPTER XII
1 — (P.A.C. Macleod Report
2 — (
3 — N.H.R., May 3, 1899
4 — N.H.R., May 17, 1899
5 — P.G., July 24, 1899
6 — N.H.R., July 26, 1899
7 — P.G., Aug. 7, 1899
8 — P.A.C.
9 — N.H.R., Aug. 16, 1899
10 — P.A.C.
11 — N.H.R., Nov. 15, 1899
12 — P.A.C.
13 — N.H.R., July 9, 28, 1899
14 — P.A.C.
15 — P.A.C. Macleod Report
16 — C.N. II, pp. 371-2
17 — C.N. II, pp. 371-2
18 — Collins' statement in Montreal Gazette reported in
N.H.R. Apr. 19, 1900
19 — N.H.R., June 21, 1900
20 — N.H.R., May 31, 1900
21 — N.H.R., May 3, 1900
22 — N.H.R., Aug. 16, 1900
23 — N.H.R., Dec. 13, 1900
24 — See #18 above.
25 — N.H.R., Apr. 19, 1901
26 — N.H.R., Mar. 29, 1901
27 — Mar. 29, 1901
28 — O.A., Apr. 18, 1901
29 — N.H.R., July 12, 1901
30 — P.G., Aug. 7, 1901
31 — N.H.R., Oct. 4, 1901
32 — N.H.R., Dec. 13, 1901
33 — N.H.R., Nov. 29, 1901
34 — O.A., Dec. 22, 1901
35 — P.A.C.
36 — O.A./P.G./N.H.R., Various documents & press reports.
37 — O.A., July 15, 1902
38 — P.G., Apr. 2, 1902
39 — P.G., Apr. 9, 1902
40 — N.H.R., May 16, 1902
41 — P.G., May 17, 1902
42 — P.G., Aug. 6, 1902
43 — P.G., Nov. 19, 1902
44 — P.G., Dec. 20, 1902
45 — P.G., Apr. 9 & interview with the late Ralph Grimmon
46 — P.G., Nov. 19, 1902
47 — N.H.R., Feb. 13, 1902
48 — N.H.R., Aug. 8, 1902
49 — N.H.R., June 12, 1902
50 — N.H.R., May 1, 1902
51 — N.H.R., Oct. 9, 1902
52 — N.H.R., Feb. 20, 1902
53 — N.H.R., Dec. 25, 1902
54 — N.H.R., Sept. 18, 1902

55 — See next chapter.
56 — W.R.H.S., 1902

CHAPTER XIII
1 — W.R.H.S., Various papers
2 — O.A. Weddell letter Sept. 20, 1900
3 — W.R.H.S., Various papers
4 — W.R.H.S., Ritchie - Bingham letter, Oct. 1, 1902
5 — W.R.H.S., Various papers
6 — W.R.H.S., Ritchie - Langmuir letter, Sept. 1902
7 — W.R.H.S., et. seq. Ritchie - Langmuir letter, Oct. 9, 1902
8 — "Evolution of Trenton" on R. Weddell
9 — P.A.C.
10 — P.A.C., Various papers
11 — P.A.C. and Various papers
12 — O.A. Evans, July 6, 1900
13 — O.A. Bingham Blackstock, Oct. 23, 1900
14 — W.R.H.S., P.A.C., O.A. Various papers 1900/1901

15 — P.A.C. Weddell, Jan. 30, 1901
16 — P.A.C. Aylesworth, Jan. 31, 1901
17 — O.A. Johnson, April 20, 1901
18 — O.A. Blackstock, Jan. 28, 1901

CHAPTER XIV
1 — N.H.R. & Stat. Hist. April 2, 1903
     N.H.R. & Stat. Hist. May 14, 1903
2 — P.A.C., Apr. 7, 1903
3 — P.A.C., May 12, 1903
4 — N.H.R., Sept. 10, 1903
5 — N.H.R., May 7, 1903
6 — N.H.R., July 16, 1903
7 — P.A.C., Aug. 26, 1903
8 — W.R.H.S., Various documents 1903
9 — P.G., Oct. 13
10 — N.H.R., Oct. 15
11 — N.H.R., Oct. 15
12 — P.G., Oct. 20
13 — P.G., Nov. 10
14 — P.G., Nov. 10
15 — N.H.R., Nov. 26
16 — N.H.R., Nov. 26
17 — N.H.R., Nov. 12
18 — N.H.R., Feb. 25
19 — N.H.R., Mar. 10
20 — Caller on phone in programme C.J.B.Q. Belleville 1978.
21 — W.R.H.S., Various documents 1903
22 — W.R.H.S., May 20, 1903
23 — N.H.R., Mar. 3, 1903
24 — N.H.R. (& Stat. Hist.) Apr. 14, 1903
25 — N.H.R., Apr. 14, 1903
26 — W.R.H.S., Apr. 24, 1903
27 — W.R.H.S., Apr. 26, 1903
28 — W.R.H.S., May 4, 1903
29 — W.R.H.S., May 20, 1903
30 — N.H.R., May 12, 1903
31 — P.G., May 13, 1903
32 — N.H.R., Apr. 28, 1904
33 — N.H.R., Apr. 11, 1904
34 — N.H.R., June 2, 1904
35 — N.H.R., Sept. 1, 1904
36 — N.H.R., Sept. 8, 1904
37 — N.H.R., Sept. 1, 1904
38 — P.G., Sept. 13, 1904

39 — P.G., Sept. 23, 1904
40 — W.R.H.S., Feb. 22, 1905
41 — W.R.H.S., Feb. 25, 1905
42 — N.H.R., Feb. 2, 1905
43 — N.H.R., Apr. 27, 1905
     N.H.R., May 18, 1905
44 — P.A.C., Various documents 1905
45 — N.H.R., July 13, 1904
46 — N.H.R., Aug. 31, 1905
47 — W.R.H.S., Apr. 23, 1905
48 — N.H.R., June 29, 1905
49 — W.R.H.S., Aug. 7, 1905
50 — N.H.R., Mar. 2, 1905
51 — N.H.R., June 8, 1905
52 — N.H.R., Oct. 19, 1905
53 — P.G., Aug. 8
54 — N.H.R., Oct. 5
55 — N.H.R., Oct. 26
56 — N.H.R., Oct. 19
57 — N.H.R., Nov.
58 — N.H.R., Nov. 9
59 — N.H.R., Nov. 16

CHAPTER XV
1 — W.R.H.S., No date
2 — P.A.C., Feb. 2, 1918
3 — W.R.H.S., Sept. 5, 1907
4 — M.H., June 4, 1906
5 — N.H.R., Feb. 1, 1906
6 — N.H.R., Mar. 22, 1906
7 — N.H.R., Apr. 5, 1906
8 — M.H., Nov. 15, 1906
9 — N.H.R., Apr. 12, 1906
10 — N.H.R., July 12, 1906
11 — W.R.H.S., No date 1906
12 — W.R.H.S., Aug. 30, 1906
13 — N.H.R., July 7, 1906
14 — N.H.R., July 26, 1906
15 — W.R.H.S., Various papers 1906
16 — M.H., May 10, 1906
17 — N.H.R., July 12, 1906
18 — M.H., June 7, 1906
19 — N.H.R., Apr. 26, 1906
20 — N.H.R., Aug. 30, 1906
21 — N.H.R., Sept. 13, 1906
22 — N.H.R., Aug. 30, 1906
23 — M.H., Feb. 21, 1907
24 — W.R.H.S., Various papers 1907
25 — W.R.H.S., Apr. 18, 1907
26 — W.R.H.S., May 10, 1907
27 — M.H., May 23, 1907
28 — M.H., June 6, 1907
29 — M.H., June 20, 1907

CHAPTER XVI
1 — McClure Heritage, Card, Picton Gazette Pub. Co. '66
2 — P.A.C., Apr. 2, 1907
3 — P.A.C., Mar. 15, 1907
4 — P.A.C., July 3, 1907
5 — P.A.C., Aug. 26, 1907
6 — P.A.C., Sept. 20, 1907
7 — P.A.C., Oct. 2, 1907
8 — M.H., May 23, 1907
9 — W.R.H.S., 1907
10 — P.A.C., Jan. 22 et. seq., 1907

CHAPTER XVII
All letters from W.R.H.S. file as dated.

CHAPTER XVIII
1 — W.R.H.S., Feb. 1908
2 — W.R.H.S., Feb. 15, 1908
3 — W.R.H.S., Sept. 1908
4 — W.R.H.S., May 1908
5 — W.R.H.S., May 1908
6 — W.R.H.S., Feb. 1908
7 — W.R.H.S., No date
8 — W.R.H.S., No date
9 — W.R.H.S., Jan. 9, 1908
10 — Mr. & Mrs. Art Young of Bancroft 1977
11 — W.R.H.S., Jan. 9, 1908
12 — W.R.H.S., Aug. 1908
13 — W.R.H.S., July 28, 1908
14 — W.R.H.S., July 8, 1908
15 — B.T., Aug. 13, 1908
16 — A.J., Sept. 10, 1908
17 — A.J., Sept. 10, 1908
18 — W.R.H.S., Aug. 4, 1908
19 — B.T., July 30, 1908
20 — P.G., Aug. 4, 1908
21 — B.T., Oct. 1908
22 — A.B.J., Sept. 10, 1908
23 — P.G., Feb. 9, 1908
24 — Regehr. Can. Nos. History
25 — C.N. Vol. II
26 — Regehr. Can. Nos. History
27 — P.A.C.
28 — Regehr. Can. Nos. History
29 — C.O.R. Timetables
30 — P.A.C.
31 — Regehr. Can. Nos. History
32 — B.T., May 27, 1909
33 — O.F. & H.S. Interviews
34 — H.S. Interview
35 — O.F. Interview 1978
36 — O.F. Interview 1978
37 — H.S. Interview 1978
38 — H.S. Interview 1978
39 — D.H. Info. 1978
40 — H.S. Interview 1978
41 — D.H. Info. 1978
42 — H.S. Interview 1978
43 — J.L.
44 — B.T., Apr. 1909

CHAPTER XIX
1 — B.T.
2 — Omer Lavallee
3 — D.H. Info. 1978
4 — Dom. Govt. Sessional Papers Vol.12, 1911
5 — O.F. Interview 1978
6 — B.T., Feb. 16, 1911
7 — B.T., Oct. 5, 1911
8 — B.T., Dec. 7, 1911
9 — B.T., Sept. 15, 1910
10 — B.T., Sept. 15, 1910
11 — B.T., Sept. 15, 1910
12 — B.T., Apr. 28, 1910
13 — O.F. Interview 1978
14 — M.H., Jan. 27, 1910
15 — B.T., Feb. 24, 1910
16 — B.T., June 23, 1910
17 — B.T., Feb. 17, 1910
18 — M.H., July 22, 1910
19 — B.T., May 12, 1910
20 — M.H., Mar. 31, 1910
21 — B.T., Apr. 7, 1910
22 — B.T., May 12, 1910
23 — B.T., Feb. 24, 1910
24 — P.A.C., Nov. 21, 1910
25 — B.T., Sept. 15, 1910
26 — Joseph Lavalley Interview 1978
27 — P.A.C., 1911
28 — P.A.C., 1911
29 — J.L. Interview 1978
30 — J.L. Interview 1978
31 — Allan Shannon Interview 1979
32 — Allan Shannon Interview 1979
33 — J.L. Interview 1978
34 — J.L. Interview 1978
35 — J.L. Interview 1978
36 — B.T., Apr. 6, 1911
37 — B.T., Feb. 23, 1911
38 — B.T., Feb. 9, 1911
39 — B.T., Feb. 2, 1911
40 — B.T., May 11, 1911
41 — B.T., May 18, 1911
42 — B.T., Mar. 23, 1911
43 — B.T., Mar. 23, 1911
44 — B.T., Mar. 23, 1911
45 — P.G., Sept. 14, 1911

CHAPTER XX
Personal and general information are from interviews with Mrs. J. Milne, granddaughter of George W. McMullen. Mary Mitchell of Picton who as a young girl worked in the McMullen home while her father worked at Beaver Meadows. Miss Naomi Macdonald of Picton who lived next door to the McMullen's and knew the grandchildren as playmates. Dr. Earl Taylor of Picton who has done much research on the McMullen family, "Down Memory Lane" an undated clipping from the Picton Gazette. And Sharon M. Reid's "The Legacy of Beaver Meadows".

1 — P.G., Sept. 14, 1911
2 — P.G., Sept. 14, 1911
3 — P.G., Sept. 14, 1911
4 — P.G., Sept. 14, 1911
5 — P.G., Sept. 14, 1911
6 — P.A.C.
7 — T.C., Feb. 8, 1912
8 — P.A.C., 1912
9 — P.A.C., 1914
10 — P.T., Apr. 28, 1914
11 — P.T., May 7, 1914
12 — P.T., May 13, 1915

CHAPTER XXI
1 — T.C.
2 — T.C.
3 — R.W. Interview, 1979
4 — P.G., July 3, 1913
5 — P.A.C., 1913
6 — T.C., June 1, 1913
7 — T.C., July 23, 1913
8 — T.C., Aug. 13, 1913
9 — T.C., Sept. 8, 1913

APPENDIX 1

18 March 1854

Original application to form a railway company in Prince Edward County.

Signed   A. McFaul, Chairman
Cecil Mortimer, Sec. Treas.
Walter Ross
J.T. Lane
Henry Dennis
John P. Roblin
Roger B. Conger
Thomas Donnelly

At a meeting on 9 June 1854 the following were elected:
John P. Roblin
Philip Low
William Proudfoot
Palen Black
D.B. Stevenson
John S. Bowes
William Johnson
James T. Lane
A. McFaul
S.G. Lynn
R.J. Fitzgerald
Dennis Kelly Feehan

APPENDIX 2

Stockholders Prince Edward County Railway
From Picton Gazette of July 26, 1878:

Walter Ross, President
S.P. Niles, Vice President
Phillip Low
W.T. Yarwood
William Delong
W.B. Blakely
C.S. Wilson (Private Banker)
J.H. Allen
John Prinyer
Robert Boyle
W.T. Ross, Secy.

APPENDIX 3

THE CENTRAL ONTARIO RAILWAY
(I. B. & O. ACCOUNTS WERE CARRIED SEPARATELY UNTIL 1914)

Year Ending June 30	Gross Earnings	Operating Expenses	Net Earnings	Net Loss	Superintendent
1884	40,486.45	50,788.29	. . . .	10,301.84	J.B. McMullen
1885	98,665.13	81,406.36	17,258.77	. . . .	D.S. McMullen
1886	81,512.26	87,488.69	. . . .	5,976.43	G.W. Dench
1887	82,387.43	78,096.96	4,290.47	. . . .	G.W. Dench
1888	80,381.78	79,598.26	783.53	. . . .	G.W. Dench
1889	100,366.72	95,925.38	5,441.34	. . . .	G.W. Dench
1890	93,816.14	91,844.65	1,971.49	. . . .	R. Fraser
1891	87,925.62	91,588.96	. . . .	3,663.34	R. Fraser
1892	103,632.53	106,249.63	. . . .	2,617.10	R. Fraser
1893	88,201.49	79,185.76	9,015.73	. . . .	J.D. Riddell
1894	76,791.44	70,125.35	6,666.09	. . . .	J.D. Riddell
1895	84,700.05	71,641.66	13,058.38	. . . .	Geo. Collins
1896	97,358.29	75,496.50	21,861.79	. . . .	Geo. Collins
1897	93,086.25	74,337.83	18,748.42	. . . .	Geo. Collins
1898	99,962.12	86,313.96	13,648.16	. . . .	Geo. Collins
1899	111,526.19	86,137.92	25,388.27	. . . .	Geo. Collins
1900	144,621.85	92,426.13	52,195.72	. . . .	Geo. Collins
1901	179,027.00	106,368.00	72,855.00	. . . .	Geo. Collins
1902	183,991.00	126,270.00	57,721.00	. . . .	Geo. Collins
1903	190,785.00	128,379.00	62,406.00	. . . .	Geo. Collins
1904	225,347.14	133,796.29	91,550.88	. . . .	Geo. Collins
1905	207,809.35	141,485.92	66,323.43	. . . .	Geo. Collins
1906	242,692.93	140,510.76	102,182.17	. . . .	Geo. Collins
1907	283,048.25	144,510.76	138,690.27	. . . .	Geo. Collins
1908	269,422.06	153,927.53	115,494.53	. . . .	Geo. Collins
1909	267,437.60	145,831.36	121,606.24	. . . .	Geo. Collins
1910	306,796.80	168,854.65	137,942.15	. . . .	Geo. Collins
1911	314,105.85	170,521.29	143,584.56	. . . .	Geo. Collins
1912	321,368.87	193,418.97	127,949.90	. . . .	Geo. Collins
1913	375,048.23	243,024.59	132,023.64	. . . .	Geo. Collins
1914	347,759.99	346,259.65	1,500.32	. . . .	Geo. Collins

APPENDIX 4a

CENTRAL ONTARIO RLY. LOCOMOTIVES
(KINDNESS A. ANDREW MERRILEES, RAYMOND F. CORLEY, R.L. & H.S. BOSTON, MASS.)

C.O. Ry.	C. No. Ry. (1912) (Class)	C. Nat. Ry.	Type	Cyl.	Driv.	Const.
1			4-4-0			
2			4-4-0			
3			4-4-0	16 x 24	60"	1879
4	35 (A-13-b)		4-4-0	16 x 24	60"	1882
5	39 (A-17-a)		4-4-0	17 x 24	57"	1882
6	40 (A-17-a)		4-4-0	17 x 24	57"	
7	41 (A-17-a)		4-4-0	17 x 24	57"	
8	42 (A-17-a)		4-4-0	17 x 24	57"	
9	43 (A-18-a)		4-4-0	15 x 24	62"	1884
10	45 (A-19-a)		4-4-0	17 x 24	62"	
11	46 (A-19-a)		4-4-0	17 x 24	62"	
12	1110 (G-15-a) 1110		4-6-0	18 x 24	57"	1902
14	47 (A-20-a) 120		4-4-0	18 x 24	63"	1904
15	48 (A-20-a) 121		4-4-0	18 x 24	63"	
16	49 (A-20-a) 122		4-4-0	18 x 24	63"	1906
17	1027 (G-3-a) 1027		4-6-0	18 x 24	57"	1907
18	1028 (G-3-a) 1028		4-6-0	18 x 24	57"	1907
19	1029 (G-3-a) 1029		4-6-0	18 x 24	57"	1907
20	1030 (G-3-a) 1030		4-6-0	18 x 24	57"	1907

	Builder	Builder's #	Name	Disposition	Can. Nat. Ry. No.	Can. Nat. Power Rating
1			"Trenton"	Sold to Gilmour Lumber Co.		
2			"Picton"	Scrapped		
3	Kingston	207	"J.B. McMullen"	Sold 1891		
4	Kingston	224	"G.W. McMullen"	Scrapped 1914		
5	Rogers (USA)	3137	"Wm. Coe"	Sold 1917 (1)		13%
6	Rogers (USA)	3138	"D.S. McMullen"	Scrapped 1913		13%
7	Rogers (USA)	3252	"H.B. Payne"	Scrapped 1917		13%
8	Rogers (USA)	3253	"D.Y. McMullen"	Scrapped 1913		13%
9	Pittsburgh (USA)	737		Scrapped 1915		14%
10	Pittsburgh (USA)	678		Scrapped 1913		14%
11	Pittsburgh (USA)	679		Scrapped 1913		14%
12	Kingston	577		Scrapped 1925		18%
14	Kingston	615		Scrapped 1925	120	19%
15	Kingston	628		Scrapped 1925	121	19%
16	Kingston	746		Scrapped 1925	122	19%
17	Kingston	785		Scrapped 1925	1027	22%
18	Kingston	786		Scrapped 1934	1028	22%
19	Kingston	787		Scrapped 1933	1029	22%
20	Kingston	788		Scrapped 1925	1030	22%

(1) Sold to Key Valley Ry.

No. 12. Her official portrait at the builders at Kingston in 1902. She was scrapped in 1925 by The Can. Nat. Rlys. as No. 1110.

Photo, Andrew Merrilees, Toronto

No. 15, 1904 Kingston Builder's Picture. Later No. 48 of Can. Nor. Then Can. Nat. No. 121. Scrapped 1925.

Photo, Omer S. A. Lavallee

No. 17, 1907 Kingston Builder's Picture. Later No. 1027 of Can. Nor. Same No. Can. Nat. Scrapped 1925. This was the first of the four most powerful locomotives of the C.O.R.

Photo, Omer S.A. Lavalee

213

APPENDIX 4b

CANADIAN NORTHERN GAS-ELECTRIC CAR NO. 500

Built 1912
Builder — General Electric Co., Schenectady, N.Y. for The Canadian General Electric Co.
Capacity — 74 passengers
Length Overall — 58' 11"
Prime Mover — 200 H.P., of unknown make, started by hand
Auxiliary Motor for lights, etc.
Baggage Compartment, no toilet facilities

LATER HISTORY

Renumbered by Canadian National Railways around 1921 as #15800. In 1923 the car was completely rebuilt with batteries as the prime mover. Not much of the original seems to have remained. The pointed front disappeared, so did the open platform at the rear, thus permitting the car to be driven from either end. The baggage compartment was eliminated and a single toilet installed. Passenger seating was reduced to 65. The overall length was increased to 59' 8".

The car was retired in 1931 to be stripped of its machinery and become trailer car #15748.

Information based Trenton *Courier* reports and Anthony Clegg's "Self Propelled Cars of the C.N.R."

APPENDIX 5

LIST OF STATIONS 1879 — 1914

Dates of opening and closing of stations are not included.
(F) Marks Flag Stations
(U) Unmanned Junctions and Timetable points
Due to many changes in opening and closing of stations, or changes to and from flag status, and for lack of data, they are listed with the status they had for what appears to be the greatest length of time. A similar problem holds with sidings and passing tracks.

The most useful document has been a Canadian Northern Working Timetable of 1914 through the kindness of Mr. H.R. Botting of The Canadian National Staff, Area Headquarters, Belleville, Ontario.

PICTON SUBDIVISION

Miles				Notes
From First	Third		Picton Stations	
3.8	4.2		BLOOMFIELD	
6.6			STINSONS CREEK (U)	
	7.6		HALLOWELL (F)	No Sidings
10.6	11		WELLINGTON	
14.1			FOUR CORNERS (F)	
	14.9		NILES CORNERS (F)	No Sidings
16.1	16.5		HILLIER	Passing Track
20.9	21.3		CONSECON	Passing Track
	24.9		GARDENVILLE	
			WELLER'S BAY	
	25.6		CARRYING PLACE (F)	
	27		CANAL/MURRAY CANAL (F)	154' Swing Bridge, No sidings
30.2	30.6		TRENTON	
31.8	32.2		TRENTON JCT. (F)	Grand Trunk Depot was used until the underpass was built, when it became a Flag Stop.

MAYNOOTH SUBDIVISION

0	TRENTON	
1.6	G.T. RY. JUNCTION	
	TRENTON JUNCTION	
4.8	GLEN MILLER	
7.9	FRANKFORD	
12.6	CHISHOLM'S (Chisholm's Rapids)	
12.9	South end of Trent bridge. Girders 5 x 50', 2 x 60', 1 x 70'.	
13.2	Steel rivetted, through truss, swing bridge over canal.	
13.6	GLEN ROSS	Passing track and water-tower.
	ANSON (F) Shown in timetables at different times as "ANSON MID. RY. JCT.", "MIDLAND JCT." (1891) and "ANSON JCT" The date of the junction's installation is obscure.	
19.9	WELLMAN (F)	
20.39	RAWDON STATION	1200' Refuge siding
22.8	SPRINGBROOK	800' Refuge siding
25	C.P.R. JUNCTION	
	BONARLAW	
27.2	BELMAR (U)	
	MARMORA JCT.	
	BRANCH	
	2.5m MARMORA (Village)	
	7.1 CORDOVA	
30.4	MARMORA STATION	Passing Tracks
36.4	MALONE (F)	
40.7	ELDORADO	
45.7	BANNOCKBURN/SUB-DIVISION	Passing Tracks,
	JUNCTION WITH BAY OF QUINTE RLY.	Weigh Scales
50.1	MILLBRIDGE (F)	
55.2	McDONALD'S (F)	
59.7	GILMOUR	
62.6	STEENBURG	
	ST. OLA (F)	
66.4	ORMSBY JCT.	
	Original terminus became	2.5 RATHBUN/ORMSBY
	ORMSBY SUB-DIVISION (F)	4.7 COE HILL
		Line was extended past the station to the iron ore mines.
67.9	BRINKLOW (F)	
	CARLOW RD. ?	
70.5	WOODS LAKE (F)	
73.2	EGAN CREEK (F)	
74.6	TURRIF (F)	
78.1	BESSEMER JCT. (U) (No Station)	
	BRANCH 4.8 BESSEMER (U)	An extension ran to two other mines and two saw mills
78.8	L'AMABLE	Passing Track
	(DETLOR)	
82.2	BRONSON (F)	
85.9	BANCROFT	Division Headquarters
88.4	YORK RIVER JCT. (U)	For I.B. & O., Wye
89.7	BIRDS CREEK (F)	Passing Track
95.8	HYBLA (F)	
98.9	GRAPHITE (F)	
101.6	MAYNOOTH	Terminus for passenger service. Wye
109.7	LAKE ST. PETER	Passing Track
113.2	McCONNELL (U) (No Station)	
117.6	WALLACE (U) (No Station)	Wye

IRONDALE SUBDIVISION (I.B.& O.)

0	YORK RIVER JUNCTION
	(2.5 miles from Bancroft)
6.0	BAPTISTE
11.7	HIGHLAND GROVE
16.0	MUMFORD
20.8	WILBERFORCE (F)
23.0	MONMOUTH ROAD (F)
26.3	TORY HILL
34.0	GOODERHAM
39.7	MAXWELLS (F)
41.7	IRONDALE
46.0	FURNACE FALLS (F)
48.0	CONWAYS (F)
51.9	KINMOUNT JCT. (GRAND TRUNK)

Index